To Victoria
happy reading.

JOY
UNCONFINED!

JOY UNCONFINED!

Lord Byron's Grand Tour,
Re-Toured

IAN STRATHCARRON

Signal Books

OXFORD

First published in 2010 by
Signal Books Limited
36 Minster Road
Oxford
OX4 1LY
www.signalbooks.co.uk

A catalogue record for this book is available from the British Library

ISBN 978-1-904955-74-0 Cloth

Text design: Bryony Clark
Cover design: Baseline Arts, Oxford
Cover images: courtesy Ian Strathcarron
Photographs: © Ian Strathcarron
Printed in India by Imprint Digital.

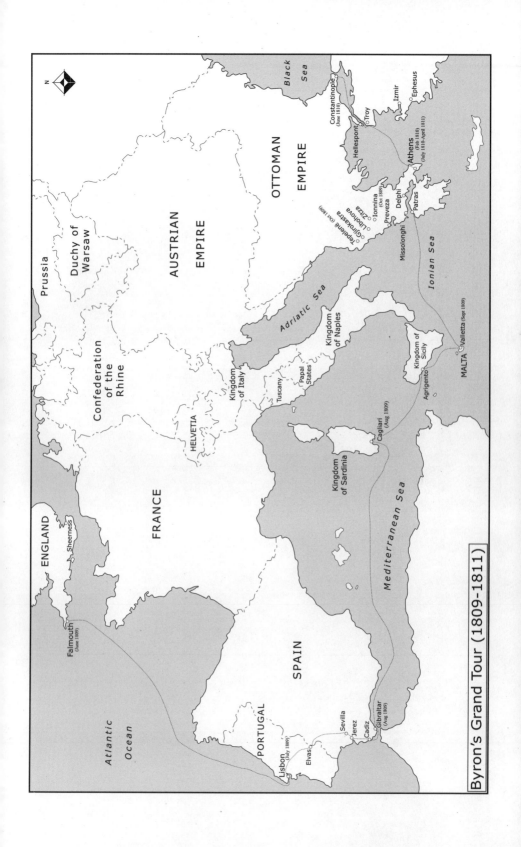

Byron's Grand Tour (1809-1811)

Contents

LORD BYRON, PRE-TOUR

George Gordon Byron, by now the sixth Baron Byron, our Lord Byron, was twenty-one and a half years old when he and his inevitable entourage left London on his Grand Tour on 19 June 1809. Byron being Byron, he did not travel lightly or without style: in tow were his best friend, his valet, the old family retainer, his pageboy, his Farsi translator and eight portmanteaux containing his library, his clothing and costumes, his bedding, his saddles and his shoes, as well as a campaign desk, two army beds and four camp beds. And Byron being Byron, he left for contradictory reasons: pulled by the promise of exotic rites of passage and a literary led yearning for the East, and pushed by the hope that his freewheeling debts would accrue more slowly in less expensive places in which to keep his camp following.

He had been born those twenty-one years earlier in reduced circumstances in lodgings off Cavendish Square, London W1, circumstances reduced by his father's determined wastage of his wives' fortunes. 'Mad Jack' Byron had been a dashing Guards Officer and then the infamous bounder who scandalised London by eloping with Lady Carmarthen to Paris before she could become the Duchess of Leeds. When her fortune, and her life, had been spent he went to Bath determined find a new heiress and duly found one in a *salon de thé*, a Georgian version of Blue Rinse Cruise Lines. There he wooed and married the Scottish heiress who was to become George's mother. He spent so profusely and borrowed so recklessly that by the time George was born he could only visit London to see his wife and son on Sundays, Sundays by English law being the only day that debtors were free from writs and harassment by the bailiffs.

George Byron's mother, Catherine Gordon, the 13th Laird of Gight in her own right, rescued what little her husband had not squandered and repaired with her young son to even lesser circumstances in Aberdeen where George spent his early childhood and schooldays learning the Bible and Latin by rote. In these constrained early days George's only birthright was a club foot, an infliction which brought him bullying at school, physical pain as various physicians tried to force it back into shape in later youth, and tenderness and sympathy from the many men and women attracted to him in later life.

When George was six, on a battlefield at Calvi in Corsica, where Nelson lost an eye, a careless cannonball killed his uncle's grandson, by which circuitous route George became the heir apparent to the Byron title and lands. His uncle, known as 'the Wicked Lord', but in reality better described as 'the Most Batty Eccentric Lord That Ever Lived' was by now 72, and helpfully died four years later. Thus in 1798, at the age of ten, George became Byron and for the first time his life took on some interest, where it would take root and flourish handsomely as legend until his death for the cause of Greek independence twenty-six years later.

Unscrambling the wayward uncle's affairs was not the matter of a moment, as he too had borrowed and loaned and mortgaged and remortgaged without recording exactly what went and came to whom and when, but doing so brought the young peer's family into renewed contact with John Hanson, a lawyer thirty years Byron's senior. For the next ten years Hanson was to become the poet's guide and mentor, his legal guardian and father figure, and he brought Byron into the Hanson family who throughout his remaining youth and adolescence took the awkward young provincial peer under their more sophisticated Kensington wings.

But Hanson could do nothing about the real state of Byron's inheritance: there was Newstead Abbey and Park and over 3,000 adjoining acres, but the park had been denuded of its trees for easy cash, parts of the abbey were roofless and the rest heading towards ruin, and the Rubens, the Titian, the Holbeins and the Canaletto had all long been sold to pay off various debts. There were some potentially highly valuable coal mines in Rochdale, as well as a farm in Wymondham in Norfolk, but on closer examination these were part of an unholy mortgaged mess—a mess still not solved at the time of Byron's death. What must have seemed like a handsome inheritance turned out to be an illusion, but the illusion was all that Byron needed to fuel his largesse. When it came to spending money he was indeed his father's son and his uncle's nephew.

Hanson did manage to arrange a place for Byron at a crammer in Dulwich and then at thirteen one at Harrow, for his mother to be supported by the Civil List, and for the Earl of Carlisle to be his guardian in the House of Lords. At his grammar school in Scotland he had learned to read and write, and to read and read and read, and here he developed his first interest in the Orient. He later wrote that 'Knolles's Turkish History, Cantemir, De Tott, Lady Montagu, Hawkins's translation of Mignot's History of the Turks, Arabian Nights, all travels, or histories, or books upon the East I could meet with, I had read, as well as Rycaut, before I was ten.'

By the time he arrived at Harrow he had already started writing poetry and it was there that he discovered Alexander Pope who was to be such an influence on his poetic values. He continued to read voraciously: Rousseau's *Confessions*, the biographies of Cromwell,

Charles II, Newton, Catherine II and dozens more; books on law, books on philosophy, and poetry, more and more poetry, poetry in French and Latin, poetry in Italian and Greek. He started writing his own poetry, private poetry about the adolescent love for the pretty boys he met in the term and the pretty girls he met in the holidays. But the private poetry remained private, and all his elders agreed his main talent lay in Oratory, a talent displayed with passion and commitment on Speech Days, and a talent that sat well with a future member of the House of Lords.

After Harrow Hanson organised a place for him at Trinity College Cambridge and in the three years there the overweight, gawky and fringed schoolboy became the reassured man, if not yet the Byronic hero, we like to think we know so well today. Yet to his surprise Byron soon became bored and disillusioned with the decadence and sloth around him at Cambridge. He found amusement in his pet bear, Bruin, acquired because the authorities forbade students to keep dogs. Furthermore he did not even study anything in particular; a chap simply didn't. An ancient rite made it unnecessary for the peerage to take exams or even attend lectures, and not too much pressure was applied to the commoners either if they chose to follow the peers' example, the peer group pressure.

What he did learn at Cambridge was to spend money famously, though this was a skill entirely self-taught. He would by now have been aware of his father's profligacy, and although he had barely met his father in person, and certainly not in living memory (his father died, by suicide it was rumoured, in poverty in France when his son was not yet three) they were reunited on the wilder shores of extravagance. Byron had arranged through Hanson an allowance of £500 a year to pay for all his expenses, plus a supplement for a servant, unnamed, and a horse, Oateater, but at the end of just the first term he had spent all that and run up debts of £1,000. He wanted, thought he needed, a carriage, so one he bought. Then the carriage needed horses, so these too he bought. Then the horses needed harnesses, so harnesses he bought. And all these needed stable lads, whom he hired. Byron was simply not interested in money—how it was accrued, from whom it came, to where it was going—in the same way other people are not interested in animal husbandry or Egyptian entomology. When a slice of money ran out one simply acquired some more, a bit like claret or a fresh horse. There seemed to him to be no end of people willing to give it away, although they did call it lending, and often against assets, but lending and assets were just concepts and details in which other people took some strange interest. The present needed funding, and being the present it needed funding now.

Meanwhile he was still reading voraciously and by now writing poetry regularly, and while at Cambridge published three collections, *Fugitive Pieces* in 1806 and *Poems on Various Occasions* and *Hours of Idleness* (his view of day to day life at university) in 1807. He was also thinking of his future. Hanson admired the poems but believed Byron's best talent lay in Oratory, and his best future lay in parliament. Byron himself was by now actively thinking about his travels. The traditional Grand Tour was impossible due to the Napoleonic Wars, but while 'Tis true I cannot enter France; but Germany and the Courts of Berlin, Vienna & Petersburg are still open...'

At Cambridge he also met those who would play a large part in his later life. John Cam Hobhouse, later the distinguished Whig peer Lord Broughton, who accompanied him on the first year of the Grand Tour and who was to be his closest friend; Charles Matthews and Scrope Davies, conveniently rich as well as talented wits and Whigs; William Bankes, 'the father of all mischiefs', who introduced Byron to the work of Walter Scott and who was later to lead such a memorable life of his own; and Francis Hodgson, the brilliant tutor in literature at King's College.

Of all these it is Hobhouse whose life is most intertwined with Byron's. They shared literary aspirations, were both widely read, by nature inquisitive and complemented each other's abilities and efforts on and off the page. Hobhouse needed Byron to give him a wing in the air, and Byron needed Hobhouse to keep a foot on the ground. They both needed Hobhouse's energy. On the Grand Tour it was Hobhouse who recorded the journey fact by fact for his own travel book, *A Journey through Albania, and other Provinces of Turkey*

in Europe and Asia, to Constantinople, during the years 1809 and 1810, and it was Byron who turned the Grand Tour into poetry, *Childe Harold's Pilgrimage.* It is often said their relationship was similar to Dr. Johnson and Boswell, or even Holmes and Watson, but it seems to the writer that it was closer to Errol Flynn and David Niven. Niven noted that the only thing you could rely on with Flynn is that he would always let you down, and loved him not for the being let down but for the friend living in another, his own, world. After Byron's death Hobhouse said: 'I know more of Byron than anyone else and much more than I should wish anybody else to know.' And just as Flynn could rely on Niven's complete discretion, so Byron knew that Hobhouse would never spread a word of his predilections, all of them surely scandalous, if not outright illegal. At Cambridge and later in London he was the greatest enthusiast for Byron's Grand Tour, but had to drop out when he argued with his father and could not pay his part; typically Byron saw this as no obstacle at all, and simply increased his own borrowings so that Hobhouse could be there too.

By early 1808, and now aged twenty, Byron had moved to London and was enjoying the city as young authors and peers sometimes do.

He rimed and dined, debauched and gambled well into the night, every night. His health suffered, severely, and then recovered. His debts grew apace and he tried a less expensive summer spell in Brighton with a pregnant prostitute he had 'redeemed' for a hundred guineas and whom he dressed as a boy, a perfect metaphor for Byronic extravagance, flourish and sexuality. He went back to Cambridge to collect his degree, writing that 'the old beldam gave me my M.A. because she could not avoid it—you know what farce a noble Cantab. must perform.' He went back to Newstead Abbey with his Cambridge friends and committed himself to its restoration—which meant more expense. He was shocked by a hostile critique of his work in the *Edinburgh Review*, and revenge spurred on even more writing into the late nights.

Yet amidst all this restless turmoil a vision of the near future was taking shape. The Grand Tour was being planned in some earnestness; he was already referring to it as the Pilgrimage. He knew that only a major break with his present wastrel life would solve the problems of debts and drift, and lately the problem of confidence in his creativity. In *Childe Harold's Pilgrimage* he wrote that his later ego:

> Stalk'd in joyless reverie,
> And from his native land resolved to go,
> And visit scorching climes beyond the sea;
> With pleasure drugg'd, he almost long'd for woe,
> And e'en for change of scene would seek the shades below.

Beyond the Grand Tour he saw his future as an orator in the House of Lords and as a poet in the world at large. He reasoned, correctly, that Hanson and his mother would be impressed if the Pilgrimage was seen as preparation for his seat in the Lords, and they were both so much of a view about his dissolute debauch that such a redeeming impression was now needed. Byron wrote to Hanson: 'I wish to study India and Asiatic policy and manners... I have no interest in fashionable dissipation, and I am determined to take a wider field than is customary with travellers... a voyage to India will take me six months, and if I had a dozen attendants cannot cost me five hundred pounds; and you will agree with me that a like term of months in England would lead me into four times that expenditure.' One can imagine Hanson exclaiming at this underestimation, for Byron had by now debts of twelve thousand pounds, and Hanson knew, even if Byron would not acknowledge it, that the inheritance would not cover these, let alone any fresh ones unless Newstead itself was sold—and Byron was determined that that would never be.

In early 1809, now of age, and six months before departing on the Grand Tour, Byron was back in London and in a less dissolute frame of mind. He had three projects: to take his seat in the House of Lords, to finish his current volume—to be called *English Bards, and Scotch Reviewers*—and to prepare for the Grand Tour. By March these first two had been accomplished, the first tentatively, the second triumphantly, and all thoughts on the third turned to a May departure.

The destination was now Persia, via the Mediterranean, but the destination was really loosely East. *Realpolitik* played its part: with the continent largely under French control, and with the Mediterranean under British control, it was by sea that he had to tour. There just remained the running problem of money, and the wrangling with Hanson and the usurers continued through the May departure date, until at just the right and last moment Scrope Davies shared a gambling win with his friend, Hanson somehow from someone topped it up, and on 19 June Byron left London for Falmouth accompanied by his entourage, what he called his suite: his friend John Cam Hobhouse, his old retainer Joe Murray, his valet William Fletcher, his pageboy Robert Rushton, and a Farsi-speaking German called Friese, of whom more later. The Grand Tour was on.

Chapter One

FROM FALMOUTH TO LISBON

2–7 JULY 1809 | 28 JUNE – 3 JULY 2008

The Grand Tour and the re-Tour both left their respective bases, London and Beaulieu in Hampshire, on 19 June; the Grand Tour in 1809 and the re-Tour in 2008. Both headed for Falmouth in Cornwall. Byron's packet ship to Lisbon left from there to avoid the long slog west against a prevailing English Channel and the running battle with French privateers who popped in and out of the Brest peninsula. Our much smaller ketch, *Vasco da Gama*, left from there to have the run south to Lisbon in the open seas outside the short-

9

tempered Bay of Biscay. All parties were looking for the mid-voyage full moon nearest the shortest night for the passage south: theirs was on 26 June, ours was on 30 June.

Byron spent nearly two weeks in Falmouth waiting for fair winds. It was more diverting than he expected. By 1810 Falmouth, with its enormous natural harbour, had become an important Royal Navy base in the Napoleonic Wars as well as the main departure point for the General Post Office's packet service. Falmouth Roads was full of frigates and packets, brigantines and fishing skiffs, as well as jolly-boats and tenders ferrying men and supplies back and forth. Ashore were inns and brothels, bakeries and chapels, the fish market and the Customs House. Byron, Hobhouse and Rushton stayed in Wynn's Hotel (where Byron wrote he was 'sadly flea-bitten'), now the site of a Co-op Bank with a fitness centre pounding away above it.

Falmouth is now also a major yachting centre, and would be even more major if they had built enough berths to cope with all the visitors such a wonderful cruising area attracts. *Vasco da Gama* arrived after a pleasant enough jaunt up the English Channel only to find the usual Falmouth bunfight around the marinas as yachts jostle for space and raft up to each other as best they can. Ashore, the streets and lanes meander around much as they would have done two hundred years ago: the inns have multiplied, the brothels have been internetted, the bakeries have gone continental, the chapels are apartments, the fishmarket a Tesco and the Customs House still a Customs House. Only the shiny new, and quite excellent, outpost of the National Maritime Museum tilts a hat towards the spirit level in the builder's toolkit.

Originally the sole purpose of a packet ship was the delivery of parcels of post, so they became known as packets from the French *paquet*. The word 'post' arose because post- was the method of charging: only at the end of its journey could the cost of sending a letter be calculated, that is after it had passed through its various toll stages. Post-payment was the only way of charging, and thus the service became generically known as the 'post', Penny Post, Post Office and so on.

By Byron's time these packet ships also took fare paying passengers, diplomats and couriers to all corners of the world: to Portugal, of course, to the Mediterranean ports of Gibraltar, Malta and Patras, and further afield to the Americas, from Halifax to Buenos Aires and the Caribbean ports in between. The captains and their packets became legends in their time, particularly Captain John Bull, who even more than his fictional namesake came to represent all that was best about sea dogs in general and British sea dogs in particular.

The sense of Destiny in Byron would no doubt have wished for a passage with the already famous Captain Bull on board his packet *Duke of Marlborough*, but instead he found his entourage under the care of Captain Kidd commanding *Princess Elizabeth*. The packets had by then reached a standard eighty-feet-long, three-masted schooner design, built around the ability to outrun privateers, pirates and what is now known as 'friendly fire'—it being a common tactic, a *ruse de guerre*, for both British and French ships to fly each other's colours in order to entrap or escape accordingly. In fact several years later the same Captain Kidd in the same *Princess Elizabeth* was engaged in a running battle with HMS *Acteon*, the resulting damage being paid for by an embarrassed Royal Navy. The packets were lightly armed with half a dozen eight-pounders, plus of course nets to repel boarders—and muskets and pikes for the crew should the repelling not have worked.

The *Princess Elizabeth* carried twenty or so able bodied crew and half a dozen officers, and conditions for the crew between the decks were as abysmal as can be imagined and for the officers above only marginally better. The captain alone had reasonable quarters occupying the stern of the packet with a large window and room to sit as well as sleep. It was a perk of the job that he was able to rent this only acceptable accommodation on board to his more solvent passengers, and he would then mess in with the other officers in the wardroom. Byron, Hobhouse and Rushton would have been in Captain Kidd's quarters, while Murray, Fletcher and Friese were down there trying to swing a cat as steerage in the hammocks. The dozen or so other passengers, British and Portuguese officers and squires and their wives, each had a tiny cabin, two metres by one metre, in which to sleep and a day mess-room to share at other times. For Byron, Hobhouse and Rushton the novelty of a packet voyage in the relative comfort of the captain's quarters would have made their five days on board tolerable, while for Murray, Fletcher and Friese below decks with the tars it was probably considerably less so.

$\sim$

I have introduced you to the cast of characters on the *Princess Elizabeth*, and now let me introduce you to those on board *Vasco da Gama*. It won't take so long as there are only two souls on board: the writer and his wife Gillian, who is also writing a book, *The Literature Lovers Cookbook*. We bought the ketch, a Freedom 40—she looks like two windsurfers mating on a caravel—a few years before when she was called *Phew!* or *Phewie!*—I can't quite remember which, either is too distressing. Well, the name had to go along with pretty much everything else; she was what the broker called 'a project' and what the surveyor called an 'are you sure?' It took as long to name her as it did the children, longer actually, until one lunchtime Gillian sat bolt upright in the bath and proclaimed: 'Vasco da Gama!', and so *Vasco da Gama* she became.

The refit continued without tearing haste with the idea that one day we would down children and tools and sail westabout into the proverbial sunset; the empty nest would become the floating nest. Part by part, cheque by cheque, her health improved and sea-trial by sea-trial, weekend by weekend, she gained strength until one autumn evening wafting sweetly home on a flood tide in the West Solent she looked over her shoulder at the self-same sunset and told us (a little warily it has to be said), 'I think, finally, I am ready.'

One evening that winter I picked up Fiona MacCarthy's *Byron: Life and Legend* (John Murray, 2002). It skipped through his life very jollily in 600 pages, but what stood out was the remarkable adventure of Byron's Grand Tour. The fact that when he left London he was only twenty-one and changing by the chapter, and that Britain's fortunes in the Napoleonic and Peninsular Wars were ebbing and flowing around him on the Grand Tour, made the adventure even more intriguing. By necessity Fiona MacCarthy had to squeeze these two years into fifty pages, but each paragraph cried out for expansion, for explanation. I then read the other biographies mentioned in the Acknowledgments and they too, for reasons of space, had to skip lightly over the Grand Tour and concentrate on the more scandalous and tragic Byron that followed. Somewhere a ten watt light bulb lit: he Grand Toured around the Mediterranean by boat, and we had *Vasco da Gama* on standby; Byron and Hobhouse were two-handed and so were we; they wrote *Childe Harold's Pilgrimage* and *A Journey through Albania, etc.* and Gillian could finish *The Literature Lovers Cookbook* and I could write *Joy Unconfined!* 'Twere as one, upon the hour, agreed, and done!, as my new best friend would have said.

Our preferred sailing regime is coastal or island hopping, so voyaging from A to Z by stopping at B, C, D and E and all the other letters *en route*. Six hours, or thirty or so nautical miles, a day is ideal, but anywhere between twenty and forty miles is fine. We don't have any particular watch system and take it in turns to doze or read or sunbathe or keep a look out. But on ocean passages of less than a week it is helpful to have a third person on board as the overnight three hours on/three hours off watch routine never provides enough sleep; on passages of over a week the mind/body clocks adjust and most voyagers sail two-handed. As this was also our first ocean passage two-handed we wanted an extra crew, and reasoned that the extra crew might as well be an experienced delivery skipper.

As luck would have it we hired Captain Terry Plumtree, an agency captain we had booked in advance and who was to be picked up in Falmouth. We meet on Sunday afternoon in the Chainlocker on Custom House Quay. A brisk northerly with some showers has got up in the morning and most people are inside. He is about sixty, large—in frame more than waist—and florid, and hale and hearty. I wonder if he is going to fit in the forepeak bunk. He looks a bit sozzled, but then so does everyone else. We introduce ourselves.

'Blowing a bit now,' he says cheerfully, 'raining too.' He has a deep lived-in voice with an officer's accent. A packet of Villiger and a rolled up *Sunday Express* lie next to his Guinness on the table. He wears two wedding rings. He bites his nails down to his knuckles.

'At least the wind's behind us. Forecast is not too good for the next 48 hours though. How's your timing?' I ask.

'I need to be in Gib in ten days, for a delivery to Mallorca. Should be OK if we press on tomorrow. Five or six days to Lisso, then I can catch the coaches down to La Linea, walk across the borders, spics permitting.'

'Well I hope the fair weather returns, I don't fancy the Atlantic in this much.'

'Oh, this'll be fine. Any special rules on board?' he asks as he gets up to buy another round.

'We don't drink on passage, but I'll leave that up to you.' He gives me an old fashioned look and toddles off to the bar.

'She'll be right,' he replies as he returns with the next round.

Two hundred years ago Captain Kidd, quite possibly sitting outside this same inn on the same quay, looked up at the western sky and saw the first traces of cirrocumulus. Time to round up the seamen and the slackers. At Wynn's Hotel Byron heard the summons and wrote a letter to his mother.

Dear Mother,

I am about to sail in a few days; probably before this reaches you. Fletcher begged so hard, that I have continued him in my service. If he does not behave well abroad, I will send him back in a transport. I have a German servant who has been in Persia before, Robert and William; they constitute my whole suite. I have letters in plenty, you shall hear from me at the different ports I touch upon; but you must not be alarmed if my letters miscarry. The Continent is in a fine state—an insurrection has broken out at Paris, and the Austrians are beating Buonaparte—the Tyrolese have risen.

As to money matters I am ruined, at least until Rochdale is sold; and if that does not turn out well I shall enter into the Austrian or Russian service—perhaps the Turkish if I like their manners. The world is all before me and I leave England without regret, and without a wish to visit anything it contains, except yourself and your present residence.

Believe me, yours ever sincerely, Byron.

The next day, while at dock waiting to cast off he wrote these playful lines to Francis Hodgson, his tutor at Cambridge:

Huzza! Hodgson, we are going,
Our embargo's off at last;
Favourable breezes blowing
Bend the canvass o'er the mast.
From aloft the signal's streaming,
Hark! the farewell gun is fired,
Women screeching, tars blaspheming,
Tell us that our time's expired.

Fletcher! Murray! Bob! where are you?
Stretch'd along the deck like logs—
Bear a hand, you jolly tar you!
Here's a rope's end for the dogs.
Hobhouse muttering fearful curses,
As the hatchway down he rolls;
Now his breakfast, now his verses,
Vomits forth—and damns our souls.

Now at length we're off for Turkey,
Lord knows when we shall come back!
Breezes foul and tempests murky
May unship us in a crack.
But, since life at most a jest is,
As philosophers allow,
Still to laugh by far the best is,
Then laugh on—as I do now.

Laugh at all things,
Great and small things,
Sick or well, at sea or shore;
While we're quaffing,
Let's have laughing—
Who the devil cares for more?—
Some good wine! and who would lack it,
Ev'n on board the Lisbon Packet?

There are no accounts of Byron's voyage south on the *Princess Elizabeth*, but he must have had a fine, fast passage as he arrived after only five days and four nights on board. Lucky him, but we had a far more torrid time battling through the Western Approaches and down the Portuguese coast.

We left Falmouth on the ebb tide to make some westing, as did half a dozen other yachts similarly bound. After two hours of being bashed about all the others had turned back, presumably to try their luck tomorrow. We sailed on alone into darkening skies and a rising wind. Apart from Terry's timetable there was another dynamic at work: I was paying him by the day, and so wanted to reach 'Lisso' as quickly as possible too. I felt like the captain of HMS *Irony* as we ploughed on in weather we would never have gone out in alone with a skipper we had only taken on to make our passage safer.

One of the many changes we had made in the refit was to sacrifice the lee berths—those berths on either side of the hull where you can rest between watches as she cranks over to one side or the other—for what seemed like a more useful use of the space. On the starboard side was our library, full of cookbooks and Byron literanalia, and on the port side our purpose built horizontal wine cellar—we are connoisseurs of cheap wine. To make matters worse, in our cabin aft the double berth lies across the boat, and at either end of the boat we had put in some rather fancy wicker cupboards. This brilliant idea didn't survive the first night: Gillian's feet went straight through the wicker into my socks on one side and my feet went straight through the wicker to Gillian's sarongs on the other.

As well as a ship's log, Gillian posted a blog so our worried friends and family could keep up with our news. They would hardly have been comforted by her first entry:

> Between midday yesterday and 4 o'clock this morning we came through a horrendous patch of rough sea. I spent the storm in our cabin, working on some counted cross-stitch embroidery to keep my mind off the towering waves and crashing noise. I was excused watch duty as it was stormy, foggy and we were in a busy shipping lane of the English Channel.

It is a truth universally acknowledged that one of the disadvantages of being cold and wet and miserable as you start the night watch is that time puts on its heavy boots and tells you straight that the feet dragging stage hasn't even started yet. From the darkness come harsh movement and harsher noise, the crashing and shrieking of an Atlantic low. In the cockpit, legs braced and wedged in a corner, you see your left self believing the logic that survival is just another storm away and your right self believing the emotion that maybe this time it's not. Searching for the bright side you lift your head up into the gale to look for lights—ships' lights, lighthouses, moonlight, any light. Now time amuses itself with another trick, the slo-mo drench as a new wave, as yet unseen, whisked up by the wind and only lately heard soaks you cold to the skin before you can duck. Now the mind games start. Byron, I thought we were friends, in this together, you on the Tour, me on the re-Tour, not with you swanning around on a moonlit deck, strolling into the captain's cabin whenever the claret glass asks you for a refill, joking with your best friend and your favourite pageboy, especially not with me on the edge of an Atlantic gale, oilskins like a wetsuit, boots squelching and body shivering, afraid and all alone in a heaving cockpit and at the wrong end of a long night of cooling soup and gallows humour.

Storms at sea are seldom dangerous in themselves, save when near land or if the boat is unsound, but they are tiring and boring. You just want them to finish, to give you a rest, so you can change into dry clothes, snatch more than the odd doze, stop being banged around. Terry and I alternated the watch every three hours. At dawn on the second day I emerged for my watch to find him in soaking oilskins, grinning inanely at the horizon and saying 'I do like a good blow.' Yes, quite. Later that day Gillian wrote:

> At about 6 pm I emerged to make some sandwiches as it was too rough to heat up the Shepherd's Pie I had made in Falmouth. On my way back into the cabin, a huge wave broke over the boat, covering the boat and me and filling the aft cabin with water. Fortunately the bed was covered with a sheepskin cover which trapped the water in a puddle and I was able to empty it, change my clothes and get into a dry bed for the night.

The next night was just as bad but in the morning:

> This morning we sailed past a pod of whales. It was a fantastic sight. They were quite near the boat, about ten of them, the largest looked about 20 feet long. They blow a spout of disgusting smelling water into the air then splash around playfully in the waves. We had another squall last night, not as bad as the first storm, but still uncomfortable. The boat was under sail and would first lurch to the left when all the bedding and I would be flung to one end of the bed. Then the boat straightened and went the other way and I would slide to the other side with my legs in the air and the blood rushing to my head. It lasted for about 6 hours until midnight, when the clouds cleared and the sky was black and covered with glistening silver stars.

Gillian's blog for the next day only reads:

> Another storm, 2 rough 2 write!

The following afternoon I looked astern and saw that a whale had eaten my Duogen, our towed generator and source of unlimited free energy. There had been a clean shear with the bracket which held it onto the transom. After a satphone discussion with Duogen it was concluded we must have hit a solid object in the night, but *Vasco da Gama* has a long and determined keel and I thought contact with a container or submarine was unlikely to have gone unnoticed. Then I remembered that that same morning I had woken up to see a whacking great whale cavorting alongside us for a good hour or so. I thought at the time he looked a bit pleased with himself but didn't like to say anything—you don't want to encourage them—and anyway was too upset about the Duogen to ask him if he had mistaken the whirring prop for convenience plankton.

On we ploughed, Terry fortified by his hip flask and cigars and anyway, literally, in his element, Gillian and I making as good a fist of it as we could. The fourth day was quieter but still wild and windy with enormous Atlantic rollers lifting us up and gently dropping us down. But that night another storm arrived.

I went back to the cabin but could not sleep. The banging and crashing, movement and noise made sleep impossible and I felt I should be on standby in case an emergency happened. This lasted through the night, the main difference with the earlier storms being that it was not cold and raining and I had the hatch open and could see stars as we see-sawed up and down. The waves were still huge but the average wind had dropped to 20-25 knots. Everything looked better in daylight and it was actually a fine sunny day. We had entered Portuguese waters at about 1 am, but we were too far out to sea to see any land. The good news is that we have made fantastic progress south and as I write we are nearly in Lisbon.

Two hundred years ago the *Princess Elizabeth* sailed up the Tagus into Lisbon to find one hundred and fifty British ships at anchor and ashore a city devastated. They had arrived in a war-zone. The ships were mostly transports carrying troops to the Peninsular War. Remembering that first impression, and adding lines reflecting his later experience, Byron wrote in *Childe Harold's Pilgrimage*:

What beauties doth Lisboa first unfold!
Her image floating on that noble tide,
Which poets vainly pave with sands of gold,
But now whereon a thousand keels did ride,
Of mighty strength, since Albion was allied,
And to the Lusians did her aid afford,
A nation swoll'n with ignorance and pride,
Who lick, yet loathe, the hand that waves the sword.
To save them from the wrath of Gaul's unsparing lord.

As we shall see, Lisbon was in a particularly sorry way in 1809, not the Grand Tour scene of exotic ribaldry and gaiety which Byron envisaged two years before at Cambridge. But he was *abroad* and the Grand Tour proper would now start.

As for the crew of *Vasco da Gama*, Terry takes his kit bag and hip flask to Gibraltar, texts us that he makes it with loads of time to spare (ha!), Gillian finds a spa, a beautician and a hairdresser and regroups looking ravishing, and the writer wallows awhile in a hot bath, sleeps and dreams of whale revenge. *Vasco* herself can't quite see what all the hoo-ha is about. But we are all *abroad* and the re-Tour proper is about to start.

Chapter Two

PORTUGAL, WAR ALL AROUND

7–24 JULY 1809 | 3–12 JULY 2008

*L*isbon has always tended towards shabby elegant rather than shiny bright, but the Lisbon of 1809 that greeted the Byron entourage found itself at a particularly low ebb. The massive earthquake of 1755 that had reduced its palaces, churches and places of government to rubble still defines the timeline of the city today, and it was then for many a catastrophe in living memory and for all a catastrophe in talking memory.

Portugal had always been one of Europe's poorest countries. The infertile land, sparse population, geographical isolation, feudal society and endless wars with Spain had held it in the Dark Ages until the great discoveries of the sixteenth century had brought it sudden and amazing wealth. But the wealth had been wasted by a series of profligate monarchs on an inbred court and idle diversions. Portugal, with a population of less than a million, could not manage the cost of maintaining its seaborne empire, an extraordinary empire which at its height in the mid-sixteenth century traded from Peru to Japan and two dozen city states and three oceans in between.

By the early nineteenth century Portugal had found itself powerless to resist the persistence of Napoleon Bonaparte and his Imperial Army. At the country's lowest fortunes of 1807, just two years before the *Princess Elizabeth* arrived from Falmouth, the Portuguese royal family, the court and government, fifteen thousand souls in all, boarded all eighty ships of the Portuguese navy and, organised by Admiral Sir Sidney Smith, upped and sailed to the safety of Brazil.

The remnants of the Portuguese forces joined an alliance with Britain and Spain and together fought The Peninsular Wars against France. But for the demoralised Portuguese their allies were cold comfort: the Spanish themselves had been allied to the French in a joint invasion of Portugal two years previously, and they had just been betrayed disgracefully at the Convention of Cintra by the British, led by, among others, the then Lieutenant-General Sir Arthur Wellesley.

The same Wellesley, well on his way to thunderbooting himself to the dukedom of Wellington and in either guise one of Byron's *bêtes noires*, had returned to Lisbon with the British expeditionary force in the spring of 1809, and quickly recaptured Oporto and promised to retake Madrid. When the Byron entourage landed just three months later, on 7 July 1809, Lisbon was in effect a British garrison under the command of General Robert Craufurd, whose Light Brigade had taken part in Sir John Moore's Corunna campaign a few months earlier.

In this war-zone atmosphere Hobhouse never really mucked in with the Portuguese; he found Lisbon 'one hundred years' behind the times. He wasn't sure what appalled him most: the fact that the retreating

French had killed ten thousand of Lisbon's dogs or that by doing so they had also ruined the city's only sanitation system. He made several notes in his journal about the life he and Byron saw:

there is a good police guard of 1,500 horse and foot to prevent disturbances in Lisbon—the police were picked out of the troops by the French, and continued by the English—but there is no *justice*, no punishment but imprisonment except in extraordinary cases, and that may be bought off; convents are supported by begging, and dead bodies are exposed in the churches with a plate on them, and are not buried until sufficient money is collected to pay the priest; the army is recruited by surrounding the public gardens and taking all the persons not married; all the equipages of the nobility have been ordered off for the army, and the articles paid for by paper money worth nothing—the best way for a traveller to buy Portuguese money is in Cheapside, London; the Inquisition is not abolished quite—twenty people lately sent there—to the dungeons under the great square Roccio; the young ecclesiastics affect levity—I saw some monks pulling about a woman in a church close to a woman praying before a shrine; married women, many of them, prostitutes for pay, which they divide with their husbands; avarice is the reigning passion of the Portuguese. Boys well-dressed attend the lobbies of the theatres for the purpose of *branler le pique aux gens polis*. Sanguinetti [their Portuguese guide for the journey to Gibraltar] told us he had seen the thing himself done in the streets—stabbing not so common, but everyone wears a knife—Sanguinetti saw a man killed by a boy of thirteen, in a chandler's shop.

If Byron and Hobhouse disliked all they saw around them, Byron also saw in Portugal one overwhelming advantage: it was *abroad*, and so was he. He wrote ecstatically to Hodgson:

I am very happy here, because I loves oranges, and talks bad Latin to the monks, who understand it, as it is like their own, and I goes into society (with my pocket-pistols), and I swims in the Tagus all across at once, and I rides on an ass or a mule, and swears in Portuguese, and have got a diarrhoea and bites from the mosquitoes. But what of that? Comfort must not be expected by folks that go a pleasuring.

When the Portuguese are pertinacious, I say 'Carracho!', the great oath of the grandees, that very well supplies the place of 'Damme,' and, when dissatisfied with my neighbour, I pronounce him 'Ambra di merdo'. With these two phrases, and a third, 'Avra louro', which signifieth 'Get an ass,' I am universally understood to be a person of degree and a master of languages. How merrily we lives that travellers be!—if we had food and raiment. But, in sober sadness, any thing is better than England, and I am infinitely amused with my pilgrimage as far as it has gone.

In retrospect he was more circumspect about Lisbon; this from *Childe Harold's Pilgrimage:*

> But whoso entereth within this town,
> That sheening far celestial seems to be,
> Disconsolate will wander up and down,
> 'Mid many things unsightly to strange ee,
> For hut and palace show like filthily;
> The dingy denizens are reared in dirt;
> No personage of high or mean degree
> Doth care for cleanness of surtout or shirt,
> Though shent with Egypt's plague, unkempt, unwashed, unhurt.

Byron and Hobhouse notwithstanding, the city still feels behind the times today, but in ways which today's times make important: it takes us two days to find a wi-fi that works, the incoming mobile phone calls keep cutting off just when you press the green button, Lisbon time is a stepping stone to Jamaica time, the 'everybody' who spoke Latin two hundred years ago were as few as the 'everybody' who speaks English today, and the disdain for commercialism is charming unless you want something to be done.

The entourage stayed at the Buenos Ayres Hotel, run by an Englishman called Barnewell, and where Hobhouse records various other English guests, Messrs. Duff, Drummond, Marsden and

Westwood, and where they dined most nights. Sadly there is no Buenos Ayres, or even Buenos Aires, Hotel in Lisbon any more, and the closest to a Barnewell in the Lisbon phone book is Gregorio Barevell. I call him on the off chance of an ancestorship.

'Hello, do you speak English?'

'Que?'

'English, the language. Do you speak it?'

'No, no inglês. Quien és?'

So much for the Barnewell lineage, but Hobhouse recorded that most nights they went to the theatre on the Rua dos Condes to see whatever was on, their favourite being an erotic Spanish revue. Local legend has it that Byron was challenged outside the theatre after the revue by an irate husband who accused the Englishman of spending more time flirting with his wife than watching the revue. There were fisticuffs, from which the amateur boxer Byron emerged the last man standing.

Be that as it may, today, there, right bang in the middle of the Rua dos Condes is the very theatre, albeit a replica rococo version having a bad hair day, but it still puts on a show at 9.30 p.m. every night, even if it is that Mousetrap of musicals, *Jesus Cristo Superstar, spectacular de Tim Rice y Andrew Lloyd Webber*. On its four corners it now has a Hard Rock Café, opposite that and behind a peeling tiled wall and rusty forlorn hanging lantern La Restaurante Chînese, then a bustling table clothed Tandoori Restaurante Indes, and the timeless ceramic and mirrored Parfumeria La Vogue.

Certain that this was the same theatre, I ask the doorman in gestures if I could have a look inside. 'Si,' he shrugs. It is mid-afternoon, and hot. The inside bears no resemblance to the façade. Contracted vandals have smoothed over the ornamental relief with plaster—already cracking—and paint—already peeling. New seats, as pressed together as on a Ryanair flight, stand straight in line not curved in elegance. Fire extinguishers abound. Strip lights are cold lights. A glance up shows three boxes mid way up each side. Byron boxes no doubt, but the doors are locked.

～

After a few days whatever novelties Lisbon on its uppers had to offer had worn thin and Byron and Hobhouse headed off to the more promising uplands of nearby Sintra. Already famous throughout Europe for its fabulous follies and palaces, gardens and aspects, it had the additional attraction for Byron of having seen recent Beckford activity.

William Beckford was an outrageously rich, flamboyant and decadent figure of the late eighteenth and early nineteenth centuries. His wealth came from the family's West Indian sugar plantations, and his decadence found its flavour in flaunting openly with young boys and in his couldn't-care-less attitude to the subsequent scandals. By 1785 even Beckford could not live with the public outrage and was forced into exile; as Byron wrote in an early version of *Childe Harold*:

> How wondrous bright the blooming morn arose
> But thou wert smitten with unhallowed thirst
> Of nameless crime, and thy sad day must close
> To scorn, and Solitude unsought—the worst of woes.

He was also an avid collector, polyglot and sophisticate who bought Gibbon's library in Lausanne and an inquisitive traveller who lived most of his life abroad in splendid palaces, between times seeing the storming of the Bastille. He was also the author of *Vathek, an Arabian Tale*, one of Byron's two favourite books (the other being *Anastasius*, by the artist Thomas Hope), and no doubt his louche and scandalous lifestyle appealed to Byron as well; he called Beckford 'the great Apostle of Pæderasty'. He eventually settled at Fonthill Abbey in Wiltshire, where he indulged his craving for beauty, whether in people or art or landscaping or theatre or architecture. Fonthill now belongs to the National Trust, and Beckford's magnificent antiquarian creations can be seen here and in his own collection in the British Galleries at the Victoria and Albert Museum in London.

Beckford's place of exile in Sintra was the magnificent palace and gardens of Monserrate, and although he had left there ten years before it was Monserrate that Byron and Hobhouse visited first in Sintra.

A few miles west of Sintra, set in several hundred acres of deliberately cultivated English romantic gardens, Monserrate is a monument to English eccentricity. Originally built for the famous Mello e Castro family of Portuguese patricians, it was rented in 1790 by the first of three immensely rich English families who between them loved and expanded it until 1947. Beckford took it for only a short time, from 1794 to 1799, but he spent money on it with a vengeance, creating the Romantic Garden that blooms so fulsomely today, carving a waterfall, a chapel and an India gateway, not to mention a cromlech and lake. In 1856 Monserrate was taken over by the equally eccentric Cook family, whose fortunes came from textiles, and Sir Francis Cook wasted no time in dubbing himself the first Conde de Monserrate; together with Lady Brenda he spent as much on the palace as Beckford had on the gardens. Today Monserrate is a UNESCO World Heritage site.

At Monserrate one sees immediately the attraction it would have held for Byron: not just the Beckford wild excess and extravagance, but the very size and shape of it, the scale of the imagination in concept and reality, the boldness of the ornate interior and with its eastern and oriental themes. Outside as well the rambling romantic landscape with its echoes of English nobility and stability tied in exactly with his own ideas of his destiny both on this Grand Tour and his life as a whole. Ten days earlier he had been in the grey, slate, workaday naval port of Falmouth, ready to leap into the unknown, and now he was already in Beckford's Xanadu with all the east, the real East, awaiting him.

Byron was immediately captivated by the rest of Sintra too, and wrote of it being a place 'Perhaps in every respect the most delightful in Europe', of it having 'Palaces and gardens rising in the midst of rocks, cataracts, and precipices, convents on stupendous heights' and in *Childe Harold* of 'The horrid crags, by toppling convent crown'd'.

> Lo! Cintra's glorious Eden intervenes
> In variegated maze of mount and glen.
> Ah me! what hand can pencil guide, or pen,
> To follow half on which the eye dilates

Through views more dazzling unto mortal ken
Than those whereof such things the bard relates,
Who to the awe-struck world unlocked Elysium's gates?

The horrid crags, by toppling convent crown'd,
The cork-trees hoar that clothe the shaggy steep,
The mountain moss by scorching skies imbrowned,
The sunken glen, whose sunless shrubs must weep,
The tender azure of the unruffled deep,
The orange tints that gild the greenest bough,
The torrents that from cliff to valley leap,
The vine on high, the willow branch below,
Mixed in one mighty scene, with varied beauty glow.

Sintra's best luck today is that it remains fairly inaccessible; it is too far inland for the cruise ship zombies, full size tour coaches cannot make the twisty, branchy climb, there is nowhere close to park a car, and the only way to reach it is by making the effort with public transport. Sintra has tourists, of course, but they tend to be the more committed type, the type who spend time looking at the sights themselves rather than walking around reading about them in their guidebooks.

The site was originally developed from the fifteenth century onwards by rich and courtly Portuguese nobles and merchants escaping the plagues and unpleasantness of the Lisbon summer. In fact Sintra does have the air of a Raj hill station about it, the smell of wood smoke, the sound of stillness, the sight of untold shades of green bathing in the light and shade. The roads and tracks meander up and down through the shrubs and plants and forests, and every turn reveals another palace. There must be more palaces, (proper palaces, not grand old houses) in Sintra than anywhere else on earth. Half of them are deserted, beyond any individual's budget to restore. The lucky ones are government- or UNESCO-run tourist sights, and the really lucky ones, like the breathtaking Palacio de Seteais, which Byron and Hobhouse visited when it belonged to the Marialva family, are being turned into five or more star hotels. And if you should chance to look up, just when you thought Sintra could not be more fanciful, there will be a surprisingly intact eighth-century Moorish castle, with full flags flying from the battlements, to put all the splendour below firmly in its place.

Does Venice meet Darjeeling in Sintra? Yes, with the great advantage that whereas Venice and Darjeeling have become hopelessly overcrowded—Venice by overloads of tourists and Darjeeling by the broad masses from the plains—Sintra remains rather stately, happily old fashioned and slightly disdainful of those that do make the effort to see what Rose Macaulay saw: 'its lush and cool verdures and grandiose battlements on wild hills'.

Byron's other port of call, the Palacio de Seteais, mentioned above and soon to be the Tivoli Palace Seteais Hotel and Country Club, from where the treacherous Convention of Cintra momentarily ending the Peninsular War was dispatched, is a construction site and so I ask the Tourist Office if there are any other Byronobilia in Sintra as Hobhouse doesn't mention anywhere else. 'Yes, of course, he stayed at the Lawrence Hotel. Beckford stayed there too.'

A short walk down the hill, on the right by a small gorge and above a stream stands a newly painted darkish yellow three-storey building with 'Lawrence's Hotel' painted high under the beam. The river rushes past below. In the shade the air is cool, blessed with hyacinths and wood smoke. We are back in the Himalayas again. The door is around the side by the stream and as you reach it a signs say 'Lord Byron stairs'. Just inside, the reception desk is newly decorated too, but in a restrained non-chain hotel way.

'Hello, do you speak English?'

'Yes, of course,' a tall, tightly drawn, close cropped lady from the Low Countries replies.

'I understand that Lord Byron and his colleague John Cam Hobhouse stayed here.'

'Yes, of course,' she agrees 'for ten days in 1809. Let me show you around.' Actually it was for only two days, but it seems churlish to interrupt her flow. 'This is where they had their Tiffin, and he stayed where we now have the Byron Suite. It's full, I'm afraid I cannot show you the room. This is our dining room, his favourite table was by the window looking south. In the library, the Byron Library we call it, is where he and Mr. Hobhouse studied and wrote their diary and poems. Outside, follow me please, is where they went down the stairs, the Byron stairs, to the Byron garden.'

'And William Beckford stayed here too?'

'I don't know about him,' she replies haughtily.

'How old is the hotel?'

'It was built in 1764 and became Lawrence's in 1780. It is the second oldest hotel in the world, after Brown's in London.'

'And why Lawrence's?'

'Nobody knows, but some people say there was a Mrs. Lawrence, a British army widow.'

I've no idea what the hotel was like two hundred years ago but now it is an absolute delight. Instead of the usual large 'coffee shop' seating area there are four small rooms, snugs, set off the main staircase, itself rich dark wide wood. Off one of these snugs there is a library, a small wood panelled room with buttoned armchairs and the smell of old reading. The rooms and meals are unashamedly expensive, yet the usual glitzy trappings of an expensive hotel are missing and not missed. The atmosphere is restrained, discreet, and courteously welcoming; the starter 'Gratinated Goat Cheese Crepe with Tomato Compote and Lime' and main course 'Braised Sword Fish with Sautey Spinaches and Lemon and Caper Sauce' are delicious even at €60 with a carafe of white wine, all served on a pressed white table cloth with full silver service.

They left the fairy tale of Cintra then, as we leave the fairy tale of Sintra now, with the promise to return, albeit the kind of promise one knows one is unlikely to keep.

After two weeks in Portugal Byron had exhausted its diversions and decided it was time for the entourage to set off on the Grand Tour proper. He found a schooner to take Joe Murray, William Fletcher, Friese and most of the baggage to Gibraltar; Hobhouse, Robert Rushton, his Portuguese guide Sanguinetti and he himself would meet them there in a week or so having ridden overland through the Portuguese plains, and skirting the Peninsular War, down to Sevilla and Cadiz in Spain and then on to Gibraltar.

At sparrowfart on Friday 21 July 1809 five horses, three men and a boy left Lisbon and set off east at a good pace across the width of Portugal. Against the intense mid-summer heat they had parasols and weak ale. The staging system was the same as all across Europe: paddocks every ten to fifteen miles provided fresh horses and refreshments for the travellers. Some were towns, most were hamlets. Rushton would inevitably get the smallest horse, the largest would take Byron's luggage and Sanguinetti would take the most rascally of the remainder. They rode long and hard; up every morning just before dawn to travel all day in the saddle and take pot luck with whatever inn they could find wherever dusk found them.

Hobhouse recorded that their first adventure came in Venta Nova, now called Vendas Novas, where they arrived in mid-afternoon on the first day. 'At Venta an old Palace—a thief, supposed a boy, whipped one of Lord Byron's pistols from the holster here—we found it after search under some dung.' The palace at Vendas Novas is now home to the Portuguese Army's 14th Artillery Brigade. In front of the main gates various pieces of rather ancient and scruffy looking artillery are on static display. One hopes NATO does not require too much assistance from the 14th Brigade. Outside the main gate is a red and white striped sentry hut and standing slackly within a gawky looking girl in an oversize, man's, uniform. One can imagine a regimental sergeant major at Aldershot going berserk as he bellows to her, his feet well clear of the ground. Inside all is quiet, as though there is nothing worth guarding anyway.

The next town east was Montemor, Hobhouse's favourite town on the journey and the traveller today could only agree. 'This stage four leagues—to Montemor, very romantic and beautiful scenery, good hard road—dark before we came in through a forest to Montemor. The sides of the road in general very green with aromatic shrubs not hilly nor level—a vast number of crosses, signs of murders, on the side of the way.' The road today is as romantic and green and shrubby—

cork and olive trees in the main—and hillocky as he described it then, except for the crosses which may have been for directions rather than the murder markers he perceived. The road is actually part of the main trunk route, the N4, from Lisbon to the old court's summer capital of Évora, and like all roads in the Portuguese countryside wonderfully wide and empty so that even my rented old 125 c.c. Honda felt it could stretch its legs.

Montemor itself is a lovely old, very old, fortified wall town topped by a magnificent Moorish castle from the ninth century. It is so out of the way that this town which deserves to be dripping with tourists has none at all. But there is a token Tourist Office in one of the old squares, which central casting has placed between a leather shop selling saddles and horse accessories on one side and a very old dusty rusty ironmonger on the other.

I duck my way in and ask the rather scraggy young henna haired young lady if she speaks English.

'That's why I'm here,' she smiles as I try to detect the accent.

'Go on, where's it from?'

'Where's what from?'

'Your accent.'

'Oh me accent, Stoke-on-Trent. You been there, have you?'

'No, unfortunately not. One day I hope to do so. What took you there, and brings you here?'

It turns out that she—Terésa—was from Lisbon and went to Stoke as an au pair; she was there on New Year's Eve as the millennium changed. She met a local lad there and they pooled resources. Then they broke up, she had long since fallen out with her parents, mostly about the shenanigans in Stoke, her grandmother was alone and poorly in Montemor and she came here to look after her and to get over the Stoke episode. As she spoke fluent English she got this job here. She asked me what brought me to Montemor.

'Lord Byron came through here two hundred years ago. Are there many hotels or inns over two hundred years old here?'

'A few, not many. Have you any clues?'

I looked at Hobhouse's notes. 'Two rooms, rather bad to sleep in.'

'Oh that'll be the Recidencial Boas.'

'It's that bad?'

'It's a shitehouse, pardon me French. Been like that for years.'

I invite her along. She doesn't bother to lock up, just leaves the door ajar. We wander through Montemor's medieval mazes and alleys with cobbles below, peeling walls and the smell of small livestock around us, walking from bright hot sunlight to deep dark shadows and back again. In a particularly attractive old square is a run down three-storey shallow light green—hospital green—building at the end. Recidencial Boas, except the 's' has fallen off Boas. Even two hundred years ago the square would have looked two hundred years old.

Terésa orders coffees and cakes. The coffee is only so-so warm and the cake nondescript. UK Health & Safety would have a fit, not least at the state of the crone who serves us. I try to imagine our party of four in their two rooms upstairs. I cannot, I don't know why, it just didn't seem like the place, although it was clearly *like* the place. I pay, it is at least cheap. Hobhouse noticed that he 'could not judge of the price because everything paid by Sanguinetti and profusely, but not so very cheap as expected.' No doubt Sanguinetti was taking advantage of his master's total lack of interest in anything to do with money. I thank Téresa, we kiss each other's cheeks goodbye. I offer to give my regards to Stoke-on-Trent, she advises me not to bother. 'The bastard (bass-ted)'.

Byron's entourage set off early again the following morning and stopped at Arraiolos. 'A good English kind of road, part very pretty, with some signs of cultivation—good horses—got a good breakfast of eggs, wine, and a little bad fruit at Arryolos, where the inn is a very neat cottage indeed. Waited upon by two neat women—(wrote this at Arryolos Castle Moorish, eleven o'clock a.m.).' Arraiolos is quite delightful, Montemor in miniature. There is just one small and very ancient square in the centre. And there, right there, on one side of the small and very ancient square is an inn which is 'a very neat cottage indeed'. This is undoubtedly the place they took their breakfast, the description is perfect, there can be no other. Outside are a few tables with people enjoying their coffee and chatting under the parasols.

Head bowed I enter the cottage/inn, now a café, half expecting to be waited upon by Hobhouse's two neat women. A charming elderly man, the owner it seems, waits on me instead. He doesn't speak English, nor I Portuguese, but there's nothing much to say anyway; the enjoyment comes from soaking up the moment and not even bothering with the 'eggs, wine, and a little bad fruit'.

Breakfasted and back in their saddles the entourage set off on the last leg of the journey to Spain. They rode through Venta de Duque, now called Vimieiro, site of the battle that led to the Convention of Cintra, and after several more hours across barren scrubland in the intense summer heat of the Portuguese plains they arrived in Estremoz.

Hobhouse recorded that 'Estremoz is a fortified walled town but not much attended to now,' and the description still holds well today. It's hard to see why it isn't better attended to; the Moors laid it out around a large open square and fortified a substantial area around and beyond, and the Portuguese then surrounded the square with attractive churches and monasteries. Hobhouse reported that there were two convents—an Iberian convent can equally well be a monastery—as well. One is now the town's museum and the other the church of St. Affonso. There is still a monastery, the Igreja dos Congregados.

They rode the next three hours to Elvas, and Hobhouse's recommendation for future travellers was to stay at Estremoz instead 'as Elvas is so bad.' They arrived in moonlight to find the town gates shutting and then had a big brouhaha getting them opened. Even worse there was 'nothing to eat at the inn—wine not allowed to be sold at inns—beds on the floor—accommodation very bad—ten at night went to bed after eating fowls just killed and boiled—which we should not have had but for Sanguinetti. N.B. it is perfectly necessary to have a man with you who can cook a little, as when there is anything to eat the people always spoil it with stinking oil and salt butter. Six dollars paid at this wretched inn next morning—very dear.' No doubt another side deal done by the guide/cook Sanguinetti.

Elvas today is remarkable only for its originality, on the way to nowhere except the border with Spain, and its significance as a staging post in the past has now been overtaken by faster means of travel. One can imagine it being abandoned altogether soon and in two thousand years time of interest only to archaeologists.

On the road again they saw Spain for the first time in the early afternoon of 24 July, and then bathed in the River Caia, which was and is the frontier. Byron was expecting the border to be separated by a proper river which he could swim across but had to make do with paddling across what is little more than a stream. They arrived at Badajoz at five and showed their passports 'to a fellow who could not read.' For the evening they 'got some boiled chickens, tolerable room and beds, and had some tunes from Sanguinetti's flute—saw a great many eating out of one bowl (as usual).' The Grand Tour had left behind Portugal and was now headed for Cadiz, Seville and Gibraltar, where they were eventually to be reunited with Murray, Fletcher, Friese, and the endless luggages.

Chapter Three

SPAIN, HEADING SOUTH

24 JULY – 3 AUGUST 1809 | 7–13 JANUARY 2009

*N*ow that he was in Spain Byron immediately noticed the increased military activity. The Battle of Talavera, on the road connecting Madrid and Lisbon and one of the bloodiest in the Peninsular Wars, was being fought barely one hundred miles to their north-east. It would be claimed as an allied victory, but one won at a terrible cost of lives. Within a few miles an officer from the Junta in Seville demanded their horses, which Hobhouse noted firmly 'he did not get.'

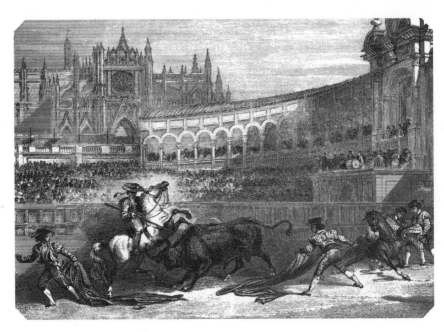

Yet by and large the entourage felt safe enough. They were skirting around the southern edges of the war and heading south, away from it. Their papers were in order; they were Spain's allies; the roads were good and progress was fast. Byron wrote that 'I had orders from the government, and every possible accommodation on the road, as an English nobleman, in an English uniform, is a very respectable personage in Spain at present. The horses are remarkably good, and the roads very far superior to the best English roads, without the smallest toll or turnpike. You will suppose this when I rode post to Seville, in four days, through this parching country in the midst of summer, without fatigue or annoyance.'

Their first stop was at Monesterio, half way between the border and Seville. Hobhouse saw the town held '2,000 patriot troops, of a decent appearance' and saw 'two French prisoners and a Spanish spy going to be hanged at Seville.' He entered 'through a barren plain, except the entrance into the town, where are hills covered with trees and a spot looking like a park.' The approach to Monesterio is exactly as described two hundred years ago, and the contrast between the flat open plains and the sudden hilly parkland reminds one of Lyallpur in northern Punjab.

Today there is no part of the town that is obviously two hundred years old. There is one old *pension*, the Pension Fenoh. Maybe they stayed there, nobody knows. Anyway it is closed, maybe for the winter, maybe forever. Even the token Tourist Office is closed when it should be open, as if it too has given up the struggle. Out and about old men sit and natter, about what new one cannot imagine. Young men loiter and chew, jeans around hips, underpants around waist. Old women wear black and stoop and nod. Young women must have fled or joined a purdah cult. Dogs lie across the pavement. Cars and buses going anywhere take the bypass. Nothing seems to smell of anything very much.

They rose early the next morning and headed south through Santa Olalla, 'a few houses' then, a few more today, not much else. The old road they would have taken now starts to rise with the Sierra Morena, and you can still see peasants being as beastly to donkeys now as they were then. On the higher ground were some artillery batteries ready to repel the French. *Childe Harold* saw:

> At every turn Morena's dusky height
> Sustains aloft the battery's iron load;
> And, far as mortal eye can compass sight,
> The mountain-howitzer, the broken road,
> The bristling palisade, the fosse o'erflowed,
> The stationed bands, the never-vacant watch,
> The magazine in rocky durance stowed,
> The holstered steed beneath the shed of thatch,
> The ball-piled pyramid, the ever-blazing match.
> Portend the deeds to come:

We are now in the area 'in the road between Monesterio and Seville', as Byron put it nine years later, which made such an impression on him that he used it as the prose preface for *Don Juan*.

The Reader is requested to suppose, by a like exertion of Imagination, that the following epic Narrative is told by a Spanish Gentleman in a village in the Sierra Morena in the road between Monesterio and Seville, sitting at the door of a Posada, and with the Curate of the hamlet on his right hand, a Segar in his mouth, a Jug of Malaga, or perhaps 'right Sherris,' before him on a small table containing the relics of an Olla Podrida: the time, Sunset: at some distance, a group of black-eyed peasantry are dancing to the sound of flute of a Portuguese servant belonging to two foreign travellers, who have, an hour ago, dismounted from their horses to spend the night on their way to the Capital of Andalusia. Of these, one is attending to the story; and the other, having sauntered further, is watching the beautiful movements of a tall peasant Girl, whose whole Soul is in her eyes and her heart in the dance, of which she is the Magnet to ten thousand feelings that vibrate with her own. Not far off a knot of French prisoners are contending with each other, at the grated lattice of their temporary confinement, for a view of the twilight festival. The two foremost are a couple of hussars, one of whom has a bandage on his forehead yet stained with the blood of a Sabre cut, received in the recent skirmish which deprived him of his lawless freedom: his eyes sparkle in unison, and his fingers beat time against the bars of his prison to the sound of a Fandango which is fleeting before him.

The 'village' is El Ronquillo, and this is surely where he and Hobhouse (the 'two foreign travellers') 'dismounted from their horses to spend the night on their way to the Capital of Andalusia.' There is 'a Posada', or inn, at the head of a cobblestone plaza. A *capilla* lies next door to the inn, convenient for 'the Curate'. The inn serves *fino*, 'right Sherris', if no longer 'jugs of Malaga' but then nobody does these days. For *tapas* they serve *guisado* or stew, descended from 'Olla Podrida'. Hobhouse is the one 'attending to the story'; and Byron 'the other, having sauntered further, is watching the beautiful movements of a tall peasant Girl.' (Funny that, wouldn't have thought it of him.) The French prisoners could easily have been nearby, and we know from Hobhouse that the night before, in Monesterio, 'Sanguinetti played his flute to a Fandango tune.'

Later that day they passed through Guillena, which they mentioned only in passing. It is now half a nondescript and dusty industrial overflow of Seville and half a dormitory town, except it is hard to imagine anyone actually wanting to work or sleep there. Even the (civil) war memorial shows little enthusiasm for its surroundings. But then there is the promise of Seville; if only we English speakers said Sevilla as it should be said. In fact, if you don't mind, from now on I will.

Byron called Sevilla 'a fine city' and 'a city of women and oranges' and neither of these has changed in the interim. I imagine he meant the quantity of women rather than the quality; not, to add immediately, that there is anything wrong with the quality, but in an age where women elsewhere were largely confined to the house one cannot imagine the feisty *Sevillanas* putting up with that sort of thing. As for the oranges: yes, the *avenidas* are indeed lined by the orangest oranges, as abundant as the women, somehow supported by the spindliest spindles masquerading as trunks.

After Lisbon the clean streets and summer awnings of this most civilised of cities pleased Byron enormously. His delight increased when he met Augustina, the 'Maid of Saragossa', the heroine of the Peninsular War who had single-handedly loaded and fired the guns at Saragossa (Zaragoza) after all her comrades had been killed. For Byron she epitomised all that was best in Spanish women: soft and alluring yet proud and steely. He elevated her to define all Spanish women:

> Yet are Spain's maids no race of Amazons,
> But form'd for all the witching arts of love:
> Though thus in arms they emulate her sons,
> And in the horrid phalanx dare to move,
> 'Tis but the tender fierceness of the dove
> Pecking the hand that hovers o'er her mate.

Byron loved Sevilla, and later even made *Don Juan* a *Sevillano*.

Apart from the women and oranges I was looking forward to meeting my collaborator Dr. Simon Hashtan. We intermet on the internet. I was researching Byron in Spain and he had been researching his family history. His task was longer, worthier than mine. A Sephardic Jew, his family had been kicked out of Spain by Ferdinand and Isabella in 1492. After what can only be thought of as biblical wanderings his particular Diaspora had fetched up in South Africa where he studied music. Now about seventy, he is still a performing classical violinist. He became a widower two years ago, was without issue and alone and decided to visit Sevilla to delve into what he could of his own and his people's ancestry. He fell in love with the city and with no good reason to go home forgave Ferdinand and Isabella and has stayed here ever since. He was brought up speaking Ladino, a Judaeo-Spanish language derived from Latin, and one which when he arrived enabled him to understand nearly all Spanish, and for the Spanish to understand 'less than half' of what he said in return. Two years later he is fluent.

He is also, and the reason that we met on the internet, a Byron enthusiast. I had sent him Hobhouse's notes on Sevilla and he had agreed to delve into the city's archives in the same way he had delved into his own. The problem is the Spanish preoccupation with place names and their uncontrollable habit of changing them. But given time and patience old maps reveal where what once was was and where what once was now is. We arranged to meet in the lobby of the Hotel Alfonso XIII.

The tiny and ancient Simon comes bundling over. His firm handshake and deep voice seem to belong to someone else, someone larger and younger. We retreat to the Café Floriana for coffee. He produces page after page of yellow pad notes. I feel guilty about all his research in Byron's cause. He won't allow an apology.

In July 1809 Sevilla was the headquarters of the Spanish Junta and its population of thirty thousand had been swollen by a further seventy thousand soldiers, officers and the other camp followers of war. The only accommodation was with families taking in guests and so Byron, Hobhouse, Rushton and Sanguinetti found themselves lodging with Josefa Beltrán and her younger sister at Callea de las Cruzes 19. All four guests shared a room; not a solution of which Byron would have approved.

We leave the Café Floriana in search of the Beltrán lodgings and head into the heart of the old city. The streets narrow and the cobbles grow cobblier with every turn. There are lots of turns. 'And now right just here,' says Simon.

I look up and see the sign for Calle Fabiola. 'This is, well was, Callea de las Cruzes,' Simon points down the alley which funnels into a passage barely wide enough to take a mule. There is no pavement. Behind us we hear an angry red scooter echoing our way. We press ourselves against a dusty wall and survive the attack; eardrums take a little longer.

The house is disappointingly dilapidated. In fact it is boarded up, declared unfit for habitation by either the local council or a property developer. Like the alley in which it lies it is tiny. There are three floors, but the top one seems to have been added more recently. There are windows to the left and right; presumably our foursome snuggled up in one of the rooms up there. The number '19' can be seen clearly, if fadedly, above the lintel.

A lock of Josefa's hair—rich, brown and curly by description—is still with us. Here's how: Josefa took a shine to Byron and invited him to her bed 'at two o'clock' (a.m. or p.m. is not known). For once in his life he declined, probably because Robert Rushton was in the same room if not the same bed. As they left she declared her undying love and gave him a lock of her hair, which is now in the John Murray archives. As Byron told his mother: 'We lodged in the house of two Spanish unmarried ladies. They are women of character, and the eldest a fine woman, the youngest pretty, but not so good a figure as Donna Josefa. The eldest honoured your *unworthy* son with very particular attention, embracing him with great tenderness at parting (I was there but three days), after cutting off a lock of his hair, and presenting him with one of her own, about three feet in length, which I send, and beg you will retain till my return. Her last words were "Adieu, you pretty fellow! You please me much." She offered me a share of her apartment, which my *virtue* induced me to decline.'

There was no food at number 19 so they ate, much to Hobhouse's disgust, at the '3 Kings' in Calle Franca.

'And you found the "3 Kings", *Tres Reyes*, in Calle Franca?' I ask Simon. 'Is that far?'

'Sígame!' says Simon with a flourish.

'Lead on McDuff,' I misquote.

We turn left and right, right and left, in quick succession and find a wider alley, a street—a pedestrian street, thank heavens—called Calle Francos. Simon declares this to have been Calle Franca. Towards the cathedral end of Calle Francos the street narrows past some spruced up yet charming neo-rococo shops: there is Casa Rodriguez selling 'Articulos Religiosos, Loli Vera, Diseñadora de Moda Flamenca selling flamenco frocks, Corseteria Peque selling corsets and Cordoneria Alba selling cordons. The colours are deep and dark in shades of blue and red. If there is such a thing as neo-medieval this must be the epicentre. As the road widens and twists right all of a sudden there are laughing tables of lunchers under parasols.

'Esto es Los Tres Reyes, señor,' Simon announces. Hobhouse's '3 Kings' has now become the Bar Restaurante Baco, and very smart it is too. They've added a portico and painted it bright yellow. Above the door a sign says MDCCLXXXII but it seems to have been added later, although that would fit in with it being the Tres Reyes. They have brasseried the interior, all varnish and brass and mirrors and bottles. In a side room where Hobhouse 'passed through the coffee room and observed a little smoking apparatus on each table' there is now a beautiful tiled private dining room, with a sign of a local Ceramica dated 1895.

It seems the least I can do to buy Simon lunch, so we lunch there and then. From his notes Simon reads: 'We went to the 3 Kings for lunch—dined on two plates of nasty pork, two meagre fowls, and dirty chops dressed in the most greasy fashion, with a poultice pudding. For this, with two bottles of good red Catalonian wine, four dollars.'

'Sounds like Hobhouse,' I reply, 'I'm sure we will do better.' We do, albeit for €35 rather than four dollars.

Like Byron and Hobhouse we spend the afternoon in the cathedral, after St. Peter's in Rome and St. Paul's in London the third largest in the world, and the world's largest Gothic church. It is as magnificent as one might hope, and only experience reveals its depth and wonder. As the poet himself said, 'Seville is a fine town; but damn description, it is always disgusting.' Byron was particularly moved by the 270-foot high Giralda with the huge statue of Faith on top of its minaret tower. Hobhouse climbed, presumably alone, to 'the highest gallery of Seville Cathedral where I wrote this.' As we had spent all day stalking him I'm sure he appreciates that I am writing this here too, most likely on the same table in the far north corner, a table which seems to have been here forever.

~

After thanking and bidding farewell to Simon the next morning, and assuring him that he had not joined some obscure footsteps cult, I set off for Utrera, where the entourage spent the night of 28 July. The town impressed them then as it would anyone now. They stayed at the Golden Lion Inn but the Posada León de Oro is no more and no one knows anything about it. Utrera is indeed a pleasant enough and unpretentious Andalusian town, but its purpose as the half-way point between Sevilla and Jerez and Cadiz has been superseded by the Autovia AP4-E5.

They left Utrera at first light in order to reach Cadiz by nightfall and to leave enough time for a long and liquid lunch en route. This was to be hosted by a distant Byron relative, James Gordon, whose family were Aberdeenshire Gordons as was Byron's mother, Catherine. The Gordons of Jerez, as they came to be known, also hosted a remarkable recent story and subsequent dynasty.

The dynasty was started by Arthur Gordon, who fearing the coming persecution of Catholics fled Scotland after the Battle of Culloden. He arrived in southern Spain in 1754 at the age of 25. He worked his way up through the wine business, buying vineyards and experimenting with new production techniques. He started his own bodega in 1787 at the age of 58. Within seven years the business was such that he imported his nephew James from Scotland to help him run it and then take it over. It was with this young James Gordon, only slightly older than himself, that Byron took lunch in the bodega Las Atarazanas, now Plaza San Andrés 7, in Jerez.

The sherry trade was established in England after Sir Francis Drake 'borrowed' 3,000 butts of sherry wine in a raid on Cadiz. The butts (a butt being a 500-litre barrel) were opened in London to great acclaim and quenching of thirst. Soon merchants were trading and it was only natural that they would later want to also control the means of production, the vineyards and bodegas. Thus, led by the Gordons, was started the great British occupation of the vineyards of Andalusia and the bodegas of Jerez, which at its peak boasted such other famous families and brands as Osborne, Sandeman, Croft, Garvey, Terry, Williams and Harvey.

Byron wrote that 'At Xeres [i.e. Jerez], where the sherry we drink is made, I met a great merchant—a Mr. Gordon of Scotland—who was extremely polite, and favoured me with the inspection of his vaults and cellars, so that I quaffed at the fountainhead.'

It was with these very words that Mauricio González Gordon, the sixth Marqués de Bonanza, James Gordon's great great grandson greets me at the bodega. 'We are particularly fond of that expression of young Byron's "quaffed at the fountainhead". Let me show you our archives, and then let's have our own tour of the vaults and cellars. I can also assure you like my many greats grandfather I am also extremely polite.'

Polite is far too modest a word to describe the hospitality they showed me that day for my own research into Byron's liquid lunch in Jerez. In the archives I learnt that through various marriages and mergers the family name became Gonzales Gordon and the company name became Gonzales Byass, most famously makers of Tio Pepe. Queen Isabel II bestowed the title of Marqués de Bonanza on the head of the family in 1860 after the family gave up some of its land in Bonanza for a field hospital. The English version of Bonanza has come to mean good fortune or windfall but it is actually the name of a Spanish port at the mouth of the Rio Guadalquivir up to Sevilla. Christopher Columbus and the New World galleons actually left from Bonanza rather than Sevilla, so when they returned laden with gold all might be forgiven for shouting 'Bonanza!'

After the vaults and cellars, and some sampling thereof, we repaired to the family home for lunch. The house is finely assembled in the Spanish grandee style, each piece austere within itself, plentifully gathered together without being overcrowded. Each room sets its own scene: the hall formal, stone floored, bare walled, rather forbidding; the drawing room with dark landscapes on white walls—for comfort modern sofas in one half, for receiving on No. 14 chairs in the other; the dining room, parquet floor, oblong and pastel with sombre portraits around a deeply polished refectory table and two dozen Charles II chairs. We sit in the middle six, the Marquésa, Milagra, on my left, their daughter-in-law Cristina on my right, with the Marqués opposite, his son Mauricio (so James's great great great grandson) on his right side and his daughter Bibiana on his left.

We talk about the Gordon dynasty. Everyone speaks perfect English, even at times to each other. The Marqués is a very sprightly eighty-five years old and officially retired, although it is hard to see any evidence of that. The younger Mauricio is now the chief executive and has the hope that his son, Pedro, now at a prep school in Suffolk, will one day take over the bodegas.

With the roast beef the butler pours a 1994 Beronia Gran Reserva from the family's vineyard in La Rioja. Quaffing at the fountainhead continues apace. There are about one thousand Gordons in Spain; everyone is cousin him and cousin her. I have actually spoken to two of them: cousin Alvaro who lives in Switzerland and who now owns Las Atarazanas where Byron and Hobhouse lunched with today's forebears, and cousin Alfonso who lives in Madrid and is the family archivist, and is my introduction to today's generosity. Every now and then groups of them dust off the kilts and reunite at Huntley Castle, near to the original family fountainhead of Wardhouse Castle, a hundred years ago the honeymoon spot for the king and queen of Spain but now in sadness neglected by the Scottish chapter of the clan.

The bodega also makes brandy, and after lunch we sample the Lepanto Gran Reserva sherry brandy. Hobhouse wrote that they enjoyed 'two bottles of most capital Sherry given us by Mr Gordon.' That was probably the same thirty-year-old Nóe that we enjoy next too. It is becoming more and more of a privilege to be carrying on the conversation and quaffing tradition with such a splendid, sophisticated and hospitable family that the afternoon soon becomes evening and with a borrowed book, *Lord Byron's Iberian Pilgrimage*, in one hand and the book *Sherry* written by the Marqués's father in the other, I feel it is time to stagger outwards if not upwards.

As I stumble across the threshold doing my best Buster Keaton impersonation I think I tell the Marqués that when I'm reincarnated I'd like to be a Spanish grandee who owns his own bodega and is *jefe* of a most extended family. To have his easy grace and natural manners would be no bad thing either, but I think that occurs to me on the Autovia to Cadiz just before I narrowly miss the police car coming in the opposite direction. Or maybe that was the absinthe from my hip flask.

Somehow or other Byron and Hobhouse and the writer all found Cadiz. Byron and Hobhouse rode as far as Puerto, now El Puerto de Santa Maria, and were sailed or rowed over in an hour to the bastion of Cadiz, sitting then on its isthmus of sand, now motorwayed, from the mainland. Hobhouse noted that there was 'great bustle at Puerto, pretty scene.' No more I'm afraid, El Puerto is now a container port. But for Byron then, and the writer now, the citadel of Cadiz more than compensates.

They 'went to Bailly's Hotel, where well served—the bog through a scullery at the top of the house with a suffocating vapour and many black beetles.' Bailly's was on the Calle de Piedro Conde, now the Calle de San Francisco, and as far as can be determined from a photocopy of a photocopy of a map from the Museo de Cadiz is now a block of offices above a KFC. The KFC was *not* intruded upon, even in the interests of research. Instead of Bailly's there is the Hotel Las Cortes de Cadiz, a little further along San Francisco. Very well served it is too, with the bog en-suite and without the suffocating vapours and or any black beetles.

While Hobhouse was busy with his notes and errands, meeting General Doyle, Don Diego Duff (the English Consul), Lord Jocelyn, the Earl of Roden, Henry Wellesley (one of Wellington's endless brothers), Mr. Terry (from the Terry bodega) and the retired Arthur Gordon (James's uncle and the Gordon & Co. founder) Byron was falling in love with Cadiz in general and the female half of its population in particular.

As he told the world: 'Cadiz, sweet Cadiz! It is the first spot in the creation. The beauty of its streets and mansions is only excelled by the loveliness of its inhabitants. For, with all national prejudice, I must confess the women of Cadiz are as far superior to the English women in beauty... —the most delightful town I ever beheld... [It is] full of the finest women in Spain, the Cadiz belles being the Lancashire witches of their land.' There was more: 'Fair Cadiz, rising o'er the dark blue sea!' 'Ah, Vice, how soft are thy voluptuous ways!' 'All sunny land of love!' 'Although her eye be not of blue/Nor fair her locks like English lasses/How far its won expressive hue/The languid azure eye surpasses!'

One could say Cadiz brought out the exclamation mark in him. Funnily enough 'The Girl of Cadiz' (from which the last quote is taken) was originally written for canto I of *Childe Harold's Pilgrimage*, but didn't make the cut and wasn't published until eight years after his death.

Meanwhile Hobhouse was taking rather a dim view of Byron in full flirt, harrumphing that his companion had become 'a little mad and apt to fall in love'. The final straw was the opera—which one is unrecorded but right there and then one presumes that *Don Giovanni* would have been Hobhouse's choice if it were his to make. Byron took up the story in a letter to his mother:

> I sat in the box at the opera with Admiral Cordova's family; he is the commander whom Lord St. Vincent defeated in 1797, and has an aged wife and a fine daughter, Sennorita Cordova. The girl is very pretty, in the Spanish style; in my opinion, by no means inferior to the English in charms, and certainly superior in fascination. Long black hair, dark languishing eyes, clear olive complexions, and forms more graceful in motion than can be conceived by an Englishman used to the drowsy, listless air of his countrywomen, added to the most becoming dress, and, at the same time, the most decent in the world, render a Spanish beauty irresistible. Miss Cordova and her little brother understood a little French, and, after regretting my ignorance of the Spanish, she proposed to become my preceptress in that language. I could only reply by a low bow, and express my regret that I quitted Cadiz too soon to permit me to make the progress which would doubtless attend my studies under so charming a directress. I was standing at the back of the box, which resembles our Opera boxes, (the theatre is large and finely decorated, the music admirable,) in the manner which Englishmen generally adopt, for fear of incommoding the ladies in front, when this fair Spaniard dispossessed an old woman (an aunt or a duenna) of her chair, and commanded me to be seated next herself, at a tolerable distance from her mamma. At the close of the performance I withdrew, and was lounging with a party of men in the passage, when,—en passant,—the lady turned round and called me, and I had the honour of attending her to the admiral's mansion. I have an invitation on my return to Cadiz, which I shall accept if I repass through the country on my return from Asia.

Hobhouse didn't know what he missed; he went off in a huff and instead of chatting up a 'sennorita' at the opera visited a *puta* in a brothel and promptly picked up an STD for his troubles.

Unfortunately the opera house is no more; likewise the bullring at Plaza de las Galeras in El Puerto, where they saw the obligatory bullfight, which is now part of the city park. On the day of the bullfight, 30 July 1809, they took their places in the governor's box. The event had a huge effect on the vegetarian Byron, who devoted eleven stanzas to it in *Childe Harold's Pilgrimage*—more than to any other event. The stanzas are full of irony against this 'ungentle sport' and about Spanish ways of spending Sundays: 'soon as the matin bell proclaimeth nine/Thy saint adorers count the rosary... then to the crowded circus forth they fare/Young, old, high, low at once the same diversion share.' Hobhouse noted dryly only that 'Four horses killed by one black bull (a priest's).' The travel writer Sir John Carr wrote that 'the death of one or two horses completely satisfied their curiosity. They looked pale and shuddered as even the young ladies continued their applause as another horse fell bleeding to the ground. One bull killed four horses off his own horns. He was saved by acclamations, which were redoubled when it was known he belonged to a priest. An Englishman who can be much pleased with seeing two men beat each other to pieces, cannot bear to look at a horse galloping around in an arena with his bowels trailing on the ground, and turns from the spectacle and the spectators in horror and disgust.'

They skulked back to Bailly's for their last dinner. No revelries were reported; maybe the bullfight had dampened their spirits. By now the HMS *Hyperion* under Captain Brodie was ready to leave Cadiz for Gibraltar. Byron and Hobhouse had booked their passage. It was time for the entourage to leave, time to enter the Mediterranean and head east and onto the major part of the Grand Tour. As Don Juan would later say when 'quitting Cadiz':

> 'Farewell, my Spain! A long farewell!' he cried,
> 'Perhaps I may visit thee no more
> But die, as many an exiled heart hath died,
> Of its own thirst to see again thy shore:...'

Chapter Four

GIBRALTAR, GOING NOWHERE

4–15 AUGUST 1809 | 16–23 JULY 2008

*Y*e gods, but Gibraltar be a dump; 'twas a dump when Byron and Hobhouse arrived there on HMS *Hyperion* from Cadiz on 4 August 1809 to start the Mediterranean part of their Grand Tour, it still is a dump when the Strathcarrons arrive there on *Vasco da Gama* from Lisbon on 16 July 2008, and would seem to be doomed to dumpdom forever and beyond.

'The dirtiest most detestable spot,' Byron remembered it, and it is hard to see now why he was so enthusiastic. The purpose of the

Gibraltar of 1809 was wholly military; the purpose of it now less clear. Then the Peninsular War was fully joined, and although the traditional Gibraltarian enemy, Spain, and Britain were allied against France, and although Nelson had made the Mediterranean safe for British shipping, Gibraltar was a place of high military activity if not actual military danger.

In fact by 1809 the Peninsular War had been a fruitful experience for Gibraltar. By the end of 1806 all the European powers had come under Napoleon's sway, either by direct occupation or forced alliance, except for Portugal and her old ally Britain. To deal with Portugal Napoleon planned a military invasion in alliance with Spain; they expected little opposition and would divide Portugal up between them. To deal with Britain Napoleon planned its bankruptcy and so devised the 'Continental System' whereby none of the countries under his control would be allowed to trade with Britain, and all British ships in these countries' ports were to be seized immediately. Britain retaliated immediately by using her sea power to blockade Napoleon's ports. The scene was set to see who would break first: Britain and her economy, the continental Europeans who would be unable to trade by sea, or the third parties, like America, who valued free trade as their country grew.

The British blockade of the Mediterranean ports under the new Commander-in-Chief Admiral Collingwood saw naval activity increase and Gibraltar became the hub not just of supplies and repairs but of resistance to Napoleon's aims. Sanctions don't work now and didn't work then, and Gibraltar was soon the staging post for British goods being offloaded onto American ships for onward passage to the continent. The British also encouraged Gibraltar as a base for privateering, or legalised piracy, to prey on any French ships that had slipped through the blockade. By the time Byron arrived in Gibraltar a major shift of alliances had taken place the year before when France, rather than simply march through Spain on its way to Portugal, decided that while it was on Spanish soil it might as well end Bourbon rule and let the Spanish rejoice at having Napoleon's brother Joseph Bonaparte, then King of Naples, as their king instead.

The Spanish disagreed and joined Portugal and Britain as allies against France, and thus began the Peninsular War.

Little of the Gibraltar that was then remains today. The Garrison Library still stands, as does the Convent and adjoining King's Chapel, the Trafalgar Cemetery, the King's Bastion and Casemates Square. The Library was created by the officers within Gibraltar, and the *Gibraltar Chronicle*, still the Rock's newspaper, was first printed from there. The Convent was built by Franciscan friars—*convento* in Spanish or Portuguese means a residence for monks or nuns—and is now the Governor's Residence and place of office as well as the King's Chapel. The Trafalgar Cemetery is where the wounded survivors of the battle, who later died, were buried after HMS *Victory* was towed into Gibraltar harbour; those who died during the battle were of course buried at sea. The King's Bastion is now a leisure centre. Casemates Square, which was the old parade ground and execution yard, is now the town's main (only) square and hosts open air events. All are well kept in a town that generally isn't, although the Library is starting to grow somewhat weary.

If Gibraltar's military purpose has long been overtaken by peace and prosperity—not to mention cruise missiles should peace and prosperity not be doing well enough—its reinvention as an offshore tax haven for spread betters and online gamblers is confounded by its seeking respectability within the European Union. The scrubby old squaddy town is not quite sure what it is these days, and so has become a cross between Portsmouth without the finesse and the Cayman Islands without the financial probity. The prints in the Garrison Library show that Gibraltar was never a place of man-made beauty, and the tradition still stands with mock Tudor tower blocks and eighties modernist office developments blotting the reclaimed land. It wants to be Dubai, but it has just reinvented Fuengirola.

Byron never willingly travelled lightly as we've seen, and having sent the bulk of his trunks and chests, not to mention Fletcher, Murray and Friese by sea from Lisbon to Gibraltar on the schooner *Triumph* he now had to wait for them all to arrive. He had expected that they would be there waiting for him, for in theory the sail down the Portuguese coast and over to and through the Straits of Gibraltar should have only taken a few days, far less time than the overland route that he, Hobhouse, Rushton and Sanguinetti had taken. But on Byron's arrival in Gibraltar *Triumph* was there none, and so the party had to find a hotel and wait, with the added anxiety of not knowing why his servants and portmanteaux had not arrived, or even if they ever would arrive. In the meantime they had to make do with The Three Anchors.

The Three Anchors is no more, hardly surprisingly as Hobhouse recorded that it was 'horrid and dirty, a shocking hotel', their two rooms 'very buggy,' and dinner 'was bad, spoilt by greasy cooking.' The owner, one Hawthorne, 'a fat, short man,' as Byron said, 'like the pictures of jolly Bacchus,' did not impress them much either. Eventually they retired to the first of ten 'horrid night(s). Bed on a little sofa.'

Without the rest of the entourage they were marooned on the Rock, and with no way of knowing what had become of the *Triumph* they passed the oven hot, dense, humid days of a Gibraltar August as best they could. In the evenings they would ride or walk to the top of the Rock and back down, making unfulfilled plans to visit the Barbary Coast so clearly seen. In the early morning they rode over to the border near Algeciras. They walked to the top of the Rock again, they rode to the top of the Rock again, but mostly they whiled away their hours and their uncertainty in the Garrison Library.

They found the library 'well-filled with good common books,' as indeed it is today. Founded in 1793 by garrison officers who donated the first five hundred books, it now has 45,000 and the shelves continue to expand with donations. Now run entirely by volunteers, it is charming and dotty, dusty and musty. The architecture is pure military Raj, two-storey, no-nonsense stone blocks and slate roof outside and cast iron pillars and wood lined walls inside. In the garden the original—so we are assured—maple tree still stands proudly to attention, now joined by subaltern palm trees and more common-or-garden shrubbery.

Hobhouse read *Life and Times of Voltaire* by Espinasse, and the two volumes of Arthur Young's *French Tour*. Both titles are still very much there in peaceful retirement high on the BB shelves in the upstairs reading room. It is easy to visualise Hobhouse reading the weighty and worthy Young, the full title of whose work was *Travels During the Years 1787, 1788 and 1789; Undertaken More Particularly With a View to Ascertaining the Cultivation, Wealth, Resources and National Prosperity of the Kingdom of France*. Hobhouse's subsequent travel book was called, equally worthily, *A Journey through Albania, and other Provinces of Turkey in Europe and Asia, to Constantinople, during the years 1809 and 1810*.

As I visit the reading room it is clear that no one has been up there for a while, and the shutters keep the room dark and cool. Two hundred years ago the officers would use the cane reclining chairs and velvet chaises-longues and whatever breeze there was upstairs to catch up on the latest news from home, although they would have learnt of the victory at Trafalgar from the *Gibraltar Chronicle* a few days before the readers of *The Times* did so back in London. The Trafalgar article has pride of place, although for reasons of preservation it is locked in the safe. I open it with white gloves, goose pimples and great care and read:

Euryalus, at sea, October 22, 1805

Sir,

Yesterday a Battle was fought by His Majesty's Fleet, with the Combined Fleets of Spain and France, and a Victory gained, which will stand recorded as one of the most brilliant and decisive, that ever distinguished the BRITISH NAVY.

The Enemy's Fleet sailed from Cadiz, on the 19th, in the Morning, Thirty Three sail of Line in number, for the purpose of giving Battle to the British Squadron of Twenty Seven, and yesterday at Eleven A.M. the contest began, close in with the Shoals of Trafalgar.

At Five P.M. Seventeen of the Enemy had surrendered, and one (L'Achille) burnt, amongst which is the Sta. Ana, the Spanish Admiral DON D'ALEYA mortally wounded and the Santisima Trinidad. The French Admiral VILLENEUVE is now a Prisoner on board the Mars; I believe THREE ADMIRALS are captured.

Our loss has been great in Men; but, what is irreparable, and the cause of Universal Lamentation, is the Death of the NOBLE COMMANDER IN CHIEF, who died in the Arms of Victory; I have not yet any reports from the Ships, but have heard that Captains DUFF and COOK fell in the Action.

I have to congratulate you upon the Great Event, and have the Honour to be, &c. &c.

(Signed) C. COLLINGWOOD

I am also hoping to find some references to Byron and Hobhouse's visit in the *Gibraltar Chronicle*, but it wasn't that type of newspaper, more a weekly digest of military matters from the major European newspapers.

Byron and Hobhouse happened to be in Gibraltar at the same time as the acting Governor, Lieutenant General Sir Hew Dalrymple, was on his annual leave (the then nominal Governor, General HRH Prince Edward, Duke of Kent was nearly always absent) and thus had no access to the social life of the Rock which then as now revolved around the comings and goings at the Convent, Gibraltar's Government House. We have no such misfortune and are welcomed most warmly by His Excellency the Governor and his wife, Lt. Gen. Sir Robert and Lady Fulton. The setting for the welcome can hardly be less formal. Gillian is in London for a few days and I am upside down deep in the engine compartment trying to mend our water maker, sweating and cursing in the darkness and humidity, in only underpants and filthy old T-shirt, the snappy temper not improved by three taps on the hull and 'Hello, anyone home?'

It is indeed the Fultons, Rob and Midge, and as I am in no condition to even shake their hands we agree to meet for a very cold beer in the harbour bar, the Waterfront, as soon as I've had a chance to scrub up a bit. After chatting for a while Midge asks if there is anything we miss on the life afloat.

'Yes,' I reply, 'a hot bath. A good long soak in a Badedas hot bath, with the heel regulating the water out and the hot tap letting a similar amount...'

'Settled,' the Governor says, 'Gillian returns tomorrow and hot baths at the Convent await your arrivals.'

'Wonderful, come at five-ish and you can have tea before the bath and something more sensible after it. Not sure about the Badedas,' Midge says.

'Don't worry about the Badedas,' I reply. 'I will provide that and furthermore insist that afterwards I invite you out for dinner at the Royal Gibraltar Yacht Club.' And so we do just that; tea and a tour and baths and drinks at the Convent and dinner at the RGYC.

The Convent is so called because that is what it once was, a convent for Franciscan friars who settled there in 1525 after the Moors had finally left in 1475. The Moors had arrived in 711, led by one Tariq Bin Zaid, and called their new possession Jebel al-Tariq (Mount Tariq) which over the years became the anglicised Gibraltar. The friars built their convent and when the British arrived in earnest after the Treaty of Utrecht in 1713 they invited the friars to invite the British to take half of the only substantial building in Gibraltar, *el convento*. They co-existed for ten years after which the friars had had enough of the military banging and crashing and left forever for Cadiz. The Victorians added to the building in a rather sombre Empire style but did include three excellent rooms: a twenty-six seat Gothic revival baronial dining room with coats of arms and pennants amid the mahogany and cornices, a very comfortable withdrawing room which can be used formally or informally, and from the top half of what is now the King's Chapel they carved out the Ballroom where investitures and royal receptions are held.

'And balls in the ballroom?' I ask

'I don't suppose the floor could stand it,' Sir Robert replies.

The Victorians also encouraged the Governors to develop the acre attached to the Convent and this has now become a trove of botanical treasures, and as Sir Robert puts it as he takes us on a tour, 'these gardens are the history of Gibraltar told in trees.'

Nearest the chapel is a form of cork tree which the friars planted five hundred years ago, now held up with a dozen wooden supports. Around this grows milkweed, which attracts the most enormous yellow and brown hand-sized butterflies. The most striking trees are the dragon trees, *dracaena marginata*, originally from the Canary Islands and most seen in the UK as a spiked pot plant but here over one hundred feet tall with a long straight trunk and cats' cradles of geometrical branches just under the leaves. Some commemorate the Treaty of Utrecht, planted in 1715, others the surviving of the great Spanish siege of 1785, yet another the visit by Queen Alexandria in 1903. The only tree not to flourish was the one planted to commemorate the visit of Prince Charles and Diana, Princess of Wales to the Convent at the start of their honeymoon on *Britannia* in 1981; like the marriage it withered on the vine prematurely and has now been replaced by a similar tree. '*Vengica camillica*,' I offer; Sir Robert smiles politely, I imagine he's heard it before.

The next morning we join them for Family Communion in the King's Chapel part of the Convent. The congregation is largely military as is the chaplain. In his sermon he tells the story of his posting in South Armagh during the Troubles, when as part of an MoD 'hearts and minds outreach initiative' the military clergy were encouraged to visit local churches. On one occasion he was seconded to a service conducted by Ian Paisley. Paisley in his most sonorous tones was quoting from Romans IV, the part about 'weeping and wailing and gnashing of teeth'. A brave man put his hand up: 'but Doctor Reverend, what happens if you have no teeth?' Paisley drew his mighty chest up to its full extent and without missing a beat thundered down, 'teeth will be provided.'

I must say the time spent with the Governor and Lady Fulton is most welcome as, like Byron and Hobhouse, I am beginning to despair of Gibraltar. In a world of upward mobility, it is for a while worth observing somewhere so relentlessly downmarket, where the *Star* outsells the *Sun*, where pink nylon cardigans and light blue acrylic slippers are stretched around muffin tops and doughnuts, many of quite repellent aspect, where soft porn calendars hang on the pub walls, where blowing bubble gum is a teenage fad from which one never evolves, where smoking is not only compulsory but competitive—with extra points for chewing gum at the same time and double extras for spitting the gum onto the pavement as you exhale the fag smoke, where the horrible little microclimate is a relief from death by open-ended two-stroke scooters, and if they somehow fail to score a direct hit there are always the pit bull terriers lying in wait in the shadow of their owners' beer bellies; all this and also where the terrible thought arises that maybe, just maybe, there is some redemption in political correctness after all.

The three immediate enthusiasms amongst Gibraltarians would seem to be the collective hatred of anything and anyone Spanish, the corresponding jingoism for a pre-service industry Britain and the subsequent careful cultivation of the bloody-minded tree. Bloody-mindedness here is a statement of identity where the perfection of placing imaginary obstacles in the way of anyone wanting anything to be done has as many precious subtleties in its rules and variations as does Mornington Crescent.

First stop after mooring was to find another connection for the hose—the taps on Gibraltar's quays being quite exceptional—and I drift into the only chandler, the famously customer averse Sheppard's, to buy same.

'Good morning, have you the marina tap-to-hose connection please?'

'No, mate.'

'Do they have them in the marina office?'

'No, mate.'

'Ah, so where do you think I could find one?'

'Don't know, mate.'

I eventually find one in British Home Stores, of all places, which still maintains its pride of place among Gibraltarian shoppers (the smart set use the Marks and Spencer). In fact Gibraltar is a Tardis of the fifties, the fifties of bread fried in the morning and thin white sliced and margerined in the afternoon, with sauces red or brown to suit, of the conscription mentality and the subsequent perfection of skiving, and of chippiness ranging from dumb insolence to outright obstreperousness.

So, enthused by the purchase of the hose connector I leave in search of the other priority, a spare boat key as I have already nearly lost our only one twice. Ah, there's the Tourist Information Office, they'll be able to help. A chubby young woman with heavy mascara, crimson lipstick and the inevitable gum in full chew, and wearing a crimson nylon cardigan—the air conditioning is maxed and deafening—deigns to interrupt her study of a glossy celebrity magazine. 'Yes?'

'Good morning, where can I have a key cut please?'

'This is Tourist Information.'

'Well, I'm a tourist and I would like some information, if that were possible.'

'We only give out tourist information, not general information.'

'Alright, so where can I find general information?'

An annoyed sigh, then 'Citizen's Advice Bureau, maybe?'

'Where would that be, as a tourist enquiry of course?'

'In Cadogan Street.'

'And the best way there?'

'It's off Pelham Street.'

'Let me ask you this: you live here, am I right?'

A wary 'Ri-ight'. She even slows down the chewing in her wariness.

'If you ever need a spare key, where do you go to get one cut?'

More cheerfully now, 'Oh, that will be Barrett's, just opposite BHS.' She looks at my British Home Stores bag, 'you know where BHS is then?'

'Just been there.'

'That's it, right opposite. Why didn't ya go there in the first place?' A shake and a tut and she returns to the intense study of *OK Heat*.

Charming parts remain in the little back alleys off Main Street—Baker's Lane, Turnbull's Lane, Cooperage Lane, Fish Market Lane—where little Moroccan grocery stores, tiny houses with an open front door, rub along side by side with Indian restaurants and Kosher markets. There's a tiny piece of history still alive and well in the non-Anglo element, the Genoese names, the Maltese Association, the synagogue and mosque and Hindu temple, the dignified dress code, but mostly they are swamped by the flabby white trash with short attention spans from the cruise ships, and by the Anglo element Gibraltarians who hold them all in such disdain.

But for Byron and Hobhouse on Friday, 11 August 1809, the Relief of Gibraltar was in sight. As Hobhouse recorded with some delight: 'Today was an important day—Byron entered in the morning and informed me with an embrace that the *Triumph* Schooner was arrived. I embraced him for his news. Fletcher came—informed me that my black case had been stolen, but recovered, at Lisbon.' The reason for the delay soon became clear: the *Triumph*'s captain Mackinnon, or in Hobhouse's view 'the wretch Mackinnon, a detestable Yankee Scot', did not leave Lisbon until six days before—no doubt waiting for a fuller cargo.

The entourage were now reunited: Byron and Hobhouse, the page Robert Rushton and the guide Sanguinetti already in Gibraltar, and the valet Fletcher, the retainer Murray, the linguist Friese and the all important trunks and chests of books and clothes and stationery and uniforms and comforts and presents needed on a Byronic baggage train. But by now Byron had decided that young Robert Rushton was not up to the rigours of travelling, and however decorative he may be he should be returned to England. Byron told Hanson it was because Turkey was too dangerous a state for boys to enter, and wrote to his mother that 'you *know boys* are not *safe* amongst the Turks' and that 'he is my great favourite'. He had already made some provision for Robert in his will, and he now increased this further—not that he had the money to do so—so that the boy could be independent. We learn that the pageboy was desperately sad to leave his master, but we can imagine the master may have been tiring of this particular pageboy with the promise of further and more exotic pageboys as they headed eastwards.

Rushton was to be accompanied by old Joe Murray, whom Byron thought too ancient for further travel, and so the one too young and the other too old were sent home from Gibraltar. The others, Fletcher and the German guide Friese, would join Byron and Hobhouse on board the Malta packet *Townshend*, due to leave in five days time. There was still idle time in the heat and dust ahead.

Chapter Five

FROM GIBRALTAR TO SARDINIA

The reduced party left Gibraltar on 15 August, 1809. The *Townshend* packet was due to deliver mail at Cagliari in Sardinia and Girgenti, now Agrigento, in Sicily and then sail on to Malta. Of course there was no timetable. The Mediterranean famously has either too much wind for sailing or too little, and in the middle of August it was always likely there would be much more 'too little' than 'too much'. The 700-nautical mile, or 800-regular mile, voyage from

Gibraltar to Cagliari took eleven days, a drearily slow average of only 2.5 knots or 3 m.p.h. Having covered the same waves at the same time of year I can report that they would have spent hours on end generally drifting followed by quick bursts of progress in the gusts and squalls.

Byron had chided Hobhouse about his 'woundy preparations for a book on his [Hobhouse's] return; 100 pens, two gallons of Japan Ink, and several volumes of best blank, is no bad provision for a discerning public.' But for reasons unknown Hobhouse put his pen away when at sea, and so we have to rely on another passenger, John Galt, for impressions of the voyage. Galt was a Scottish businessman who was in the Mediterranean looking for ways to break Napoleon's embargo on British goods. When that failed he became an author of sorts and twenty-one years after their short voyage together and six years after Byron's death he suddenly had a rush of rather patchy recollection and published his *Life of Lord Byron*. Personally I don't much like the cut of the Galt jib, and not just because of the self-aggrandisement after this fortuitous meeting with Byron on the *Townshend*. Galt remembers Byron being aloof from his fellow passengers and spending only one evening conversing and playing cards in the mess area with the others. Byron would just stand outside throughout most of the night, leaning on the rigging and gazing at the moon and stars. This at least certainly has the ring of truth, as Byron was famously nocturnal throughout his adult life.

What was he doing, what was he thinking, leaning back on the rigging, gazing at the sky and sea through the night? Was he being a lord spiritual or a lord temporal? Seers, if not most peers, know that it was not through the individual mind, through thinking, that the miracle of life was created or is being sustained, but through a far greater intelligence or imagination.

As with life so with art. The seer, the lord spiritual, looks to the sea and sees the sea as an almost perfect metaphor for eternity. There is the one substance, water, the metaphor for One, the Absolute: '*That* which can have no name because it cannot be limited by description or definition.' The sea is still when it is deep, it is just the sea being the sea. On the surface there are waves, with the illusion of movement, just as man identifies with the illusion of change rather realising the constancy of *That*, but the waves are still the sea. On the waves are ripples, just like man's lives—lasting mere moments and seemingly of dubious consequence—which miraculously arise from *That*, are sustained by the will and circumstance of *That* and return inevitably to *That*, yet they too are still the sea.

But the seer will know that the sea is *only* a useful metaphor because ultimately, no matter how seemingly timeless, it must have had a beginning and eventually it will have to have an end, and so can never be eternal, Absolute, *That*. For the seer *That*—the ultimate Existence, Knowledge and Bliss, the *Sat, Chit and Ananda*, is real; thus the finite universe is not real but merely existing for now. *That* and *Atman*, the cosmic mind resting and awaiting realisation in each of our souls, are one. '*Thou art That*'. One only has to look, as did another poet, T.S. Eliot: 'The river is within you; the sea is all around you.'

Yet although Byron's words could take some readers beyond the literal and transcend the labelling limitations of the intellect, he himself was not remotely religious, let alone spiritual. Catholic theologians recognise a quality called 'gratuitous grace' as an aspect of cosmic consciousness. Gratuitous grace—the power of healing or prediction, or spiritual insights—can descend on anyone. One thinks of Mozart, or indeed Wordsworth. One walks on cut glass to judge another's spirituality, but as Aldous Huxley has observed, there is no biographical evidence that Byron developed his gratuitous grace, his theophany, beyond his poetry: 'Byron was as fascinatingly Byronic after he had beheld the One in all things as he was before.' As he wrote to Hodgson, the latter starting to wear his religious tendencies on his sleeve:

I will have nothing to do with your immortality; we are miserable enough in this life, without the absurdity of speculating on another. If men are to live, why die at all? And if they die, why disturb the sweet and sound sleep that "knows no waking"? I am no Platonist, I am nothing at all; but I would sooner be a Paulician, Manichean, Spinozist, Gentile, Pyrrhonian, Zoroastrian, than one of the seventy-two villainous sects who are tearing each other to pieces for the love of the Lord and hatred of each other. Talk of Galileeism? Show me the effects—are you better, wiser, kinder by your precepts?

If Byron was 'none of the above', what, if anything was he?

Leaning back on the rigging looking out to the moonlit sea, he would surely have reflected on destiny, elevated it to Destiny, and if anything he would be a Destinyist. One image of his life which stays in the writer's mind is of him, aged ten, looking through the gates at Newstead Abbey and its Park for the first time and seeing somewhere from a dreamy planet far, far away. What an extraordinary and random change, and a change for which there had been no preparation. Up until then he had lived with his tiresome mother and sexually abusive Calvinist maid in humblish circumstances in Aberdeen, learning Latin by rote by day and hearing his mother bleat on about how grand her family used to be before she met his father by night. She would remind him that his father was from grand stock too when she married him, but look at them now! All around Aberdeenshire were her rich relations, relations she was too embarrassed to visit, a precept with which she burdened her son frequently too.

Then suddenly, out of nowhere, came an event which changed everything. He had, in effect, won the lottery of life. An obscure relative, one he had never met, died on a battlefield somewhere equally obscure and wee George not only became Lord Byron in title but the owner of 3,000 acres of parkland, an abbey and at first sight much else besides. The story is told of his mother and him arriving at Newstead for the first time. Their carriage pulled up to the gates and his mother asked a passer-by who lived in such a magnificent mansion. The reply was: Lord Byron, but he is dead. We hear it now belongs to a young boy in Scotland. 'This is he!' squealed his mother in excitement, preening herself through her son.

The image of the ten-year-old looking through the gates at Newstead for the first time is made sharper by the lack of preparation. Hereditary peers by and large know they are going to inherit from the earliest age, and by tuition or observation know what to do and when to do it; equally what not to do and when not to do it. When their predecessor dies they seamlessly slip into their new role, knowing—we hope—full well that it is just a role. If there is land too, they will know how to husband it; if there is politics or clergy or regiments too, they will know the rungs on the ladders and the lairs of the snakes. But young George Byron had none of this preparation, and it showed to his disadvantage throughout his life. He took his status as a peer as automatically entitling him to jump hierarchies and insist on protocols where he had no business to do so. If he had earned his peerage, or even paid or whored for it, one might understand this grandstanding, but the fact that he won it in a hereditary lottery he didn't even know he had entered should have attracted more modesty, less self-importance.

It is an irony of his life that although in his poetry he seemed instinctively to understand that in reality 'all the world's a stage and all the actors in it only players', in the illusory world we take for real he should conduct himself so self-seriously just because of an arbitrary title—and that is another contradiction to add to the long list that made the man.

Destiny, bordering on Serendipity, gave him two roles: peer and poet, and if he loved being a peer, he adored being a poet, and especially the adored poet he was to become. 'I awoke one morning and found myself famous,' he said after the first edition of *Childe Harold's Pilgrimage* was published. He had been reading poetry studiously in classical and modern languages since he was ten, and writing it seriously since he was thirteen. He knew from sixteen that he could summon words and turn them into verses, and that when poems they had the power to take the reader somewhere beyond the original words.

> But words are things, and a small drop of ink,
> Falling like dew, upon a thought, produces
> That which makes thousands, perhaps millions, think.

He may well have already known on those Mediterranean nights that it would not be just poems but epic poems that would fulfil his concord with Destiny. And Destiny would serve him well as after the Grand Tour and the publication of *Childe Harold's Pilgrimage* it was his celebrity as a poet rather than as a peer which made him compulsory company in the best drawing rooms in London.

Resting on the rigging, gazing at the moonlit seascape, hearing the rush and settle of the bow wave, smelling the salted timber, I imagine he was just 'letting go' and allowing the words, the phrases, the lines and the verses to come to him as they may. There is active authoring and passive authoring. Byron, when on active duty, would write deep into the night and often until dawn. His manuscripts are a scribbling mass of revisions and alterations. He called himself 'the mighty Scribbler'. On passive patrol he would just let the words come on the breeze, love them and discard them for the ethereal notions that they are. Phrases or passages with meaning would be retained and brought back to light later. *Childe Harold's Pilgrimage* was written in Spenserian stanzas: eight lines of doubled iambic pentameter followed by a doubled alexandrine, with rhymes *ababbcbcc*. Byron composed by phrases, usually mid-line or bi-line. There cannot be a more natural rhythm to rhymes composed than the steady sound of a boat plying a sea, so the Spenserian stanza structure flows:

> The free, the easy flow of bow on wave
> The voice beyond the silence prompts to hear;
> From where the rolling word becomes a stave
> To phrases, which within themselves are clear
> Intent of what the stillness tells the ear.
> Moon too! and timeless stars and wake combine
> With phosphorescence prompting well the seer.
> I do nothing, forsaking me and mine;
> I just observe! and let Life's rhythm be the shrine.

Eight years after those Mediterranean nights he published *Manfred: a Dramatic Poem*, and this passage about Manfred at the same age as Byron was when en route to Malta must have been self-reflective:

My spirit walk'd not with the souls of men,
Nor look'd upon the earth with human eyes;
The thirst of their ambition was not mine;
The aim of their existence was not mine.
My joys, my griefs, my passions, and my powers,
Made me a stranger. Though I wore the form,
I had no sympathy with breathing flesh.
My joy was in the wilderness—to breathe
The difficult air of the iced mountain's top.
Where the birds dare not build, nor insect's wing
Flit o'er the herbless granite; or to plunge
Into the torrent, and to roll along
On the swift whirl of the new-breaking wave
Of river, stream, or ocean, in their flow—
In these my early strength exulted; or
To follow through the night the moving moon,
The stars, and their development; or catch
The dazzling lightnings till my eyes grew dim;
Or to look listening on the scatter'd leaves,
While autumn winds were at their evening song;—
These were my pastimes—and to be alone.
For if the beings, of whom I was one—
Hating to be so—cross'd me in my path,
I felt myself degraded back to them,
And was all clay again.

As Byron's thoughts turned from poems to passion it is also quite possible that he was pining after his pageboy Robert Rushton. At the start of his third seven-year cycle Byron was as casually bisexual as he was ever going to be. He loved beauty in the round, as a unity; dividing beauty into male or female entities, limiting it thus, was not in his nature.

From his own letters and earliest biographers one can sense that he was bimental as well as bisexual; in fact the former would surely have caused the latter. His vegetarianism, vulnerable limp and dandy style with cloaks and scarves would have added to the hermaphroditic quandary experienced by those he met. His first biographer, Thomas Moore, who knew him well and sympathetically, noted that he talked like a man and thought like a woman, and others had commented to him on his 'soft, voluptuous character', and 'that there was a great deal of the woman about Byron, in his tenderness, his temper, his caprice, his vanity.' Hobhouse from Malta noted that a female friend had 'picked out a pretty picture of a woman in a fashionable dress, and observed she was vastly like Lord Byron.' Sir Harold Nicholson in his biography notes that his subject held 'a catalogue of false positions. His brain was male, his character was female.'

Lady Blessington, who was to know him well—but only socially —after the Grand Tour, observed that 'his voice and accent are particularly clear and harmonious, but somewhat effeminate; his laugh is musical,' and that his feminine side encouraged 'the perfect abandon with which he converses to recent acquaintances, on subjects which even friends would think too delicate for discussion.'

The historian George Finlay, writing in relation to later events in Greece noted that: 'it seemed as if two different souls occupied his body alternately. One was feminine and full of sympathy; the other masculine, and characterised by clear judgment. When one soul arrived the other departed. Hence he appeared in his conduct extremely capricious, while in his opinions he had great firmness. He often, however, displayed a feminine turn for deception in trifles, while at the same time he possessed a feminine candour of the soul, and a natural love of truth, which made him often despise himself quite as much as he despised English fashionable society for what he called its brazen hypocrisy.'

Later on the Grand Tour in Istanbul an anonymous Englishman saw him in the souk. In a long description of Lord Byron he noted that 'his features were remarkably delicate, and would have given him a feminine appearance, but of the manly impression of his fine blue eyes... and head of curly auburn hair, which improved in no small degree the uncommon beauty of his face. The impression which his whole appearance made on my mind was such that it has ever remained deeply engraven on it.'

He appealed to the woman in a man, and the man in a woman; if these qualities in others were repressed he brought them nearer openness. If already open, a flirtation, dalliance or affair would have seemed only natural. Other, more sensitive conventions such as the taboo of incest were sacrificed to the gods of beauty, a trait he and his sister Augusta inherited from their father 'Mad Jack' Byron and their aunt Frances.

Nowadays men—New Man, Metro Man—are encouraged to listen to women and empathise accordingly. Self help books and glossy magazines shout it from the rooftops. Emotions are to be discussed. Tone down those solution orientated instincts. Relationships are to be explored. Sex is to be shared. Cherish is an idea whose time has come. Understand her pain; give reassurance; commit, devote, care. We all do our best, some more reluctantly than is wise in these troubled times. But two hundred years ago men and women inhabited exclusively male and female worlds, and Byron and his bimentality and bisexuality must have been a rare bird to traverse so freely and seamlessly between the two worlds.

~

Back on board the *Townshend*, now nearing Cagliari, the south coast of Sardinia would have reminded Byron then as it does the writer now of the west coast of Scotland. Barely inhabited, with wide open rugged bays for lochs, one has the feeling of sailing in ancient seas where galleys, caïques and brigantines have plied before. The fishermen then still used dhows, a throwback to Carthaginian days, and these beautiful lateen sailed craft would have been Byron and Hobhouse's first sight of anything Eastern. Now the few fish left are chased by the few fishermen who can be bothered roaring around in dayglo RIBs with screaming outboards. Many of the sailing dhows themselves have been beautifully restored, or even more encouragingly recently built, for the pleasure of the newly affluent Sardinians.

Typically, as any yachtsman will confirm, the only wind of any use came as they turned north for the destination and it came right on the bow. They had a long day tacking across Cagliari Bay, as indeed do we. Nowadays the western shore is blighted by the obligatory oil refinery and tanker terminal but then it would have been just marshes. For us there is hardly any wind at all. We see wind farms on the northern shore going lazily through the motions, and Mr. Perkins, our third crew member whose quirk it is to dress up as a diesel engine and live in the dark, is not discouraged to bring these two souls more swiftly in to Cagliari, just as patience brought the eighteen souls on board the *Townshend* safely to port two hundred years ago.

Chapter Six

SARDINIA, SHORE LEAVE

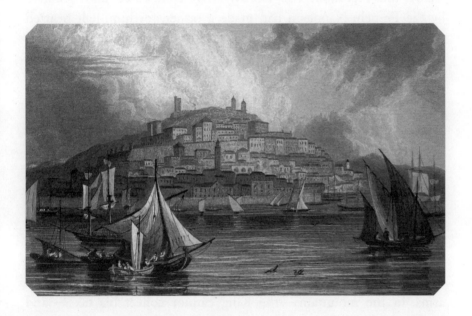

The *Townshend* packet only spent two nights and a day—Sunday 27 August 1809—in Cagliari, and the passengers fairly raced off board after being cooped up for eleven days on the slow drift over from Gibraltar. Byron and Hobhouse had every expectation of being presented to the royal family, and had had appropriate outfits made in Gibraltar for the occasion. From there Byron had written to his mother: 'My next stage is Cagliari in Sardinia, where I shall be presented to his Sardinian Majesty, I have a most superb uniform as a court dress, indispensable in travelling.' As usual, that which to our poet is 'indispensable' is to everyone else a mad extravagance, but then most would not see themselves on a 'stage' in the first place. Whereas Byron had spent £50 on a suit of full regimentals and regalia, Hobhouse had had himself tailored a more modest bright red morning suit—itself an act of derring-do sartorial extravagance from our fogeyish diarist.

And why should they expect to meet the King of Sardinia, Vittorio Emanuele I? So far Sardinia had escaped involvement in the Napoleonic wars, whereas Vittorio Emanuele's dukedoms of Savoy and Piedmont had already been confiscated and denuded by the French. Napoleon had made a rather, for him, half hearted attack on Sardinia, and as Hobhouse later observed: 'The (Sardinian) army is in a deplorable state, with officers for 30,000 men and only about 2,000 soldiers; yet the French attacked this place without effect, landing in two places, and fighting each other in the night.' Further attacks were unlikely as long as the English navy controlled the Mediterranean, and it has to be said that, then as now, Sardinia for all its size and beauty and secrets is of no great strategic, cultural or prestigious importance. Its neutrality evolved not as part of some grander treaty but from its sleepy irrelevance to grander designs.

Yet there was a more prosaic reason for Vittorio Emanuele to receive his English visitors. As Hobhouse further noted: 'At this time there are seven or eight hundred men, bands of robbers in arms, in the mountains—the King cannot collect his taxes—and is chiefly supported by £12,000 per annum, which he receives from England. He is next Catholic heir to our crown.' And so he was, being directly descended from Charles I. Luckily for him, in 1800 George III had granted Cardinal York, the Jacobite heir, a pension of £12,000 a year. The cardinal had died in 1807, and by the labyrinthine legacy of Catholic succession it was Vittorio Emanuele I, who took up George's pension, a pension without which his court could not function.

In the event Byron and Hobhouse were not presented to the royal family personally, probably because their arrival and very short stay could not have been anticipated, but there were royal family sightings at the royal church for mass and later at the royal theatre for an opera. Hobhouse became quite the court reporter. Apart from the king there was the queen, Maria Teresa, daughter of Archduke Ferdinand of Modena and Maria Beatrice, Duchess of Massa and Princess of Carrara. There was also 'their daughter Madame Beatrice, rather pretty', and the king's brother Carlo Felice, who later took over the throne when Vittorio Emanuele abdicated. Hobhouse noted that Carlo Felice looked 'very like the Duke of York (that The Grand old Duke of York, second son of George III). The Duke of Orleans, I was told, observed the same thing.'

The visitors' first impressions of Cagliari were favourable: 'Cagliari, from the shore, looks like Lisbon in miniature—it is a fortified town, and the King's house is situated on the higher part of the hill on which the city is built. The streets are narrow, but have no unpleasant stench in them, at least not very generally diffused.' Sailing into Cagliari today one has the same impression, and the city has spread surprisingly little in the last two hundred years beyond the ramparts, now known as the Castello district, which defined it then. Hobhouse 'walked out to ramparts on both sides of the city—saw a country divided into gardens well-cultivated, which, however, Lord Byron, who rode into it, told me was not so agreeable, he having seen nothing particular but three heads nailed to a gallows.'

Between Castello and the shore is Marina, where all the expensive shops and the more intriguing restaurants lie, and around Castello some small suburbs made worse by the usual hideous sixties tower blocks. The main development in Sardinia has been away from the capital, in the tourist resorts around the coast, most famously in the Aga Khan's exclusive and sympathetic development of the Costa Smeralda on the north-east of the island. Sailing around the coast as we did, the remarkable point is how little it has been developed, especially the south coast which has the grandeur and emptiness of the Scottish isles and lochs, but without the midges, mist and chippy locals.

If an ambassador is no longer needed here in Cagliari, the theatre at which he arranged for his visitors to see the opera is still very much alive and thriving. Now called the Teatro Civico in Castello, it has recently undergone a major refit, or rather de-fit as it no longer has a roof or boxes but is a beacon to democracy with open brickwork, unscrubbed floorboards, sky above, hard single seats in the stalls and sumptuous sofas in the gods above. The director, Marcello Borhy, had arranged for me to have a guided tour by his assistant, the amply bodied and named Leonora Pelicciotti di Castellammare. 'Just say Lea,' she advises, advice upon which I readily agree.

It takes only a few moments to tour the new fresh air theatre and considerably longer to view Lea's archives, a process I'm not in a mood to hurry. From the earliest photographs and contemporaneous sketches it is clear that the theatre which Byron, Hobhouse, Galt, the ambassador and the royal family attended has only the same floor area in common with today's theatre. The seating area in the centre occupied only a third of the floor area, with an equal amount given to twelve large boxes on two levels along each side. From the evidence it seems that audience participation was part of the proceedings.

The opera that night was *La Nina (o sia La Pazza per Amore)*, the first time Byron had heard an opera in Italian. *Nina (or the girl driven mad by love)* was written by Giovanni Paisiello twenty years previously. The writer has not been able to find anyone who has seen it, but Ogden is rather sniffy about it, describing it as an over-sentimental comedy without humour, which may explain why no one known has seen it.

In the days of the Napoleonic Wars Sardinia merited a full ambassador, in this case The Hon. William Hill. On landing Byron and Hobhouse headed straight for his residence, described as a rather splendid Spanish-owned house in Castello, now sadly unidentifiable. Not expecting them, he too was away but later sent word back to the *Townshend* that they should all attend the opera that evening.

Mr. Hill evidently had two boxes as he placed Hobhouse and the others in one of them and took Byron as his personal guest in the other, smarter, one next to the king's box. However Byron and the king did not seem to meet; I'm sure we would have heard if they had done so.

Nowadays Sardinia does not merit an ambassador, nor even a consul, but an honorary consul, so I contact our man in Cagliari, Andrew Graham, MBE, and we arrange to meet. Not having an office as such—we are represented from his home, which is out of town—we meet at the Ristorante Italiano on Via Sardegna in the Marina district. I ask him if there is much call for Byron research.

'None at all,' he replies. 'Quite frankly, until you enquired I didn't even know he had been here.'

'Well, it was only for a day,' I offer defensively. 'Which Brits do people enquire about?'

"Nelson, of course. Benjamin Piercy. D.H. Lawrence. Those are the big three.'

'Benjamin Piercy?'

'Yes, he's an interesting one, he built the Sardinian railways. He had been building railways in India, and there he married an Indian lady called Chilivani. The railways here are a miracle of engineering through the mountains. It's hard to think of worse ground. They named a village in the mountains along the route Chilivani out of respect for them both.'

'And D.H. Lawrence?'

'To hear people here talk about him you would think he had spent his whole life here. Actually it was just a week, but he did write *Sea and Sardinia*. It's well translated in the Italian, very popular.'

'By yourself?'

'Unfortunately not.'

I ask him about himself, and his work as an honorary consul. He met and married a Sardinian girl when she was a language student in London twenty-five years ago, and jumped at the offer of working in Cagliari for a multinational construction company building the new container port. The company went bust, but by then he had fallen in love with Sardinia as well as his wife and he took up work where he could find it. A series of coincidences and retirements found him in Rome being offered the job of honorary consul in Cagliari, 'Our Man in Sardinia'.

He is responsible for the welfare of Brits on his patch. Before the advent of cheap flights there was not a lot to do, the odd lost passport, the odd wedding certificate. But since Ryanair and easyJet have arrived the quantity of British visitors has increased enormously. I ask about the quality. Mostly educated, he's pleased to say, and I'm pleased to hear, both of us having been embarrassed by the stag and hen party brigades throwing up all over each other in Mallorca, Prague or the Baltic states. The cruise ships have brought in many more visitors too, and with them hospital visits to these more ancient mariners who have fallen ill on passage. It's clearly a job he loves, and does with pride and care. 'Although job is not exactly the right word as it implies a salary and pension, some continuity.'

'But you must be paid, surely?' I ask.

'Honorary consuls receive an honorarium. £2,700 is the current figure…' I do a quick calculation and think that thirty odd thousand a year ain't too bad. '…plus expenses, of course. Not a lot in a year.'

In spite of this derisory figure he is fiercely defensive about the Foreign Office and all who sail in her, so I bite my tongue about Margaret Beckett. I show him Hobhouse's report of Ambassador Hill's views on Sardinia:

At Mr. Hill's I learnt that the property was feudal—that murders were every day committed and often by men of rank, that one seigneur would often steal three or four hundred sheep, and shoot the horses of another—as formerly in the highlands of Scotland—that no man therefore travelled, not even five miles from the town, without a gun, which is a weapon at which they are very expert. He said that men procured their pardons by the distribution of money, which they all kept for these occasions.

Hobhouse added from his own observations:

I saw a low cart drawn by oxen surrounded by six ill-looking fellows with guns—two prisoners from the villages were tied in the cart. Executions are frequent—the manners of the women very licentious, so much that there are no common whores. Money is scarce, but provisions exceedingly cheap—beef two pence a pound, and a bushel of grapes for a dollar—bread exceedingly fine, three times as cheap as in England—the appearance of men and women and houses and of everything most miserable.

Andrew smiled at the familiarity of then and now. 'Italian politics have always been rugged. Don't forget it's a very well paid job here, starting around €25,000 a month, plus plus plus, and the corruption is open and expected. Just last week the local strong man, Renato Soru, who made his fortune starting and selling Tiscali, stood up in parliament in front of all the public and media and openly told his MPs that if they didn't support his two-kilometre coastal development exclusion zone he would make sure they all went back to their previous clerical jobs at €1500 a month. With that reminder they all voted for him.'

'Funnily enough I had lunch with Prodi in Bergamo last May when he was still prime minister. He had the personality of a stick. And now Berlusconi is back.'

'Yes,' says Andrew, 'and you know you will never find an Italian who will admit to voting for him. But clearly a lot of them did. The most interesting person in politics right now is Beppe Grillo. Have you heard of him?'

'Only in the headlines,' I reply, 'what's the small print?'

'A third of all politicians have been convicted, and that's just the ones that have ended up in court. There's at least another third who should have ended up in court, but the system is paralysed. He wants them limited to two terms. But he's banned from state TV, and of course Berlusconi's channels too, so he does it all through his website and blog. It's the most popular one in Italy.'

'So why doesn't he stand himself?

'He did, but lost badly.'

'How come?'

'It's the Berlusconi syndrome in reverse. Everyone says "oh yes, I voted for Beppe," but clearly no one did. In the dark of the voting booth they want a fixer. Welcome to politics Italian-style. Hard not to love it though.'

'And them.'

'Quite.'

To settle our stomachs we drank a glass of myrto, a local liqueur made from myrtle. I hope never to fall ill, or be in prison, or need a certificate of birth or death or matrimony in Sardinia, but if I do I cannot think of a better person to take care of me than our honorary consul in Cagliari, Andrew Graham MBE.

Chapter Seven

MALTA

31 AUGUST – 19 SEPTEMBER 1809
29 SEPTEMBER 2008 – 23 MARCH 2009

'*I*n the act of addressing you for the first time, it is with the greatest pleasure that I have to inform you that His Majesty takes the Maltese nation under his protection. He has authorised me, as his representative, to inform you that every possible means shall be used to make you contented and happy.' With these words Major-General Henry Pigot, on 19 February 1801, confirmed to the inhabitants of Malta and Gozo that they were indeed now, as requested, under British rule.

Napoleon had stopped at Malta on his way to Egypt on 9 June 1798, and sent an ultimatum to the Grand Master of the Sovereign Military Hospitaller Order of St. John of Jerusalem of Rhodes and of Malta, Order of St. John, Knights of Malta. After a rude exchange of messages the Knights Hospitaller, half of them French and many too old to fight, surrendered three days later. Napoleon immediately started the process of *département*-alising Malta. A bureaucracy was established and the theocracy abolished. Houses were to be numbered so taxes could be collected. Three thousand French troops under General Vaubois were to stay behind to form a garrison. All the gold and silver in the churches and hospitals was to be removed and melted down for Napoleon's war machine; a potentially enormous haul of 3,500 pounds of bullion. A week after arriving, satisfied with such an easy and succulent conquest, Napoleon resumed his quest for Egypt.

On the island the French behaved appallingly and with due arrogance. They tried to impose their language and revolutionary mores on the Maltese who in defiance closed ranks behind their religious institutions. Matters passed mutual accommodation when two years later the French tried to auction the contents of the Carmelite church in Mdina; the outraged Maltese threw the French chief of militia out of a window. The French retreated to Valletta and from then on were effectively under siege. Meanwhile a Maltese delegation had found its way to Nelson who obliged by sending a dozen ships and 1,500 troops to blockade the Grand Harbour. Vaubois held out for a while, but with rations low and morale lower he eventually accepted surrender in 1800, after only two years of French occupation.

By the time Byron and his companions sailed into Grand Harbour on 31 August 1809 most of the strategic Mediterranean had followed Malta's example and settled under British control. The exceptions were the Ionian Islands, stretching from Corfu in the north to Kythira in the south, whose recent history had been confused by events and decisions in Venice, Moscow, Paris and Constantinople.

It is probable that on arrival in Malta Byron and Hobhouse were not abreast of these recent developments further east, yet it was the preparations in Malta to retake the Ionian Islands which played the pivotal role in their Grand Tour, diverting them from their intended destinations of Greater Arabia, Persia and India to countries that would later become Greece, Albania and Turkey. By the time Byron reached Malta the Ionian Islands were again under French control, Napoleon having first inherited them as a Venetian colony when he took Venice herself in 1797. Since then they had been taken over by the Turco-Russians, had been formed into the Septinsular Republic, were retaken by Russia acting alone and then in 1807 in a secret clause in the Treaty of Tilsit handed back to France.

Two days after arriving in Malta Byron and Hobhouse had the good fortune to meet a remarkable gentleman called Spiridion Foresti; or more precisely the day after arriving in Malta they were sought out, then later charmed and seduced by a remarkably successful British consul and secret agent called Spiridion Foresti. They were to leave the island nineteen days later on a secret mission for what then passed as British Intelligence.

Foresti was 57 years old when he recruited Byron; I say Byron rather than Byron and Hobhouse because it was specifically the 21-year-old peer on whom he had set his sights. Foresti would later become popularly known as 'Nelson's spy', although in fact he was at least as useful to Collingwood. His first posting for the British had been in his native island of Zakynthos in 1783 and he was to serve the cause in the Ionian Islands throughout the Revolutionary and Napoleonic Wars. He was imprisoned by the French, exiled to Venice, but found his way back to the Ionian Islands to help the English cause by joining the Russian fleet. Throughout his time as consul or resident, prisoner or sailor, he maintained his network of scouts and sneaks, runners and rubbernecks and reported to the Admiralty accordingly. Nelson attested that Foresti was one of only two consul 'I have found who really and truly do their duty, and merit every encouragement and protection.' After imprisonment by the French Nelson wrote to him: 'Give me leave to say, that throughout my command in the Levant seas, you have done yourself the highest honour, and rendered, as far as was possible, the greatest service to your Country. This public testimony, from a stranger to everything except your good conduct, will, I trust, be not unacceptable.' In all nearly one hundred pieces of correspondence between Nelson and Foresti are held in public archives, as indeed are further testimonials from three other Mediterranean Naval Commanders, Jervis, Keith and of course Collingwood. He was knighted in London by the Prince Regent in 1817, on the specific recommendation of the Foreign Secretary, George Canning; and of Canning more later.

The Treaty of Tilsit had put this perfect spy out of work, however, and he had repaired to Malta where from August 1807 he was employed as Minister at Large. In fact he ran British Intelligence on the island. Malta was a hotbed of French-sponsored espionage, the *Treason Harbour* of Captain Jack Aubrey and Stephen Maturin's adventures. (As an aside Patrick O'Brien based Aubrey's character on 'Dauntless' Cochrane and 'Foulweather Jack' Byron, our Byron's grandfather.) It was Foresti's task to control as best he could French espionage activities and at the same time build his own espionage and counter-espionage networks, as well as plan for the covert British re-taking of his native Ionian Islands.

In 1808 Foresti had persuaded Collingwood that the islands could be retaken without too high a price being paid. Except for Corfu they were poorly defended, and the French had managed to upset the islanders as convincingly as they had done the Maltese ten years previously. But, as always, there was a problem. On the mainland opposite the islands ruled one Ali Pasha, a particularly unpleasant mass murderer who ruled his fiefdom as a despotic tyrant under the diplomatic cover of the Ottoman Empire. With memories of one time's Mujahideen being another time's Taliban springing to mind, the British had promised Ali Pasha their assistance in taking at least the northern Ionian Islands as a way of making trouble for France. Now that the British were able to take the islands directly themselves Perfidious Albion would break the promise made to Ali Pasha, and an unhappy Ali Pasha would at best be an unpredictable neighbour.

Foresti calculated that Ali Pasha could huff and puff, but without a navy could only take his vengeance out on his own people, which he was inclined to do anyway. The rewards of taking the islands outweighed the risks of having Ali Pasha as a disgruntled neighbour. Collingwood agreed, and on Malta a troop of 1,900 men from the 35th and 44th Regiments, the 20th Dragoons and Corsican Rangers under Major-General Sir John Oswald was assembled as an invasion force. The navy was ready. The moons *en passage* made 22 September the ideal day of departure. Spiridion Foresti was to sail with them as Special Advisor, with a particular responsibility to pacify the troublesome Ali Pasha.

The preparations on Malta were done as secretly as conditions would allow. There were at any time dozens of ships in Grand or Marsamxett Harbours and a dozen more did not necessarily arouse suspicion. There was also a military garrison, so soldiery aplenty, and the extra troops who made up the invasion force were camped and trained in the north of the island near the beaches of St. Paul's Bay. Foresti must have hoped that any reports back to France of a build-up would have yielded more questions than answers, but still through habit and necessity he ensured security was as staunch as it could be.

It was into this complex and secretive military adventure that the Byron party stumbled unknowingly when they disembarked on 31 August. Hobhouse, like the Phoenicians, Carthaginians, Romans, Byzantines, Normans, Spanish, Knights, French and British before him was impressed by the majesty of the entrance into Malta. He wrote that 'the entrance of the eastern harbour of Malta is very grand, and surpassing every conception of that place', a good way to describe the grand harbour that is Grand Harbour. The awe still arises as one passes under proud St. Elmo's Fort and enters the magnificent embrace of its sweeping sandstone arms, arms which offer the promise of safety at last and an end for now to the random perils of the sea. One presumes that even the latest invaders who come in cruise ships not war ships must sense it 'very grand, and surpassing every conception of that place', although the likelihood is that they are down below stuffing their faces in the endless buffet.

The *Townshend* anchored off the north side of Valletta. Then as now the fairway was kept clear and boats anchored in one of the southern creeks, most likely what was then called Angelo's Creek. Over time this anchorage, being the one best protected from all weathers and yet the one nearest to Valletta, was increasingly commandeered by the Royal Navy, until it became known as Dockyard Creek and the name still stands today thirty years after they left. Guarded by St. Angelo's Fort at its entrance and with the original Maltese city of Birgu on its northern flank and Senglea to its south, this was the scene of the Great Siege of Malta in 1565. Today the site is the decidedly upmarket Camper & Nicholson Grand Harbour Marina where we moored for our time in Malta. Ancient History walks the streets ashore. To go to Valletta, a few hundred metres across the Grand Harbour, one hails a *dghajsa*—pronounced 'dee-sa', thank heavens—a sort of Maltese gondola. Nowadays they fire up a Yamaha and outboard you across; Byron and Hobhouse would have been sculled over in less of a rush.

On the *Townshend's* arrival Captain Western attended firstly to the mail, and delivered by hand correspondence from Sir Richard Bickerton, Commander-in-Chief of the Home Fleet to the Governor. Byron and Hobhouse dined on board, dinner in those days being taken much earlier than now. After dinner they made their first foray into town. Valletta is steep-to with endless stairs. Byron must have struggled up and down, as even with abled legs progress is halting, as the steps are spaced inorganically one and a half paces apart, ideal for horses and so fit for purpose. Over time they have worn down and are treacherous in the rains, and most are without wall banisters. Later Byron was to write of Valletta:

> Adieu, ye cursed streets of stairs!
> How surely he who mounts you swears!

The not yet portly Hobhouse however was impressed and pronounced the city: 'very clean with streets broad enough'; both Byron's couplet and Hobhouse's comment still sit well today. After a quick tour around the city they took a *dghajsa* back to the *Townshend* and spent the night on board.

The first sight tourists then and now seek is the magnificent Cathedral of St. John the Baptist, the patron saint of the Knights

Hospitaller. The visitors rose early, at nine o'clock, uncommonly early for Byron in particular, breakfasted on board and made for the cathedral in its pride of place on the promontory of Valletta. From the outside it looks rather austere, and in fact the inside was austere too when it was built after the Great Siege of 1565. My guide suggested that they did not want to attract the attention of the Ottomans again, so 'played it cool for a while'. The layout that stands today was established then: a nave the size of that in Christ Church Cathedral, Oxford, with a higher barrel vault overhead and eight chapels or *langues* equally spaced off the nave, one for each of the lands from which the Knights' families originated. As lesser contributors the English and Bavarians share a chapel. An oratory was added a generation later for instructing pupils in the papal processes.

Slowly the Ottoman threat receded and the Reformation took hold on the continent. Knights' families who felt constrained to spend freely in France, Spain and Italy in particular felt no need to hold back on Malta and within a hundred years of its foundation the cathedral had started to assemble some of the opulence it has today—and indeed which it had in full measure when Byron and Hobhouse visited it two hundred years ago and when baroque was in more recent memory. The guide suggested it was best not to ask from where the money came, churlish but true. Of course, Byron would not have had to put up with the crowds of today clogging up the aisles—one is well advised to be there at opening time, 9.30 a.m.—nor the black mats which protect the ornate inlaid marble Knights' tombstones which, stunningly, make up the floor. They would also have seen Caravaggio's *St. Jerome* in its original position in the Italian *langue*, whereas today it is rather obscurely displayed, if well lit, in the Oratory. The artist's *Decapitation of St. John the Baptist* remains displayed distantly in the Oratory, but with the benefit of modern lighting. The image is chilling and current; one presumes a decapitation is done by a quick clean guillotine or axe stroke, but the instrument used was little more than a knife, and similar to that used by Islamists today when they behead their hostages. The dress and expressions of those attending unites those times and these as well.

The writer must confess to being a cathedral enthusiast, one who has spent many still and happy hours in Chartres and Ely and others along the way, but the impression of St. John's is that it is not really a place of worship, rather the opposite: it is so splendid that one feels as if God was being invited to worship at the shrine of the Knights. It is, however, a quite magnificent place, the very definition of baroque, a testament to the confidence that this particular religion would be eternal, as would the enormous amount of funds needed to glorify it further and further.

Be that as it may; Malta was not specifically expecting Byron's and Hobhouse's arrival, and in those days a member of the House of Lords could not simply be ignored or detained for the three weeks needed until the invasion fleet departed. The first reaction of the governor, Rear-Admiral Sir Alexander J. Ball, and the Commander of the British forces, Major-General Hildebrand Oakes, was to persuade them to leave the island as quickly as possible. In two days time a convoy was leaving for Smyrna—now Izmir—and Constantinople and they should join that. But Foresti, who would have known of their arrival almost as soon as they stepped ashore, immediately saw a better use for them. Ali Pasha, among his many other virtues, was a societal fascist and aggressively bisexual with pederast tendencies. This Lord Byron, who had suddenly been delivered by the graces into Foresti's lap, was a beautiful young aristocrat with a ready made entourage and no direction home. After the diplomatic double-cross Ali Pasha would need consoling. Could young Byron be his consolation? Would the worldly-wise and wily Spiridion Foresti not have smiled to himself, laid the sign of the cross in the air and schemed his trap?

Back on board Hobhouse found they had received a dinner invitation to join the governor at his country house in San Anton. The dinner was clearly more than sociable, as Hobhouse recorded that they were advised to leave Malta as soon as possible, in fact to take the convoy that would leave for Turkey in three days time. Later he noted that there was a 'perpetual recommendation to go instantly to Constantinople'. After dinner they returned to Valletta in a trap, 'a neat carriage with two seats, two wheels, one mule, and the man running by the side', and found some excellent hospitality, as well as accommodation, from a merchant called Chabot. No trace of any of his time there remains today.

~

I think by now it is time to issue a dinner invitation of my own. Before leaving on the re-Tour, as part of the preparation for this project I had joined the International Byron Society, and without any great expectations I contact a gentleman the Society had listed as the Malta local branch secretary, one Professor Peter Vassallo. He sounds interested in the project over the phone; we arrange to meet for dinner the following week, and he agrees before then to cast his eye over an early draft of the chapter you are reading now, and I think no more of it.

A day or two later I am in the National Library in Valletta and ask about Byron's time in Malta, and if they have anything relevant. 'Ah, you'll want Peter Vassallo's books,' the librarian replies straight away. She volunteers to retrieve them, pulling her long skirt down even further as she shuffles away. While she raids the shelves in the dungeons I Google 'Professor Vassallo Malta' on the library's grubby old Mark 1 PC and up pops:

PETER VASSALLO is Professor of English and Comparative literature and Head of the Department of English at the University of Malta. He also is Director of the Institute of Anglo-Italian Studies in this University. He is the author of *Byron: The Italian Literary Influence* and editor of *Byron and the Mediterranean*. Peter Vassallo is the editor of the Journal of Anglo-Italian Studies and has published various articles on Anglo-Italian Literary relations in the nineteenth and twentieth century.

I spend the afternoon reading *Byron and the Mediterranean*, and find a treasure trove of information, learning in the preface that the author had also hosted the 10th International Byron Society conference in

Malta. Clearly Professor Vassallo is an all round Byron brain box, and a brain box I'm looking forward to unlocking.

Byron and Hobhouse weighed up taking the next day convoy to Turkey, and decided to spend some more time in Malta instead. All the signs of their intentions still pointed to Arabia and beyond. They were in no rush, and it wasn't—and isn't—an uninteresting island. In particular for Hobhouse it was an untapped mine of historical majors and minors, and for Byron the British expatriate society had not yet had enough time to amuse him. They visited the public library, now the National Library on Republic Street, and found it as excellent then as it is evocative now. They came across there an Arabic Grammar which Byron bought for a dollar, and they discovered that the chief librarian, Abbate Giacchino Navarro, spoke Arabic and gave Arabic lessons; he gave them their first one there and then. They had found a lovely place to stay, 'capital lodgings' as Hobhouse had it, a proper palazzo at 3 Strada di Forni—now at the top of Triq Il Fran or Old Bakery Street—belonging to an absent Dr. Moncrieff. Like much of Valletta the palazzo was bombed in the Second World War. It is now a block of a dozen apartments needing at least an external wash and brush up. Later they dined with General Hildebrand Oakes at his country house, and a likeness of the general can be found next to the dominant lion and unicorn motif in the National Library. Above the portrait a sign announces Hildebrandus Oakes, and I don't suppose anyone has told him but hand-on-hip he looks remarkably like Bill Clinton.

Sunday was Malta's day of rest, and is still well observed, but by now Spiridion Foresti would have been fully informed of Byron's movements and circumstances and it was time for him to play his first ace. He arranged for his son George, only slightly older than Byron and Hobhouse, to be at the Chabots for dinner that night. George had clearly been taught well as his mixture of salacious gossip and inside knowledge of a wider world clearly had the visitors impressed and intrigued. Hobhouse could not wait to record all the juicy details: the anecdotes of Buonaparte, tales of an assassin and what happened when Napoleon sent Ali Pasha his portrait in a snuff-box, how Napoleon's brother-in-law demanded a loan from the Hamburgers who spilled the beans on the Danes, how Napoleon said he would overrun Holstein with five hundred French grenadiers, the time when Bonaparte made King Maximilian I of Bavaria and the Viceroy of Italy wait standing behind his chair, of the immense expense of keeping Capri, all the news of Sir William Drummond's strange behaviour at the court of Sicily, the moment Young Wellesley Pole bullied the Divan and got Wallachia for the Russians, who then got him appointed Secretary of Embassy at Constantinople where he had to do everything, as Arbuthnot did nothing. Then there was the time when Sir George Rumbold disguised himself as a sergeant and tried to seduce Danish soldiers at Altona, and as for Spencer Smith—certainly guilty, and didn't they know that the famous diva Angelica Catalani was previously a whore in Milan?

We presume that Foresti *fils* reported back positively to Foresti *père* because the next night at the theatre the latter not only introduced himself to the visitors but he played his second ace: he introduced Byron to Constance Spencer-Smith. Mrs. Spencer-Smith to be exact, but never mind, she was alone, tall, pretty, well built ('fat arms, well made' being Hobspeak for amply breasted) and the most exotic creature Byron had ever met. He, in turn, was the most beautiful man she had ever met, a poet, a peer, charming and courteous, four years younger than herself, and like herself a soul in transit. Soon they were inseparable.

Her story alone was enough captivate him. Her father was Baron Herbert, currently the Austrian Ambassador to Constantinople. Her brother-in-law was the celebrated swashbuckler Sir Sidney Smith, burner of Toulon, hero of Acre, saviour of the Lisbon court, and of whom Napoleon was later to declare 'that man has cost me my destiny'. Her husband was the British Minister in Stuttgart and while away from her duties there on a cure at a spa near Vicenza in Italy the French army captured the town. She fled to Venice to stay with her sister Countess Attems, but the *Grande Armée* caught up with her again. She was soon arrested by the gendarmes, trussed up and sent off to prison in Valenciennes. Her fate reached the ears of the young

Marquis of Salvo, who having met her determined to rescue her. He intercepted the prison convoy at Brescia, spirited her down a ladder from the top floor of an *auberge*, whisked her across Lake Garda on a skiff, dressed her as a boy and they made their way perilously through French territory to the safety of her other sister, Countess Strassoldo, in Graz. To add further to her glamour Napoleon personally had paid her the signal honour of placing a reward on her recapture. She was in Malta on a roundabout tour back to the solidity of Stuttgart, skirting the French-held continent, but she seemed to be in no desperate hurry to reunite with an arranged husband old enough to be her father. She was to become his 'new Calypso' in the second canto of *Childe Harold's Pilgrimage*, and remembered in 'Lines Written in an Album at Malta', 'Stanzas Written in Passing the Ambracian Gulf', 'Stanzas Composed During a Thunderstorm' and 'To Florence', from which:

> But wheresoe'er I now may roam,
> Through scorching clime, and varied sea,
> Though Time restore me to my home,
> I ne'er shall bend mine eyes on thee:
> On thee, in whom at once conspire
> All charms which heedless hearts can move,
> Whom but to see is to admire,
> And, oh! forgive the word—to love.

Byron wrote of her to his mother: 'Since my arrival here, I have had scarcely any other companion. I have found her very pretty, very accomplished, and extremely eccentric. Buonaparte is even now so incensed against her, that her life would be in some danger if she were taken prisoner a second time.' To the young and as always passionate Byron a more appealing set of attributes would be hard to imagine.

By their second week in Malta Byron and Hobhouse had settled into a routine. Up late morning, a stroll to some sights, an Arabic lesson in the afternoon, and the theatre in the evening. In between times Hobhouse would browse the library and Byron would browse Constance Spencer-Smith. Either George or Spiridion Foresti was never far away; helping them find La Pietà baths, accompanying them to the theatre, running into them at dinner, dropping in at Constance's salon, and gossiping about him and her and this and that.

By the end of that second week Foresti played his third ace and took them on a private tour of the island. They went to Mdina, the walled city and oldest part of Malta. The writer's wife spent years of her childhood there—her father being a latter day Spiridion Foresti—and remembers it as a lively lived-in village, a village but within city walls. In Byron's time it would have been even more so, but its closed walls, determined moat and squeezed alleys held little allure for the expansively-minded poet, and neither the memorable Mdina nor Malta at large find their way into *Childe Harold's Pilgrimage*. And he was in love, his mind not on the capitals but on Constance. One has to feel he would like it even less now it is an uninhabited well scrubbed tourist attraction, the grocer's a gift shop, the butcher's a pastiche boutique, the post office a glass blowing outlet. Mdina has become a museum, pleasant enough for a thoughtful stroll and expensive lunch if one is lucky enough to find a break in the loudhailed tour groups from the dreaded cruise ships.

After Mdina Foresti took them to visit St. Paul's catacombs, which Hobhouse found 'very spacious and tolerably perfect—bats chasing in clusters to the cave', but they were looted thoroughly later in the nineteenth century and the space is now just a mouldy dungeon, although still 'tolerably perfect' for potholing enthusiasts. Nearby they visited St. Paul's cave. The priest who showed them around assured them that St. Paul had lived there for three months. Our guide was more mutant than priest, but he had shrunk St. Paul's residence there to a more explicable one month. Perhaps St. Paul was an early potholer himself, otherwise it's hard to see why he grottied in the grotto at all. Seeking fresh air they visited Buskett Gardens with its 'large neat palace, gardens of pomegranates, orange and lemon, and fine fountain of clear water where the citizens of Valletta take cold dinners.' The gardens are still fine, and even more abundant, but the palace has long been closed, but it is a pleasant enough picnic spot—on weekdays.

Foresti had their ears all day and in between sightseeing and gossiping—did they know that Lord Valentia had caught the shitten pox in Egypt? For sure, Foresti had heard it from his own surgeon—this is when he first planted the seed of their going to Albania instead of Arabia. Being Foresti the seed would have been of the subtle variety, planted so that it grew more questions than answers, and ready to sprout within a week. Foresti knew the convoy to Patras and Preveza, within easy reach of Ali Pasha's fiefdom, was due to leave in eight days and that he could arrange space for the Byron party on board the naval escort *Spider*. He knew too that his own invasion fleet was to sail for the Ionian Islands three days after that. He needed Byron on board the *Spider*, and Byron pacifying at Ali Pasha's court as the Ionian Island invasion was unfolding. By now he might even have had the further idea of passing Byron off as George III's nephew, for that was the rumour that followed Byron around the less well-informed Ottoman lands; it had the ring of truth, was impossible for Ali Pasha to disprove, and would appeal to the tyrant's sense of self-aggrandisement. Foresti might even have had the less charitable thought of it appealing to Byron's sense of self-aggrandisement as well. But all this, and the talk of secret missions, would be for later. In the evening he took Hobhouse to the theatre again, 'Lord Byron gallanting at Mrs Fraser's'—Constance Spencer-Smith's safe house.

~

By now it is time for us to have dinner with Professor Vassallo. We meet at La Borga, a waterfront trattoria near where *Vasco da Gama* is resting in Malta. With Peter is his equally brainy wife Madeleine. We all have pasta of various distinctions and local Delicata white wine—very crisp it is too, at least in Malta. Thank heavens he quite likes the direction of the early draft but then says:

'I think you have missed out the duel.'

'I have?' I reply, 'what duel?'

'Towards the end of his stay a Captain Carey—Alexander Ball's *aide de camp*—made some snide reference to his affair with Constance

Spencer-Smith. So Byron challenged him to a duel. He told Carey he would not tolerate the marked insolence of his behaviour.'

'What did Carey actually say, what was the snide remark?'

'It's not recorded. Byron later wrote that he was a grinning and insolent oaf. Carey appointed a Captain Waddle as his second, and he seems to have gone to see Hobhouse to see if they could talk Byron out of the duel. Hobhouse didn't need much encouraging, I can tell you.'

'Let's call the whole thing off.'

'Exactly. Just as they were boarding the ship to leave for Greece, Carey wrote apologising and Byron swore to keep the supposed scandal secret. Of course he did no such thing, far too juicy a story to stay out of his letters.' After dinner we agree to stay in touch, which indeed we do. Peter is also behind most of the useful information for the chapter on Byron's return to Malta, 'Malta, Heading Home', found later in the book.

Byron and Hobhouse's routine of Arabic lessons, bathing, dining and theatre—and in Byron's case consorting with young Constance—took up the next three days. One or both of the Forestis was always close at hand. The next day at dinner Spiridion Foresti played his fourth ace. The talk was now directly of Ali Pasha. A pretty picture was not painted. They discussed his war with the Souliotes, how on their expulsion from Souli five years previously sixty women with their children had thrown themselves over a precipice rather than be captured alive. Six months later a hundred and thirty women, again with their children, threw themselves into the River Achelous. Such was his reputation. The twelve-year-old son of the chief Souliote was captured and taken before the son of Ali Pasha in Ioannina. The young Pasha said, 'Well, we have got you and we will now burn you alive.' 'I know it,' replied the prisoner, 'and when my father catches you he will serve you in the same manner.'

These were not pleasant people; barbarous people in a lawless land. No doubt Foresti added weight to the bait with stories of how Ali Pasha enjoyed pleasuring himself on boys as much as girls when he was not murdering their mothers and fathers. But, Foresti explained, however horrific he may be the British government still had to deal with him as a neighbour, as an Ottoman pasha and one not without influence in Constantinople. The British government required a mission of the utmost delicacy. A diplomatic despatch was needed to neutralise any unpleasantness that might soon arise between our countries. A visit by an aristocrat who was, in the Pasha's eyes, of equal social standing to himself to deliver the despatch would be decidedly advantageous. The invasion of the Ionian Islands had to be seen solely as being to Napoleon's disadvantage, not a slight against Ali Pasha or his fiefdom. They would not be alone; he had an English consul to Ali Pasha at Ioannina, Captain William Leake, who knew the country and the court. A Royal Navy ship was being readied right now, and discreet arrangements could be made for it to take them to Preveza. Britain would be grateful. Britain expects. He hoped he could count on them serving their country.

It is hard to see Byron putting up even a veil of resistance; it is hard to imagine him not smiling ear to ear. The clandestine mission appealed to Byron on any number of levels: they had no firm destination or travel arrangements from here, and this decided that particular dilemma for them, and at His Majesty's expense; as an aspiring politician in the House of Lords this would do his future career no harm, might even open many a door he didn't even know was closed; Ali Pasha might be the mass murderer depicted, and worse, but it wasn't every day one supped with one of those; boys were clearly not a crime; he had had a full set of regimentals made in Gibraltar in which he would look quite splendid, just the part; it was *terra incognita*, exotic and dangerous—and none the worse for those—to his friends in London; and it was in the final consideration his duty to serve his country, and if Hobhouse thought that pompous, well then Hobhouse didn't—couldn't—understand.

The next day they stopped taking their Arabic lessons, no need of these now, and the Farsi-speaking Friese was dismissed, no need for him either. They started instead making hurried preparations for the voyage. The brig-of-war was HMS *Spider* under the command of Captain Oliver. The Governor advised them to take extra provisions.

Spiridion Foresti was arranging despatches, and unknown to Byron and Hobhouse, arranging for another agent to accompany them with a further despatch to his consul, Captain Leake, advising Leake of the Byron mission and George III nephew cover story. Hobhouse took care of their private provisioning. Byron was in passionate farewells with his *amorosa* Constance Spencer-Smith; they arranged to meet again right there in exactly a year from then, and in the meantime, no doubt, both agreed to remain devotedly chaste. Luckily Byron didn't have the last-minute duel with Captain Carey as Peter Vassallo related earlier.

Hobhouse's last entry from Malta reads: 'Tuesday September 19th 1809. Got up nine. The *Spider* and convoy under weigh very early, firing guns.' And so the Grand Tour moved on; next stop Patras, one week later, in what would become Greece.

Chapter Eight

FROM MALTA TO IOANNINA, PRIVATEERS ALL

19 SEPTEMBER – 10 OCTOBER 1809 | 4–10 FEBRUARY 2009

*𝒰*nfortunately—and most unusually—the actual log of HMS *Spider* is not to be found at the UK National Archives. From other records there it seems she was built in September 1802 and served in the Baltic until 1808, and so had only recently arrived in the Mediterranean by the time she escorted her convoy from Malta to Patras in September 1809. The last record of her is in October 1817, and the short life and lack of logbook would suggest her eventual capture or shipwreck.

What was she? Well, one hates to engage in pedantry with HMS Hobhouse—one would strike one's colours at the first puff of his well-considered cannon smoke—but she wasn't a ship. A ship needs a bowsprit and three masts, each stepped mast carrying a topmast and a topgallant mast, and with yards carrying square sails across those masts. Ships of war were nothing less than floating fortresses, and battle joined by lining up one's own ships opposite those of the enemy and trading broadsides, pdq. Ships suitable for this strategy were classed from first rater to sixth rater, but in practice only first to fourth raters could muster the firepower needed for this blunderbuss approach to war at sea. They were known as line-in-battle ships, or more easily 'ships of the line'.

After a sixth rater, which would be a frigate, ships stopped being ships and became barques and barquentines, brigs and brigantines, sloops and cutters, and these latter non-ships made up the quantity of naval vessels. HMS *Spider* was technically a bark-rigged sloop-of-war, known more conveniently as a brig-of-war. She was near the bottom of the naval hierarchy of vessels, displacing about 250 tonnes, carrying sixteen six-pounder guns on one deck and enjoying a crew of 120 souls; for perspective HMS *Victory* displaced 2,200 tons, carried one hundred 32-pounders on three decks and enjoyed a crew of 900 souls.

As we have seen before, Hobhouse tended to put his diary away at sea, and Byron makes no specific mention of the voyage on the *Spider*, and we are hence unsure of how they fared for most of their week on board. At least the entourage was easy to accommodate, being now just the ever-faithful and ever-complaining William Fletcher—a dangerously low suite by Byron's standards—so we can assume the long suffering valet squeezed in below decks with Jack Tar, and Byron and Hobhouse each bought space in an officer's cabin. It would not have been particularly comfortable, but the voyage appears to have

been leisurely, its progress being dictated by the speed of the slowest member of the convoy. One can imagine keen young Captain Oliver of the speedy *Spider* cursing the over-laden and ill crewed merchantmen that caused him to take a whole week to voyage the 350 miles in the breezy September winds.

One must put one's hand up here and declare no such open sea bravery on the part of *Vasco da Gama*'s crew of two, who took a month to sail from Malta to Gozo to Sicily to Calabria to Corfu and the southern Ionian Islands before re-joining Byron's route at Preveza; in defence of such abrogation of duty one can only say how pleasant the ambling jaunt across the Mediterranean islands was at the time.

But for Byron and Hobhouse it wasn't all wallowing merchantmen and endless horizons by day, and cramped quarters and brig's biscuit at night; there was sport to be had, privateering sport, and very well they privateered too.

While it might at first sight appear that one man's pirate was another man's privateer, there were distinct and proudly held differences. Piracy was simply illegal and there was only one penalty: hanging, there and then. Privateering was legal, even if its practitioners were subject to civil rather than naval law, and only vessels belonging to, or trading with, enemies of the state could be attacked and taken as prizes. The captured crew were not to be harmed. A complication was the common practice of flying other countries' ensigns as a *ruse de guerre*, either as a discouragement from attack or as an encouragement to relax defences. As captured vessels were routinely pressed into the victor's fleet, appearances were deceptive enough for even the expert eye, and the trick was to guess, or double guess, the true identity and intentions of the other vessel. No doubt Captain Oliver explained the sea rules before letting Byron and Hobhouse loose on passing shipping.

On 21 September 1809, two days or a hundred miles off the Greek coast, just as the British fleet carrying 2,000 men was leaving Malta to invade the Ionian Islands, they saw their first sail on the horizon. Captain Oliver put the *Spider* on full alert, only for the stranger to identity herself as Greek and returning from a corn run to Sicily; as

Greece was under Ottoman control and Sicily a Spanish colony, no enemies of England were involved and no privateering allowed. A pirate would have had no such restraints of trade.

Other coastal shipping soon appeared. They chased a small galliot—a rowed sailing boat—and found her to be trading fruit with French controlled Ithaca. She was taken as a prize and the crew of three brought onto the *Spider*. Then they chased another galliot, but found her only to be coastal trading and under the Turkish flag and so had to let her go. Captain Oliver must have deemed the *Spider* could not be a convoy escort and privateer at the same time and thus ordered the captured prize and the *Spider's* jolly-boat—its launch—to be turned into privateers. They fitted the former with a two-pounder cannon, which Byron called Murphy, rounded up ten beefy volunteers (you, you and you, look lively!) to be oarsmen, and with the *Spider's* surgeon Mr. Swann as captain, the teenage midshipman Mr. Parker as helmsman, and our heroes as accessories, off they went looking for trouble.

They were by now just south of Kefalonia. Byron's privateer rowed or sailed into an inlet to wait in ambush for whomsoever might pass. Before long they saw one sail pursuing another, and without looking too closely they joined in the chase and fired on the first vessel. Looking more closely they discovered they had just friendly-fired on their own jolly-boat which was merely towing a prize of its own back to the *Spider*. They then hounded two coastal dhows, one of which had 'women sleeping', and the other 'a Turkish soldier with a firman', but both were Turkish flagged and so unable to be prized. They rowed and sailed back to join the jolly-boat on the *Spider*.

The next morning at first light saw them well inside the Gulf of Patras, which leads into the Straits and the Gulf of Corinth. They rose at dawn, and to the sound of 'sail ahoy!' from the *Spider's* crow's nest took to their privateer and set off in pursuit of the day's first quarry. In the early morning still air it took two hours of sweaty rowing to come close to the becalmed merchantman, a seventy-ton, ten-manned Turkish-flagged brigantine called *San Marco Fortunato*. The English privateer did not believe the brigantine was flagged correctly, hoisted her own colours and fired Murphy across the suspect's bows in an invitation for the brigantine to heave-to. The brigantine replied with lively musket shot, directed at the privateer, at which point of conflict protocol deemed a proper engagement could start. Murphy and the English muskets then replied in quick fire, and so for half an hour quite a small naval battle raged. One bullet went 'within an inch' of Hobhouse's ear. Then, of all the cheek, Hobhouse saw that 'a man, a foreigner, shot the next man but one to me in the thigh about four inches from the knee.'

Just as the English privateer was about to win the Battle of Hobhouse's Ear a breeze perked up and the much larger merchantman was able to put some distance between herself and her pursuer. Then the same breeze reconsidered and the English were encouraged to make 'one last try'. They loaded up Murphy and the muskets and were soon alongside. As they were ready to take their prize three of the brigantine's crew jumped on board the privateer but were overpowered and forced into the hold.

On board the *San Marco Fortunato* they found a cargo of iron, coffee, sulphur and raisins, the latter belonging to a Greek whom Hobhouse found to be 'the most timid sneaking fellow I ever saw'. The Turkish captain said that they too were from Malta, and had fired on them because he thought the English were French—in spite of flying British colours. But as Swann, and excited opinion on board determined they were sailing for French-controlled Parga the brigantine was taken as a prize.

Soon Swann and the privateer veered off in search of more prizes, leaving the *San Marco Fortunato* under the command of young midshipman Parker (quite a first command), half a dozen stout English sailors and Byron and Hobhouse, while the Turks were kept below and told to man the pumps. They soon came across a suspicious looking dhow with twelve men on board, hoisted their newly captured Turkish colours and boarded her, 'but finding nothing French let her go.' By the evening a wind and swell had built up and Parker chose to anchor in a bay south of Patras. At two in the morning they saw a boat approaching and prepared arms, but it was only Swann in the privateer; he 'had driven two French boats on shore but taken nothing.' And thus a memorable day's privateering (not least for young Parker) had come to an end.

On board the *Spider* Captain Oliver decided that as it could not be proved that the *San Marco Fortunato* had been trading with the French she had to be let go, no doubt to much disappointment from Parker and our literary London heroes. One presumes gifts of compensation from the freed Turks' cargo hold were not discouraged.

Later that morning Byron and Hobhouse set foot on Greek soil for the first time, but within an hour they were summoned back on board as the *Spider* had completed her whistle-stop mission to Patras: delivering the secret despatch from Spiridion Foresti in Malta, via the English consul in Patras, Mr. Strané, to Captain Wilkes in Ioannina informing the latter of Byron's forthcoming visit to Ali Pasha. Neither Byron nor Hobhouse knew of the contents of the despatch. Later that evening they sailed past the salt flats and marshes of Messolonghi, where Byron was to die fifteen years later.

But their adventures afloat were not over. On the way north to Preveza a Turkish galliot was rash enough to 'salute' one of the convoy with a live shot, and soon the *Spider* was alongside her. This time Captain Oliver found them with a smoking cannon: the galliot had sailed from Dulsinea, a French-occupied port, and so was made a prize and the crew put below in the *Spider*'s reeking hold. Byron and Hobhouse were sent to rummage through the galliot's cargo, and found small arms and the cannon primed for another 'salute'.

On their way into Preveza they sailed over the site of the Battle of Actium, the Roman name for Preveza. It was here 1,840 years previously that Mark Antony had broken off his engagement with Octavian's squadron to pursue the fleeing Cleopatra on her purple-sailed treasure ship, completing his transformation from Roman warrior to love-lost Egyptian puppy in front of the legions watching from the hills behind Preveza—soon to become the sight of Nicopolis—and by his downfall reshaping the course of Roman and Mediterranean history. As usual Shakespeare captured the moment perfectly, as when Antony's friend Scarus says:

She once being loofed,
The noble ruin of her magic, Anthony,
Claps on his sea wing, and like a doting mallard,
Leaving the fight in height, flies after her.
I never saw an action of such shame,
Experience, manhood, honour, ne'er before
Did violate so itself.

They rose early the next morning to visit nearby Nicopolis. Built by Octavian to celebrate his victory over Mark Antony, and named after Nike, the goddess of victory, the polis covered a vast undulating stretch of land, a most glorious setting worthy of the king of the world, that covered the breadth of the isthmus north of Preveza, with the Ionian Sea on its western shore and the Gulf of Amvrakia to its east. Little remains today except the perimeter foundations, not in dissimilar repair to Hadrian's Wall, but spread over so large an area that a colony of thirty thousand souls settled there. There is no trace now of the famous 27-mile aqueduct which brought water down from the Prevezan mountains. The stadium is a hollowed mound, although the mound itself is the size of a hillock, and the amphitheatre large enough to entertain the colony's easily distracted citizens.

These scattered remains confirm the wonderful advantage for a man with Octavian's vision, the advantage of an unlimited supply of free labour; not such an advantage for the slaves, it has to be said. But civilisations breathe in and out like the rest of us and what with the Goths and the Slavs and the Turks it was sacked and taunted and used as a builders' yard until the glory that was Rome was rubble. Even two hundred years ago there was precious little to see, and Byron and Hobhouse were unimpressed: 'they are nothing magnificent, all that remains being broken walls with here and there the vestiges of a house. We saw the masons cutting up antiques from Nicopolis for the building of some paltry house in Preveza—but yet the Turks seem aware of the value of these curiosities.'

Preveza then, and Preveza now, seemed and seems rather unsure of itself. Just twelve years before Byron's visit the French had stumbled across it when they took over the Venetian empire along with La Serenissima. Five years later Ali Pasha had taken it from the nonplussed French, and made the still-imposing Venetian castle into his palace. Byron and Hobhouse visited the residence and were shown around by the Albanian governor, 'a most merry man who laughed much, and *avec un sourire impudent*, told them that one of the rooms was for the "boys".' No doubt Byron, out of amused curiosity, popped his head around that particular corner.

The town they found to be 'very dirty, with narrow streets, low houses, wooden roofs stretching out forming a wretched colonnade.' The population were half Greek and half Turkish, so half Christian and half Muslim. The Venetians and French would have favoured the Christians, and now Ali Pasha would have made sure the Muslims' version of one god, and their rights and privileges held sway. Since then Preveza has been racked by earthquakes and wars, and is trying to reinvent itself as a sailing centre and now has an impressive town quay with the usual amusements ashore and afloat. But a street or two back the town reverts to type, and the disappointment of seeing the Venetian castle going the way of Nicopolis is metaphor enough.

They cheered themselves up that night with an enormous feast at their host the consul's house. Although they soon surmised the consul to be a rogue, they dined famously, especially after a week of the *Spider's* fare, on 'first a tureen of rice soup, fowl boiled to rags, mutton seasoned high, fish broiled, goose, fish roes, fruit, all brought in separately—decent wines of the country at dinner, and a bottle of good port after by way of a *brune bruche.*'

~

The pains and pleasures of Preveza were but a mere pit stop on their way north to Ioannina to meet Ali Pasha. The consul arranged for them to be rowed to Salaóra, two hours to the north-east, and to pick up some horses for the journey north. But ready horses were there none, and Byron was forced to spend the first of many exotic nights in the company of an Albanian guard, this one of ten soldiers and this time in the old Venetian fortress at Salaóra. Byron smoked 'the long pipe and gave the captain a glass of *maraschino* from the canteen.' The Albanians then produced a bottle of aniseed aqua vitæ and Byron and Hobhouse had their first taste of ouzo. They were served by 'a pretty boy, one of the soldiers, about fifteen and for the public good.' During the course of the evening Byron also picked up his first dragoman, Georgiou, of whom Hobhouse noted ruefully 'he never lost an opportunity of robbing us.' The exotically dressed and wildly mannered Albanian soldiers, the hookah, the ouzo, the open sexuality, the new servant, the Venetian castle, the initial tension and its easing with good company were Byron's first taste of his Orient, with no English society close by to judge or impress, and for the first time he must have felt the Grand Tour had found its bearings.

They rode through the plains up to their first stop, the country town of Arta. Hobhouse found it a 'better-most sort of town, the streets partly paved and sufficiently wide, and not having any unpleasant smell.' Which is more or less as it remains today, a once is enough, no harm done, just passing through type of town, whose highlight remains its many-legended bridge. Byron and Hobhouse rode out to the old castle on a hill just to the west of the town, and noted that it was 'still fortified, badly built on the declivity of the hill.' Well, in the meantime the hill has won and now there are only ruins, hardly justifying all the brown and yellow tourist signs pointing its way.

It was in Arta that they came across the first murmurings of what would become an increasingly anti-Albanian chorus as they headed north. Travel from town to town was by staging post, the Pony Express system, where one rode from post to post, paid for the stage just ridden, collected a fresh horse, and set off again. In Arta they had to pay in advance, 'a circumstance that astonished us, because many travellers, Albanese merchants, &c., galloped off without payment.' The antagonism towards Albania remains today. When in Salaóra I rented the Smart car now below me in the hotel car park in Arta. I had asked for it for two weeks but was absolutely forbidden under any circumstances to take it to Albania. 'First time stop, ba-zoom!' and a short sharp clap explained their thinking.

The next night found them at an *osteria* on a summit half way between Arta and Ioannina, at a spot then called St. Demetre, now called EL-VO Truck Stop. Not having a truck I didn't comply and anyway was keen to reach Ioannina.

It was on Thursday 5 October 1809 that the entourage rode through Ioannina's southern city gate. It did not take long for them to see they were in the capital of Ali Pasha's fiefdom: riding through the outskirts of town, near where now stands the Archaeological Museum, they saw a man's arm with half his torso still attached dangling from 'under a tree, hanging to a twig'. It had clearly been there for several days and was not in good condition, and Hobhouse noted that 'no pleasant impression [was] made by this—Lord Byron and myself feeling a little sick.' They were later to find out that his arms had been tied to the end of a horse and his legs to another, and the horses encouraged into a tug of war. The 'legs' horse had won and that half of the equation was hanging from another tree at another entrance into town. It was their first contact with the ruthlessness with which Ali Pasha ruled; worse was to be seen soon. At their first meeting he boasted to Byron that he had personally killed 30,000 people; as he was seventy at the time and had been killing voraciously for fifty-five years one can 'do the maths' (ten a week) and not disagree with his tally.

His Excellency Ali Pasha, to whom they were bound on His Majesty's business, was the worst possible type of monster. A cross between Robert Mugabe without the agrarian acumen and Saddam Hussein without the love for humanity, he was the sort of despot that gives tyranny a bad name. He was also, as already remarked, an enthusiastic pederast and paedophile, and when six years before their visit to Ioannina he had become bored with his harem he had sewn the then-current incumbents up in a giant sack and chucked them wriggling and screaming over the ramparts into the lake.

In 1740, when he was born, all of what are now the new Balkan countries plus Albania, Greece and Turkey were part of a decaying Ottoman Empire still governed from Constantinople. Power was bought and sold from the Grand Seigneur to Viziers and then to regional Pashas. Ali himself was born in what is now southern

Albania. He was the son of the village chieftain, and this grasp on the first rung was all he needed to loot, betray, torture, steal, liquidate, starve, terrorise and bribe his way to run his own and his sons' private fiefdoms. This nepotocracy controlled an area which stretched from south-western Greece to Macedonia in the east and to the southern half of Albania to the north.

Ali Pasha was above all a natural Machiavellian who believed that all his subjects were beastly and the only way to rule them was to be correspondingly more beastly. He did not want them to love him, let alone fear him, but just be terrified of him.

Although Byron did not yet know it Ali Pasha was expecting him; they may or may not have already heard that he himself was upcountry, engaged 'in a small war' to the north with the last of his rivals, Ibrahim Pasha. Ali Pasha's knowledge of their arrival can only have come through Captain Leake, the English consul at Ioannina, and he would have known of it from the despatch brought from Malta by the *Spider* and given to his fellow consul Strané in Patras. As was Foresti's design their importance had become exaggerated and Ali Pasha was under the impression that Lord Byron was no mere humble peer but a nephew of King George III.

They settled in a substantial house belonging to a Greek trader called Signor Niccolo. Even Fletcher had his own room. The house is now on Lord Byron (Lordou Vironus) Street, a busy pedestrian cobbled affair lined with boutiques; funnily enough the house that gave the street its name is the only one that has not been developed, being still unkempt and decorated with anarchist graffiti. The house is midway on the right hand side walking north, just opposite the very chi-chi Venetian pink 'Lord Byron Fashion House'. In this old part of town the cobbled streets are laid out just as they were in Byron's day, and the two- or three-storey houses, with many old ones interspersed among the new, can give one a fine idea of how the visitors found Ioannina two hundred years ago.

Spies ensure news spreads quickly in a dictatorship and they did not have to wait long for Ali Pasha's delegation to arrive. Byron and Hobhouse dressed to meet them; Byron in his full regimentals and Hobhouse in his best red suit, the ones they had had tailored in Gibraltar. Ali Pasha was represented by his secretary, Spiridion Colovo, and Ioannina's primate, its mayor. The guests were invited to join Ali Pasha in his provincial capital Tepelenë, several days ride to the wild and mountainous north; in the meantime they were to be the vizier's most honoured guests here in Ioannina, forbidden from paying for anything, and with all of Ioannina at their disposal. Between them Byron and Hobhouse, Captain Leake, Signor Niccolo, Spiridion Colovo and the primate spoke an impressive array of languages: apart from all of their native tongues, they had between them Latin, Ancient Greek, Italian, Turkish, French and Albanian—the latter being described by the fogeyish Hobhouse as a 'mixture of Greek, Italian and a country language', As everywhere Latin prevailed, the Esperanto of the times.

They were to spend the next five days in Ioannina preparing for the trip to Tepelenë and waiting for the weather to improve. In the meantime they had tailored Albanian costumes 'as fine as pheasants'— quite likely Byron's being the one in which he was painted by Thomas Philips in 1814, versions of which are now in the British Embassy in Athens, the National Portrait Gallery and the John Murray archive. They learned about local courtship practices—a subject never far from Byron' heart. Husbands never saw their wives until the wedding ceremony, so an affair had to be either with a married woman, or one of easy virtue, or with a man—or better still a boy. Hobhouse reported that all 'this is some excuse for pæderasty, which is practised underhandly by the Greeks, but openly carried on by the Turks.' They saw a Greek wedding, with its raucous music and lights, its jewels and pistols, its chanting and praying, its bride 'waddling from side to side like the Virgin'. They witnessed the start of Ramadan, when all concerned let off their pistols and guns firing live ammunition, two balls of which narrowly missed Hobhouse on the loo. We can be sure Byron—never slow to fire his pistols, real or metaphorical—joined in too, but not usually fired at Hobhouse on the loo. They went shooting themselves, wildfowling on the lake, without any great success. They tried out Ali Pasha's horses, and were favourably impressed.

But the highlight of their stay in Ioannina was a visit to one of Ali Pasha's sons', Mouktar's, palace. Ioannina is dominated by the bluff which juts out as a promontory into the restful and reflective Lake Pamvotis. It holds a perfect defensive position, the far lakeside end of which was originally built as a fortress in the sixth century by the Byzantine emperor Justinian. Since then it has expanded and contracted with the ebb and flow of cultures and invasions. Ali Pasha saw its potential immediately and three hundred slaves died in his rush to re-enforce and expand the whole promontory from a castle into a citadel.

The promontory is now called Its Kale and it houses not just Ali Pasha's and his sons'—like Saddam Hussein he bred two (legitimate) sons who were just as ghastly as their father—palaces, his tomb, his mosque, and his treasury but the city's Byzantine and Municipal Museums. Outside the inner citadel but still within Its Kale's walls the area is called Kastro and is peacefully residential with one or two hotels and bars in converted houses. I stayed in, and can recommend, the Hotel Kastro. One can look over to the small island opposite where Ali Pasha met with a sticky end at the hands of the Ottoman army twelve years later at the age of 82. Fittingly, the Church of St. Nicolas nearby is adorned with graphically gruesome depictions of martyrdoms. His head was paraded through the streets of Constantinople on a pike—he would not have had it any other way.

At Mouktar's palace they took coffee and were introduced to Mouktar's handsome young son. Byron noted that he was 'a little fellow ten years old with large black eyes as big as pigeon eggs, and all the gravity of sixty.' They were shown around the palace and were impressed to see English carpets and a large painting of Constantinople. No mention was made of his harem, or of the story of how Mouktar had taken a shine to a married Christian woman and ordered her to attend his harem. Him being a Pasha, and his father being the Pasha, she had to take the offer seriously. The family convened and realised they had to obey, and so she submitted to his demands and her family fled the city. But Mouktar went further and fell in love with her; the other *haremistas* complained to Ali. Ali knew exactly how to put a stop to this; he rounded up the wives of the fifteen most prominent Christian families in Ioannina, tied them together and drowned them in the lake as a warning to other Christian wives to leave his poor sons alone.

There were always Ali family squabbles in the palaces. A year or so before Byron's visit, when Ali Pasha's other son Veli was away on another war, Ali raped one of his daughters-in-law, who subsequently had Ali's baby. To keep it quiet before Veli returned Ali had some slaves strangle the wife, baby, doctor and midwife in return for their freedom. He then had the slaves beheaded by his black mutes, who knew, if nothing else, how to keep a secret. Inevitably Veli found out, and on hearing the news shot the hapless messenger.

By 11 October it was time to leave Mouktar and Ioannina and seek the real thing in Tepelenë. The rains had stopped, the horses were gathered, supplies were saddled, the escort assembled, the entourage in place. They left Signor Niccolo's house, rode out past the main gate without noticing any fresh semi-torsos and headed north. Ahead of them were the gentle forested hills of Epirus, rising to the holy mountains of northern Greece and the badlands of Albania and the breeding land of *Childe Harold's Pilgrimage*.

Chapter Nine

FROM IOANNINA TO TEPELENË, AND BACK

11–26 OCTOBER 1809 | 12–24 FEBRUARY 2009

*L*ord Byron and the writer both left Ioannina, now in Greece, for Tepelenë, now in Albania, on diplomatic missions. Byron was to take Spiridion Foresti's reassurances of His Majesty's good intentions to His Excellency the Ali Pasha in the hope of pacifying him in the wake of previous, now broken, promises to give him the Ionian Islands in exchange for allying himself with Britain against France. If he could not be pacified, and a torrential rant if not bodily harm would be far from unexpected, Foresti hoped that Byron's embassy could at least keep Ali Pasha from allying himself with the French.

The writer's version of Spiridion Foresti was Professor Afrim Karagjozi, head of the Albanian Byron Society, whose university was organising a conference in the capital, Tirana, to celebrate the 200th anniversary of Byron's visit to the country. Via the professor's powers of persuasion, and the good offices of the Albanian Ambassador in London, my mission was to request King Leka I of the Albanians to invite the Marquis of Lansdowne to lend Albania Lord Byron's famous Albanian costume—as Byron is wearing in the National Portrait Gallery—to be the central display at the anniversary celebrations.

The Byron party left Ioannina on 11 October 1809. At its core were of course Hobhouse and Fletcher, with an outer ring of the dragoman

Georgiou who had joined them in Preveza, and a new servant, courtesy of Ali Pasha, an Albanian warrior called Vassily who was to stay with Byron for the duration of the Grand Tour. Accompanying the group were Ali Pasha's secretary's priest and the priest's servant, as well as eight of Ali Pasha's janissaries as their escort and six horses for the baggage. With sixteen men and twenty-two horses the Byron entourage had grown into the Byron battalion. The writer left Ioannina alone in the worn and rented Smart car, but we live in straitened times.

What a wonderful sense of exhilaration, of freedom and adventure, the young Byron must have felt as he led the colourful and eclectic group that left Ioannina that autumn day. Beside him rode his best friend whom he knew was recording the great adventure day by day, behind him was his valet to keep him looking spruce, around him came a Greek guide and an Albanian guard to smooth the way in this strange and savage land, and all escorted by heavily armed, white kilted

soldiers of the fiercest aspect with direct orders from a tyrant who 'requires and requests' their safe passage 'without let or hindrance'; all this, and on a secret mission for his king and country, and riding through wild and open autumnal landscapes that reminded him of his childhood Scotland. We know he was already spending more and more time writing, or scribbling, as he would have put it. Twenty days later, back in Ioannina, he would be inspired by what he had just seen and done and noted to unpack his sheaves, shuffle and shake them and start creating the first draft of his first epic *Childe Harold's Pilgrimage*. The Albanian adventure eventually stood out as the most vivid part of the more melancholy second canto.

Byron's king, Ali Pasha, and the writer's king, Leka I, are both prime examples of the art of power and survival. Ali Pasha and power understood each other perfectly, and he played the English off against the French, the Muslims off against the Christians, and the Turks off against the Greeks. He himself was a Bektashi, a most interesting branch of Islam which mixes local folklore and animism with the mystical aspects of Sufism. It was brought westwards to Albania by eastern dervishes in the sixteenth century, and settled in southern Albania by Ali Baba when Ali Pasha was in his twenties. When the Maoists made Albania the world's first atheist state in their cultural revolution of 1967 they made a particular point of trying to wipe out Bektashism, partly by shooting the babas. (It's fair to say they shot most of the imams and priests too.) The Bektashis disguised their religion by reverting to their folkloric tradition, and having weathered the ungodly storm Bektashism is now practised openly in *teqes*, these being more like retreats than mosques.

King Leka I of the Albanians is an interesting character too. He was two days old when the Italian fascists invaded Albania in 1939. By then his father, King Zog, who promoted himself from prime minister to president and then invented his own monarchy, upped with as much gold as his entourage could carry and fled to France.

It was a rare triumph for the Italian military. The Albanian army took one look at the Italian army and, using best Italian tactics, headed for the hills. Their leader King Zog, his Queen Geraldine and their new Crown Prince Leka arrived in Paris in the scarlet supercharged Mercedes cabriolet that Hitler had given them as a wedding present. When the self-same Hitler approached Paris Zog fired up the Merc again and spent the rest of the war in the London Ritz—not on the top floor, one imagines. The wartime Home Office rather unkindly called the royal family and their countless retainers 'King Zog's Circus'.

But the king, clearly nobody's fool, had the presence of mind to make King Faisal of Saudi Arabia and King Farouk of Egypt—the latter himself Albanian—the infant Leka's godfathers, and then the further presence of mind to send him to the Sorbonne and Sandhurst. The young adult Leka then had his own presence of mind to put his family connections, multilingual education and military knowledge together and develop a thoroughly respectable career as a renowned arms dealer. Along the way he reminded Richard Nixon they were distant cousins and befriended Ronald Reagan, giving him the present of an elephant.

But for Crown Prince Leka, by now in the mid 1960s King Leka I, it wasn't all plain sailing. Early in his career he was arrested in Thailand with an arms cache; then he had to leave Spain in a hurry when, in spite of being a guest of the newly restored monarch Juan Carlos, the Spanish secret service found a small arsenal in his compound. He escaped to Rhodesia and when that became Zimbabwe to South Africa where he stayed until he was busted there too with an even larger arsenal after the apartheid regime fell. He returned to Albania on a passport issued by his own court-in-exile; at the border he filled in a form and under 'occupation' put down 'King'. In the post-Hoxha chaos they let him in. His effects arrived soon afterward, and included eleven containers of arms 'for my personal use'. Once back on the home soil he had known for only two days he narrowly lost a referendum to restore the monarchy. That was fifteen years ago. Since then, though not exactly content, he has become resigned to being the symbolic King of the Albanians rather than outright King of Albania. It's a large diaspora, with Albanians all over the Balkans, in Turkey, Greece, Egypt, Italy and now in England too.

To reach Albania from Ioannina one needs to travel through to Zitsa. Zitsa, still being in Greece, is only thirty or so miles, and the track then, and the road now, winds slowly up to the mountains to the north-west of Ioannina. Yet it was on this comparatively easy stretch of the journey that the company managed to find itself scattered in a tremendous storm. When the heavens opened an advance guard of four of the janissaries went ahead to Zitsa to secure lodgings. This was simple enough; all villagers were obliged to house and feed any of Ali Pasha's men whenever they passed through, so the guard would just have found the village primate and told him to arrange lodgings and food for sixteen men and twenty-two horses. At dusk and in a ferocious downpour with thunder and lightning exploding over their heads, Hobhouse, Vassily and the secretary arrived in the village. But of Byron and his group—Fletcher, the secretary's valet and priest and the other four soldiers and the six pack horses—there was no sign. In the pitch dark, on the slippery track, with panicky horses in the fury of the storm they had become lost.

Byron had not been cowering from the storm; the sense of adventure, of being somewhere so different, so exotic, and right now so dangerous, simply inspired him. They found shelter in a hovel and lit some torches. Byron took some paper from his satchel and started composing what would later be polished into 'Stanzas Composed During a Thunderstorm', in which his thoughts turned back to Malta, and to Constance Spencer-Smith, his 'Sweet Florence':

> While wandering through each broken path,
> O'er brake and craggy brow;
> While elements exhaust their wrath,
> Sweet Florence, where art thou?
>
> Not on the sea, not on the sea—
> Thy bark hath long been gone:
> Oh, may the storm that pours on me,
> Bow down my head alone!

Full swiftly blew the swift Siroc,
When last I pressed thy lip;
And long ere now, with foaming shock,
Impelled thy gallant ship.

Hobhouse and the secretary sent out a search party, lit some fires and set off some guns in an effort to guide them in. Eventually at about 3 a.m. the Byron party arrived. Hobhouse was not amused: 'The party had been for nine hours in total ignorance of their position, notwithstanding the three guides belonging to the horses, a priest and the secretary's valet, who, I was informed, knew every step of the way.' Fletcher was not amused either: at the height of their peril, just after two of the horses had slipped down the mountain, Byron started laughing and Georgiou panicked, 'stamped, swore, cried and fired off his pistols', which only made poor Fletcher think they were being ambushed by robbers.

No one in Zitsa today knows exactly where they slept, unusual itself in Greece as these Byron visitations are normally so well celebrated, even quite often with a Hotel Lordou Vironus on the supposed spot like so many splinters of the Cross. In fact the writer managed to cause quite a ruction in the Tourist Office by asking where they lodged, at which point in translation two Zitsanites fairly flew at each other before declaring by way of a truce that no one was sure. The only hotel is the Aganti, a new three star on the hill opposite Zitsa, with a fine view of the town and up to the mountains where they were, and the writer is, all heading, and from where some of these words are being written this evening.

The next morning they explored Zitsa and walked up the hill behind the village to the Monastery of Profitis Elias. Byron was moved that it lay 'in the most beautiful situation I ever beheld.' Hobhouse wrote that 'This monastery of Zitza perhaps is the most romantic spot in the world.' It's hard to disagree now. Arriving at the peak of a sizeable hill, in the scent of a light forest of eucalyptus, surrounded below by a moat of valleys and then towered over by snowed mountains beyond, the visitor is serenaded by goats' bells and rushing water, and beyond that only silence, stillness and the constancy of patient time.

After a bit of banging on the iron gate Byron and Hobhouse persuaded a monk to let them in. The writer was more fortunate and pushed on an open door; inside the cleaner was sweeping the refectory. All of us found 'panels covered with red pictures, particularly of Elijah.' The monastery is now used only as an occasional retreat, but still kept in pristine condition. Above the entrance, carved in stone, is written:

12th–13th Ocktober 1809.

Monastic Zitza! from thy shady brow, thou small but favoured spot of holy ground!

Byron.

The lines are from the second canto of *Childe Harold's Pilgrimage*.

They spent a second night at Zitsa and the next day headed north-west again but had to call a halt at Mazaraki because of more storms. From Zitsa to Mazaraki the road descends steeply into a valley, from goat country to sheep country, and now some vineyards and orchards. Mazaraki is still a small village, no more than a hamlet. There were only scattered hovels and so among the hovels they scattered themselves. All of them spent the night hunting fleas, but at least Byron, Hobhouse and Fletcher had the army travelling beds which the latter laid for them every night. The construction was 'sapper simple': the four sides of the frame and four legs slotted together in moments, and the slats of the base laid into a groove along the frame—typical examples can be seen in the Imperial War Museum.

The track continues to rise as it heads north-west up to the next stop, the village of Delvinaki, just shy of the Albanian border. On the way the track that was, and road that is, climbs steeply and there are still the 'tremendous precipices beneath and grand prospect to the left of a thousand woody hills'. There is now a fence of sorts along the road, but it seems so flimsy that it would only prevent a bicyclist from taking the quick route down the 'tremendous precipice'. This is a prosperous little town without it being immediately obvious why it should so be. There is a taxi rank, with taxis thereupon, a new three star hotel and whitewashed houses. The streets have just been swept. The flags are new. A taxi driver explains Delvinaki's good fortune: there's a famous spring in the mountains nearby, and the spring begat a health farm and the health farm begat the B&Bs and the B&Bs begat the taxi rank and his taxi thereupon. Does he take the waters himself? He does not, rubbing his thumb and forefinger together: the water is expensive. More than the wine? More than the wine!

From here to what has become the Greece/Albania frontier the Byron battalion's route has become the victim of geopolitics. There are now only two official border crossings, one to the north and one to the south of the track that was the old way into Albania. But here on this Michelin map I am looking at there is a dotted line that joins Orino in Greece and Radat in Albania; clearly the old crossing has to be attempted.

Straight after Orino the road loses its tarmac. A few miles further on it goes from gravel to grass, and then reduces to two lines of rutted earth or mud. I press on, the Smart hire car being ideal for this sort of off road work. Suddenly, after a few kilometres the track stops at a rampart. There's a feeble wire fence with large gaps underneath it. Fresh footprints are on the earth, heading south.

I was just thinking it would take more than this to keep the poor Albanians out when a helicopter, an angry helicopter clearly on full revs or whatever it is helicopters are full of when angry, appears fast and low over the treetops. It is blue and white with POLICE under the doors. Thank heavens the photographs of the frontier are safely on the flash card. It flies over, banks tightly and descends. Just when you need a Stinger one is never to hand. Does a man alone in a bright red oilskin standing next to an electric blue and dayglo Smart two-seater in the early afternoon look as suspicious as he does conspicuous? He could hardly be a people trafficker, or at least not a very tactical one. The man on the ground opens both doors and the tailgate, and gives the helicopter some gentlemanly English body language. The helicopter hovers just above the ground, not sure of its quarry.

The ground shakes, the dust attacks. The driver shrugs and waves, and the car gingers its way back along the track. The helicopter follows, but now higher and better tempered. The car stops outside Orino, and the driver shows more signs of peace. The helicopter turns sharply about itself and flies off without a proper goodbye.

And so to the official southern border. It has been clear for a while that Greeks and Albanians cannot stand each other, in a deep Greco-Balkan kind of way that is hard for others to follow. The Balkans seem prone to finding new ways to divide and loathe each other. You can forget Forgive and Forget, they are just not on the menu; memories are as long as blood feuds. The closer to the border, the shriller and more alarming the warnings. Never go out at night. Never go out alone. Keep your hands in your pockets. Never wear your watch. Everything for sale has been stolen.

The resentment needs no encouraging, but the role reversal they each find themselves in reinforces the mistrust. Under the Ottomans the Albanians had converted to Islam and paid their dues if not their taxes. To the Greeks they had become quasi-Turks. For them the Greeks, the slaves and infidels who had always been nothing but trouble, had somehow wangled their way into the European Union—the underbelly to milk and honey—and now it was the Albanians who had to cross the border on their hands and knees in the middle of the night and work for half the Greek wage. To the Greeks the Albanians are what they always have been: inherently dishonest, congenitally disingenuous, downright disagreeable and much as their own King Zog had described them: 'a primitive and backward people'. And now millions of them were racketeering in Greece. *And* they were still camping in the north of Greece's Epirus—the 'land without end'—and calling it southern Albania.

The car has to spend some time in the car park on the Greek side of the border as no Greek car hire company will allow their charges into Albania. Both sides are mighty suspicious of this lone traveller on foot. The Greek customs asks why my two bags were so heavy.

'Mostly my books,' I reply.

'Open,' he snarls. Many of the books are those mentioned in

Acknowledgements later in this volume. On three covers were pictures of Lord Byron. Others had his name on the cover.

'I'm writing a book about Lord Byron, when he visited here. In Ali Pasha's time.'

'Byron good Greek,' he says, smiling. 'Be careful. Albania strange country. Your case not locked?'

'Well apart from the books there are only clothes,' I reply.

'Albanians steal clothes.'

'They are old clothes, and some dirty washing.'

'Albanians like old clothes. Better for them,' he laughs out loud, then turns back into his office and I presume repeats my story and his joke to his colleagues to much shaking of heads and general merriment.

I wheel the two bags through no man's land, about three hundred metres uphill. Either side of the road are barbed wire fences on top of concrete blocks. There are watchtowers on the Albanian side. I feel as if I am to be an extra in an old John le Carré film. Looking up and beyond the fences, the mountains either side are crisscrossed with paths and tracks. Greece is full of illegal Albanians working where they can. One wonders why no one down here realises what is going on up there, and then the climb over, one knocks on Albania's door.

The hotelkeeper in Zitsa had warned me that the Albanians would not let me through until I had paid a bribe. How much? €10, but he wasn't sure. But I have all afternoon and am quite as interested in observing the comings and goings at the border as I am in reaching Libohova, Byron's and my first overnight stop. The rummage through the big bag reveals nothing but the books and clothes.

'Import tax.' The officer wears an oversized and overbraided concave cap. His face looks small and pinched below the adornment above.

'No imports,' I reply.

'Import tax, €20,' he insists.

'No,' I say, and sit down pointedly.

He walks off and some minutes later a more senior braided cap approaches. His face is fuller and kinder. 'Where you go, my friend?'

'Libohova,' I smile.

'Taxi here, come,' he gestures me to repack and follow. Outside is the first of very many old Mercedes that are seeing out their days to the roads of Albania. 'Pay taxi now,' says the customs man, '€20.' Seems a bit high but not worth the argy-bargy. I hand the taxi driver a twenty note, and ease into the back seat. I see the taxi driver give the customs man some lek notes. I suppose I have just paid the €10 after all.

We reach Libohova late in the afternoon. In Byron's day there was no official difference between what is now Greece and Albania, except as one crossed the Epirus the ethnic Greeks gave way to the ethnic Albanians. Once down on the plains of Albania Hobhouse noted the well-cultivated land with 'English-looking divisions and rivers running through the hills'. There were tobacco fields and snuff factories, fortresses on hills all around them. They rode the fifty kilometres from Delvinaki to Libohova in one day, and stayed in the house of a relation of one of Ali's wives, the house being set aside for receiving Ali's guests. Ali's nephew was the governor, an absent governor that night, and he resided at the castle which sits atop Libohova with his mother, Ali's sister, of whom more later.

There is a path up to the castle but it has been washed away, reclaimed by a greater Albania. One has to clamber up the last fifty metres, but it's dangerous underfoot and there is nothing up there but stubs of walls and tangled weeds, and the clamber not really worth the mud and scrapes and bother.

The prosperous town that was is more or less deserted now, and just a dirt-poor village remains. Only the name is the same. The few people there are very old, mostly women, mostly in black, mostly stooping. The only paved street is littered and worn and just behind the street, in the shrubbery, are layers of dirty and dusty plastic bottles and bags. There was a hotel, the one at which the writer was planning to spend the night, but it is closed and doesn't look like reopening, ever. There is a café serving Nescafe and Chinese wheat biscuits. The owner speaks a little English. Where is everyone? 'Olympic! Building London Olympic!' he declares proudly. There is no bed for the night. 'Nothing here,' he says with a shrug. The

Vasco da Gama downwind in a squall off Lisbon

Cascais, Portugal, first landfall, flat land at last!

The *plaza* at El Ronquillo, exact birthplace of *Don Juan*

James Gordon's bodega in Jerez 'where the sherry we drink is made' and where Byron 'quaffed at the fountainhead'

^

The now smart Bar Restaurante Baco, Sevilla, the site of the old Tres Reyes, where the Grand Tourists ate 'two plates of nasty pork, two meagre fowls, and dirty chops dressed in the most greasy fashion, with a poultice pudding. For this, with two bottles of good red Catalonian wine, four dollars.'

> The Beltrán sisters' 'B&B', Sevilla

Gillian takes away at Mumtaz Curry House, Gibraltar

Vasco da Gama near Agrigento, Sicily

Captain on watch

Byron Research Team Executive Board Meeting

Grand Harbour Marina, Malta. *Vasco* resting centre left

Senglea, Malta, early morning peace

∧ Ali Pasha's HQ at
Its Kale, Ioannina, Greece

∧ Signor Niccolo's house
in Ioannina, now in
Byron Street...

> ...right opposite Lord
Byron's Fashion House

∧ The mountain village of Zitza
  in northern Greece

∧ The monastery above Zitza,
  where Byron wrote…

> '…Monastic Zitza! from thy
  shady brow, thou small but
  favoured spot of holy ground!'

Byron's badlands
track from Greece
to Albania

US warplane atop
Gjirokastra castle, Albania.
Heaven knows how…

Plaque to Byron's visit to
Tepelenë castle, Albania

Roma hovels now inside Tepelenë castle

Tepelenë castle's grand entrance. Byron wrote: 'I shall never forget the singular scene on entering Tepelenë at five in the afternoon, as the sun was going down'

The man himself – 'the sort of despot that gives tyrants a bad name'

Author with King Leka I of the Albanians

∧ At Delphi before the excavations, where Byron carved his name in a pillar

Anything he can do…

Fities, Greece: 'This house in which we are lodged is like
a squire's house in the Wiltshire downs, a little in decay'

Byron outside Byron House, Messolonghi, Greece

^ The last one standing – the Temple of Thesium, Athens

< Pendeli Monastery, now home to resting monks and a smudged lipstick coloured Datsun Cherry

The Temple to Olympian Zeus, with its chopped-up sausage pillar

Izmir, 'the Nuneaton of Asia Minor'

Byron swam across the Hellespont, now the
all-day and all-night Dardanelles tanker rush hour

The Beyazit Tower, Istanbul,
where 20,000 janissaries lost
their heads

The infernal oven:
the Lazaretto, Malta

nearest one is in Gjirokastra, the capital of the province, just five miles across the valley.

It wasn't always thus; in Byron's day, in Ali Pasha's day, this used to be a thriving town, made more so by it's most famous resident, Ali Pasha's sister and the governor's mother, Chainitza. She was a proper Ali, a true chip off the old block. After a feud with a neighbouring village she borrowed some of her brother's brigands and ordered them to massacre all the men and children there and drive the women to her at Libohova castle. She had them stripped, their hair cut and stuffed into her new mattress and then told the brigands to describe, slowly, one at a time, how they had killed the women's families. She then turned the women over to the brigands' amusement and issued an order that they were not to be provided with clothes or shelter, and had them driven naked into the woods to be eaten by bears and wolves.

Two hundred years ago Gjirokastra belonged to Ali Pasha's only local rival, Ibrahim Pasha. In fact it was against the latter that the former was 'in a small war' when Byron and Hobhouse came to find him in Ioannina, and this 'small war' was the reason they had to make the journey to Tepelenë if they wanted to see him. A short time after they left Albania Ali Pasha would duly capture Gjirokastra too and set about fortifying, and presumably terrorising, it. Visitors wishing to follow Byron's route now have to divert to Gjirokastra as the track from Libohova to Byron's next stop, Qestoral, has been washed away and there is no need to replace it as the farms are deserted and the land fallow.

Although Enver Hoxha died in 1985 the Maoists hung on as best they could until 1990. In 1991 the country reacted to the release from communism with anarchy, led by the peasants who had been used as slave labour. They owned nothing, were paid nothing and kept nothing. The punishments for failing to meet targets were descended on extended families; the sentence for owning any form of livestock or taking part in any free trading was an extended visit to the camps. Living had been just plain hard until 1960, but when Russia denounced Stalin Hoxha aligned his country with Mao. He even had his own

Cultural Revolution and purges of imaginary class enemies. By 1991 the peasants decided no one should ever be used as field slaves again, and trashed the land so that it could never happen.

Now the towns are spreading as the farmland is returning to from whence it came. One can drive for miles and not see anyone working in the fields. Trees have been felled for fuel and the land washed away in the rains. There are no birds. The land has turned an insipid shade of pale green and looks sad, dejected, defeated by decades of greed and gross stupidity. In many ways a feudal system would be better as at least someone owned the land and was responsible for it. Now no one owns it, or more precisely no one knows who owns it: the communists nationalised it all and since then there have been endless and unsolvable disputes, claims of original and often undocumented ownership complicated by the traditional Napoleonic system of inheritance. As the Gjirokastra hotel owner said, 'every house and field is owned by a hundred people, and so is owned by nobody.'

Back on the road to Tepelenë, Gjirokastra has recently become a UNESCO World Heritage site and is dominated by Ali Pasha's enormous citadel which sits brooding over it. The rest of the town spreads down steeply from the citadel. From a distance the setting of the citadel beyond the lake with snow capped mountains looks enchanting, but close up the town is shabby; St. Moritz or Vail it ain't. There are a number of well-priced hotels in converted houses. It is wise to eat near your hotel at night as a pack of wild dogs roam the streets, and this can be somewhat unnerving. Torches are useful as there are frequent power cuts and the streets are not blessed with neighbours or names or numbers.

The citadel is massive, worthy of its UNESCO status, and hidden in the nooks and crannies are Hoxha's tanks and guns and Ali's cells for the prisoners and animals. This is where he liked to keep his menagerie, whose main purpose was to eat the prisoners. One tigress became so sated with human flesh that she lost her appetite so Ali Pasha let her free to hunt in the town as her appetite dictated; apparently the bears weren't so fussy and their appetite never diminished. He kept his hunting dogs here too, and fed them on boiled prisoners. Even the prisoners unwittingly ate other prisoners, disguised in the stew. Word around the campfire was that the Italians tasted best, but that's just a rumour the writer cannot verify.

Byron and Hobhouse could not stay in Ibrahim Pasha-held Gjirokastra and instead stayed in Qestoral and then the next day Ereend, about fifteen kilometres further on. I left my bags in the hotel in Gjirokastra, took the bus to Qestoral and walked to Ereend and hitched a ride back. The villages are more or less deserted: there are only old men, old women and 'honorary men', these being women who refused their father's choice of husband and so were obliged to spend the rest of their lives as spinsters, or 'honorary men'. People are living in hovels, dressed in rags, with a standard of living barely higher than the chickens that cluck around them. In the fields you see what you think is a scarecrow, then it starts to move; but there are no crows to scare anyway; even the flies have stopped bothering to breed.

The country has been ravished but the setting remains magnificent. One is in a valley alongside a careering river and on either side hills unfolding higher and higher to become mountains. Back in the day, with the moors and lakes and kilts and clans and the music and food, it again reminded Byron of his childhood Scotland. King Leka had once described Albania as being 'like Scotland in the Middle Ages'. The following week I was to ask him if the description still held good.

'Yes,' he replied thoughtfully, 'although the communists destroyed a lot of our traditional life. Purges, forced movements, gulags. Hoxha was as much of a mass murderer as his mentor Mao. The last seventy years have not been kind to Albania.' Indeed they haven't. History has passed them by and not even noticed.

By the end of the next day, 19 October 1809, they were approaching their destination, Tepelenë, and Ali Pasha's palace there. Byron himself now takes up the story:

I shall never forget the singular scene on entering Tepelenë at five in the afternoon, as the sun was going down. It brought to my mind [Sir Walter] Scott's description of Branksome Castle. The Albanians, in their dresses, (the most magnificent in the world, consisting of a long white kilt, gold-worked cloak, crimson velvet gold-laced jacket and waistcoat, silver-mounted pistols and daggers) the Tartars with their high caps, the Turks in their vast pelisses and turbans, the soldiers and black slaves with the horses, the former in groups in an immense large open gallery in front of the palace, the latter placed in a kind of cloister below it, two hundred steeds ready caparisoned to move in a moment, couriers entering or passing out with the despatches, the kettle-drums beating, boys calling the hour from the minaret of the mosque, altogether, with the singular appearance of the building itself, formed a new and delightful spectacle to a stranger. I was conducted to a very handsome apartment, and my health inquired after by the vizier's secretary!

Unfortunately the castle is no more, and just the base of the walls that used to surround it remain unreclaimed or unplundered. At its peak it must have been magnificent as it takes a full ten minutes to walk around its perimeter. On one corner is an unpolished plaque to commemorate Byron's visit. What was once a glory is now but a shell, and the shell is populated by hovels and surrounded by mounds of rubbish. The structure of the main northern gate can still be determined, but access is restricted by heaps of used plastic and tin. The hovels house reluctant gypsies, who would much rather be out and about but have been told to stay put. I paid an urchin 50 lek to show me around, as much to ward off the others as to enquire within. Actually the Roma in the castle lived in better shacks than the Albanians in the countryside around, and were more cheerful too.

The main point of interest now in Tepelenë is the enormous statue of a reclining Ali Pasha, its most famous son. He is seen with pistols and daggers in his belt and an unforgiving scowl on his face. Behind him is a communist-brutalist hotel which is open but empty and decomposing. The main street sells only oversized bright plastic flowers for the road death shrines. Ali Pasha and Lord Byron, even the less fanciful John Cam Hobhouse, even the reluctant Fletcher, would be heartbroken to see what humankind—the Italians, Germans, Stalinists, Maoists, anarchists and now the gangster 'democrats' have done to their beloved Tepelenë in particular and Albania in general.

But let's cheer up for a moment. Two hundred years ago the two legends, Lord Byron and Ali Pasha, did meet right here in this castle. The evening before Byron had met one of Ali Pasha's secretaries called Ioannis Colletti, whom Hobhouse rather breathlessly reported as fluent in German, Latin, French, Italian, Greek and Turkish. Colletti would have prepared Byron for the meeting, the procedures extant, the courtesies to follow. Ali Pasha would be using his physician as his interpreter, addressing them in Turkish, which the physician would translate into Latin, the language Byron would use. Byron took considerable trouble with his preparations. He was clearly nervous: he even ticked Hobhouse off for not being respectful enough of the British nobility. He was here on a diplomatic mission, an important and secretive affair of state. It had to be done correctly. This was his maiden voyage as a diplomat, his first time doing anything responsible, consequential, like this at all. Ali Pasha's reputation alone demanded caution. The tyrant was almost fifty years older and in total control. Byron had no political weight to throw around, and had to win the day by his personality and bearing alone.

They met in great luxury and splendour. One can sense Byron's excitement from this letter to his mother:

> The next day I was introduced to Ali Pacha. I was dressed in a full suit of staff uniform, with a very magnificent sabre, etc. The vizier received me in a large room paved with marble; a fountain was playing in the centre; the apartment was surrounded by scarlet ottomans. He received me standing, a wonderful compliment from a Mussulman, and made me sit down on his right hand. I have a Greek interpreter for general use, but a physician of Ali's named Femlario, who understands Latin, acted for me on this occasion. His first question was, why, at so early an age, I left my country? (the Turks have no idea of travelling for amusement). He then said, the English minister, Captain Leake, had told him I was of a great family, and desired his respects to my mother; which I now, in the name of Ali Pacha, present to you.
>
> He said he was certain I was a man of birth, because I had small ears, curling hair, and little white hands, and expressed himself pleased

with my appearance and garb. He told me to consider him as a father whilst I was in Turkey, and said he looked on me as his son. Indeed, he treated me like a child, sending me almonds and sugared sherbet, fruit and sweetmeats, twenty times a day. He begged me to visit him often, and at night, when he was at leisure. I then, after coffee and pipes, retired for the first time. I saw him thrice afterwards. It is singular that the Turks, who have no hereditary dignities, and few great families, except the Sultans, pay so much respect to birth; for I found my pedigree more regarded than my title.

His highness is sixty years old, very fat, and not tall, but with a fine face, light blue eyes, and a white beard; his manner is very kind, and at the same time he possesses that dignity which I find universal amongst the Turks. He has the appearance of anything but his real character, for he is a remorseless tyrant, guilty of the most horrible cruelties, very brave, and so good a general that they call him the Mahometan Buonaparte. Napoleon has twice offered to make him King of Epirus, but he prefers the English interest, and abhors the French, as he himself told me.

He is of so much consequence, that he is much courted by both, the Albanians being the most warlike subjects of the Sultan, though Ali is only nominally dependent on the Porte; he has been a mighty warrior, but is as barbarous as he is successful, roasting rebels, etc., etc. Buonaparte sent him a snuff-box with his picture. He said the snuff-box was very well, but the picture he could excuse, as he neither liked it nor the original. His ideas of judging of a man's birth from ears, hands, etc., were curious enough. To me he was, indeed, a father, giving me letters, guards, and every possible accommodation. Our next conversations were of war and travelling, politics and England.

Hobhouse thought that Ali Pasha was behaving rather 'leeringly' towards Byron, and it is common currency in Albania that Byron and Ali Pasha had been sexual partners. Although both actively bisexual and quite capable of said romp, I think it unlikely: Byron at 21 was too old for Ali Pasha and Byron's gaydar was alerted by beauty alone, not masculinity or femininity as such. In addition he knew he was there on business, diplomatic business he was taking seriously and had to perform correctly, and an impromptu liaison with his objective might open too many unexpected doors.

From their respective letters and diaries one can see that Byron met Ali Pasha at least once without Hobhouse, and one presumes that Byron and Hobhouse had agreed that Byron on his own would be a better conduit for Spiridion Foresti's message of diplomacy. Neither refers in any specific detail to Ali Pasha's reaction, but as the latter had just heard, and had the pleasure of breaking the news to his visitors, the British had just taken the Ionian Islands, except for Corfu. If nothing else they must have hoped that Ali had appreciated the courtesy of a personal explanation and perhaps an unsaid apology from one of King George's nephews for Perfidious Albion's treachery.

They spent two more days in the splendour of Ali Pasha's court and castle at Tepelenë. The experience of his time there, of his mission and of the journey made an enormous impression on the 21-year-old Byron. *Childe Harold's Pilgrimage*, for which he was by now nightly writing notes, fairly bristles with his experiences from his time in Albania, centred around the visit to and from Tepelenë.

~

It only took them four days to return to Ioannina, and I don't intend to follow them closely as the route back to Ioannina was the same inbound as outbound. The return journey only took four days instead of nine, the fine weather making the difference. But the writer still had his own mission to complete, also with an Albanian chieftain, but any similarity between Ali Pasha and King Leka I of the Albanians ends with this sentence.

First I had to reach Tirana, a greater distance than the local hops already made to reach Tepelenë. Luckily you have to let someone else do the driving in Albania. Prices of taxis, in fact of everything, are half of those in Greece, and buses or minibuses are plentiful, very cheap and more atmospheric—the seats being better dressed than the passengers. Driving is not for the fainthearted; blind corners and roundabouts are particularly fraught. India without the horns comes mind, although that is a touch harsh on the Indians. There is no great compunction to take a driving test, and the multitude of road death shrines along the road warn one of the dangers. One junction had all the makings of a small cemetery. All along the roads are stalls selling replacement hubcaps, bumpers, and light clusters, but not mirrors, as one doesn't miss what one doesn't use. Maps were illegal until 1995, and no two agree with each other; printouts from Google Earth are the answer.

Strangely enough although the roads are quite full there do not seem to be any car dealers, new or used. All the cars have been 'personally imported' and most of them are middle-aged Mercedes; the later models with immobilisers aren't so susceptible to this type of 'personal import'. Whether by bus or taxi progress is slow as every few miles there is a police roadblock where the drivers help to top up the officers' wages. Nevertheless six hours later the writer's shaken bones were in Tirana.

King Leka's Old Palace is in the centre of Tirana, nestling among the embassies. In fact it is like another embassy, a kingdom within a republic, with its own grounds, wrought iron spiked railings, a fleet of long black Mercedes, armed guards and walkie-talkies. Once through a semblance of security, mostly being thoroughly sniffed at an awkward height by the most boisterous of the royal boxers, one is ushered by the chamberlain to a large square room with a long L-shaped sofa on one side and matching armchairs opposite. The man who would be king, all two metres and blue safari suit of him, bears more than a slight resemblance to another old Africa hand, Tiny Rowland. Scattered around the chairs are a pack of boxers, all apparently related, one hopes not too related. Behind the armchairs a gas heater is on full blast. Behind the sofa a hot air blower is also on full blast. The air is hot and dry and stale and decidedly doggy, made more palatable only by the smell of accumulated cigarette smoke. The king looks annoyingly chipper, and I regret my recent conversion to the ranks of the non-smokers.

Apart from the chamberlain he is alone. His Australian wife Queen Susan died five years ago; in her obituary the *Daily Telegraph* noted that she and her king had a very close relationship and that 'both shared a keen interest in smoking.' I know what it meant; my wife and I both share a keen interest in wines from Burgundy.

I had taken the precaution of swotting up on the protocol with an old *Debrett's Etiquette*. Should you find yourself in similar circumstances you 'shake his hand while bowing from the neck, not the waist, and with the weight on the *front* foot greet him with "Good day (etc.) Your Royal Highness."' That was done, but then the king is clearly a man who believes in getting his retaliation in first.

'Do you know Jeremy Paxman?' he growls.

'Aaargh...' I parry.

I know what this is about though. Five years previously the grand inquisitor had come to Albania to interview the king for his book *On Royalty*. Although he didn't actually sneer 'Oh, come off it, king' as he would have done to some hapless political lackey the questions were somewhat more rough and tumble, more Paxotic than those to which the king was used.

To divert from this potential unpleasantness I reach into my bag and with some trepidation hand over my present. It's not quite what I had in mind: due to the 'snow event' in southern England in early February I had not been able to do the usual last minute raid on the House of Lords gift shop and instead asked my wife to have a forage in Fortnum & Mason. She had chosen a tin box of Duchy Originals Organic Highland Shortbread, with view of the Highlands 'reproduced from a watercolour by HRH The Prince of Wales' on the lid.

The king huffs. 'Do you know Prince Charles?'

'Better than I know Jeremy Paxman,' I offer weakly.

He puts out one Rothmans Imperial and lights up another. 'Do you smoke?' he asks. 'I didn't,' I reply, taking one. 'They are real,' he confirms. I'm relieved: fake fags are confusing in Albania. The only discernible difference in a new pack is the price: 100 lek for a real pack of Marlboro and 50 lek for a fake one. There's a factory up in Pogradeç, makes all the top brands. I had asked how one can tell which is real and which is fake. 'The price, of course.' Ah, yes, silly me.

The king maintains a keen interest in Albanian politics, and is clearly popular with the run of Albanians. At the airport I had been searched by customs and they had asked about Prince Charles's bickies. I explained it was a gift for the king. A gaunt young man with an unhappy face topped by a deeply concave and braided cap told me to 'Vait' and beetled off behind closed doors. A minute later a happier, chubbier man with even more braid had me repeat the story and then nodded approvingly and told me I was 'Velcome, velcome in Tirana. King good.' It was the same in the taxi: 'King good, quiet man now, drink beer. We don't like Greeks.' The hotel receptionist agreed when I asked her to show me the Old Palace on the map: 'Old Palace here. King Leka good Albanian man. I like, yes.' And Greeks? 'I don't like.'

The chamberlain coughs discreetly and looks at where a watch should be on his wrist. My time is up. He has agreed to help with Byron's costume but before I go I have to ask two questions.

'Do you know what happened to the supercharged red Mercedes?'

'Only up to 1972. We gave it to the British Red Cross. There were three identical ones. Hitler's own car, and then those he gave to my father and the King of Romania. I don't know where it is now.' Later I traced it to a private collection in California.

'And is the Gabon story true?' I should explain: in every article about King Leka there is a reference to his refuelling stop in Gabon. After the Spanish had started asking too many questions about his arms cache he thought it best to fast forward and loaded up his plane and headed for Rhodesia/Zimbabwe. The Spanish found out just after he had taken off, saw from his flight plan he was refuelling in Gabon and asked the Gabonese to arrest him. The Gabonese army duly surrounded his plane at which point, the story goes, he appeared at the aircraft door with a bazooka and the Gabonese army scurried off back into the jungle.

'Of course it's not true,' he replies. 'Bazookas! We had 40 mm grenade launchers. All sixteen of us on board had them, even my wife had one. We told the Gabonese that if we saw a single soldier again we would blow up the airport. What was our alternative? The

Rhodesians were supposed to send a plane for us, but then changed their mind unless we gave them $250,000. We had to take the plane ourselves, what else could we do?'

What indeed? One last question: 'are you writing your memoirs, an autobiography?' He isn't, he says, 'some stories are better left untold.' I say it's a shame and give him my card—in case he changes his mind.

Like Byron I had come to like the hospitable and fierce, warlike and kind Albanians. Byron saw them in their prime, when their leader ruled as much of the world as any of them was likely to see. Of the Albanians he wrote a year later that they are:

Brave, rigidly honest, and faithful; but they are cruel, though not treacherous, and have several vices but no meannesses. They are, perhaps, the most beautiful race, in point of countenance, in the world; their women are sometimes handsome also, but they are treated like slaves, beaten and, in short, complete beasts of burden; they plough, dig, and sow. I found them carrying wood, and actually repairing the highways. The men are all soldiers, and war and the chase their sole occupations. The women are the labourers.

No nation are so detested and dreaded by their neighbours as the Albanese; the Greeks hardly regard them as Christians, or the Turks as Moslems, and in fact they are a mixture of both, and sometimes neither. Their habits are predatory; all are armed, and the red-shawled Arnaouts, the Montenegrins, Chimeriotes, and Gedges, are treacherous; the others differ somewhat in garb, and essentially in character. As far as my own experience goes I can speak favourably. I was attended by two, an Infidel and a Mussulman to Constantinople and every other part of Turkey which came within my observations, and more faithful in peril and indefatigable in service are no where to be found.

The writer saw them soon after their nadir, and time had not yet had a chance to loosen the pain. Unfortunately he also did not persuade or cajole any Albanians to join his entourage, so will have to take Byron's word for their suitability as servants. The women's lot has certainly improved from Byron's day, and although the country is nominally

Muslim it seems to be so with no great enthusiasm and so one can see women out and about and dressed as women. Most of the men work abroad, and the economy is supported by their remittances.

One cannot help being sympathetic for the Albanians' plight, as though for a whole century the gods have unwrapped all the evils of the world, played with them in one land alone and called it Albania. Unfortunately it is going to take generations to unbreed the corruption, especially now the gangsters have taken over. In the meantime—and as a result—there are less interesting, and certainly less hospitable, places to visit.

And so we all found our way back to Ioannina. Byron and Hobhouse were to spend a further week at Signor Niccolo's house, doing nothing in particular, before retracing their steps to Preveza. The writer drove his no longer quite-so-smart-Smart back to the hire company, also in Preveza, and so we will resume the Grand Tour and re-Tour there.

Chapter Ten

FROM PREVEZA TO MESSOLONGHI

7–22 NOVEMBER 1809 | 26 FEBRUARY – 4 MARCH 2009

When Byron and Hobhouse left Ioannina on 3 November 1809 Ali Pasha had undertaken to give his guests safe passage as far as Patras, where they would be under the protection of his proxy, his son Veli Pasha. Byron's battalion was still recruiting new members: the first escort, which was to take them as far as Preveza, was formed of fifty Albanian soldiers, in addition to which Byron led his core entourage of Hobhouse, Fletcher, Georgiou, Vassily, a new Albanian dervish called Tahiri—who like Vassily was to stay with Byron throughout the Grand Tour—and now two unnamed Athenians and a Greek priest. The plan was to retrace their steps with the escort as far as Preveza, then sail from Preveza to Patras on one of Ali Pasha's galliots. Unfortunately, as we shall see, they encountered foul weather in an ill found boat with ill trained crew and were nearly shipwrecked. They eventually arrived in Patras overland.

We will pick them up in Preveza as the journey south from Ioannina to Preveza was much the same as the journey north, and they stayed in the same places in St. Demetre, Arta and Salaóra as they had on the journey upcountry. The journey south sped by; riding at escort speed, and with little new to see, they arrived in Preveza in only four days, and stayed there only for one night.

They left Preveza on 8 November in one of Ali Pasha's four-gun galliots. A galliot was, as it sounds, a small galley, usually single masted, built to be rowed as well as sailed. They were the standard lightly armed merchant ships of the time in the eastern Mediterranean. The skipper was Albanian, a Captain Dulcigniote. The ship's crew were twenty Turks and five Greeks and, although not specified, there would typically be about a dozen Christian slaves—captured enemy men, in that area probably Souliotes—for the oars. Hobhouse described the captain as 'a mild mannered man', seldom an encouraging sign with a mixed crew, and not all of them volunteers.

The problems started as soon as the galliot tried to leave Preveza harbour. They nearly ran aground in a gust as they weighed anchor, whereupon the captain asked them if they would prefer to wait until later before setting off. Byron would have none of it: the winds are fair, let's away. Instead of insisting on his captaincy, Dulcigniote concurred and at 1 p.m. off they set.

All was well as they sailed past the site of the battle of Actium, the Roman name for Preveza. Apart from Mark Antony and Cleopatra's sea battle with Octavian here, more recently, in 1538, at the battle of Preveza the Ottoman navy under High Admiral Barbarossa (like Drake the famous corsair had become a poacher turned gamekeeper) had defeated the allied fleet of Emperor Charles V under Admiral

Doria. Doria, with a far superior fleet, had seen his stragglers harried and hounded by the ferocious Barbarossa's galleys but rather than regroup and attack he posed up and down the Ionian coast with all colours flying to preserve *intacta* the papal flagship. As Admiral de la Gravière pointed out in his *Doria et Barberousse*: 'For far less than this the English shot Admiral Byng in 1756.' Doria remains an Italian national hero, Andrea Doria the most common name seen on Italian fishing boats.

Within moments they were in the Ionian Sea and by 4 p.m. a determined south wind had risen to greet them. About fifteen miles offshore and heading due west the captain decided to tack to the south-east towards Patras, half way through which manoeuvre the main lateen sail split asunder. The galliot could not now even resume its westward course and was unbalanced, and I imagine, almost unhelmable, and being blown northwards by the gathering wind alone towards French-held Corfu. The Turkish crew promptly leapt below and the captain 'wrung his hands and wept.'

At this point the main yard broke and with no power in the sails the ship would soon have been floundering, and the floundering would then have caused the 'cannons to roll' and loose cannons rolling from bulwark to bulwark across the deck would soon be smashing through the topsides. It needs little imagination to see the danger they were in: apart from the hull being in danger, the frantic flapping of the split sail, the flaying of the unstayed rigging ropes and the wielding giant's club of the broken yard would have imperilled any soul still above decks.

The five Greeks now took over the ship. While one wrestled with the helm, the others jury-rigged a staysail and they slowly brought the galliot back under command, albeit heading still further north, but at least under some degree of control. As Byron wrote a few days later to his mother:

I was nearly lost in a Turkish ship of war, owing to the ignorance of the captain and crew, though the storm was not violent. Fletcher yelled after his wife, the Greeks called on all the saints, the Mussulmans on Alla; the

captain burst into tears and ran below deck, telling us to call on God; the
sails were split, the main-yard shivered, the wind blowing fresh, the night
setting in, and all our chance was to make Corfu, which is in possession
of the French, or (as Fletcher pathetically termed it) 'a watery grave.' I did
what I could to console Fletcher, but finding him incorrigible, wrapped
myself up in my Albanian capote (an immense cloak), and lay down on
deck to wait the worst. I have learnt to philosophise in my travels; and if
I had not, complaint was useless.

By the evening the wind had subsided as it is apt to do in the Ionian
Sea and early the following morning the Greeks brought the galliot
into Fanari Bay, still in Ali Pasha's territory, but they had been blown
twenty-five miles off course, twenty-five miles north of Preveza.
Fanari Bay is today still sparsely populated, and we spent a pleasant
night at anchor bobbing up and down under a waxing moon. At the
south end of the bay is the mouth of the River Acheron, and a not
too unreasonably drafted boat can navigate a mile or two upstream.
We can presume that Byron and the entourage disembarked from
their wounded galliot in the Acheron rather than the beach. Thus
they abandoned Captain Dulcigniote and his stricken galliot and
made their way back to Preveza by land, for as Byron wrote two days
later: 'I shall not trust Turkish sailors in future. I am therefore going
as far as Missolonghi by land, and there have only to cross a small
gulf to get to Patras.' As it happens, he had to embark on one of Ali
Pasha's galliots again two days later, but this time one under Greek
and Albanian supervision.

Although safe from the sea and on dry land the entourage were
not totally out of danger. They were in Souli territory; and the
Christian Souliotes were a fearsome race, if for now subdued by Ali
Pasha's garrisons. (It was Souliote mercenaries whom Byron hired
for his private guard fifteen years later at Messolonghi, and in his
final days there they proved to be an uncontrollable, unpredictable
band of robbers in uniform.) To reach Preveza they had to ride near
the gorge of Zalongo where two hundred Souliote women saw Ali
Pasha's brigands slowly massacring their men in a convent while they

were forced to wait outside. They knew they had only been saved for slavery and debauchery. Grabbing their children in their arms, reciting psalms and singing hymns, they ran to a nearby cliff and threw themselves off in one of the strangest hetacombs in history rather than meet their fate as playthings of Ali's brigands.

Furthermore, to ride the two days back to Preveza they had to bypass the port of Parga, also still held by the French. There was now no official escort, although the second-in-command from the galliot offered to accompany them. They set off inland, riding through the forests of Acarnania and spent the first night at Dolondoracho. The land is dominated by the Souli castle which took Ali Pasha thirteen years to capture. As they rode they picked up further soldiery, and by the time they arrived at Kastrosikia the next evening the entourage had grown to fifteen strong.

Soon they were back in Nicopolis, just north of Preveza, and Byron and Hobhouse 'trotted off to pay another visit to the ruins.' They spent two nights in Preveza, again at the consul's house, but by 13 November had found another galliot, albeit commanded by the same hapless Captain Dulcigniote, who had somehow navigated himself back from Fanari Bay. Someone somewhere organised another escort, this time of thirty-five Albanian soldiers under a Captain Lato. The Byron battalion had now become the Byron brigade, a precursor to the more famous officially named Byron Brigade which he was to lead fifteen years later at Messolonghi in the War of Independence.

The first destination was Loutraki in the far south-eastern corner of the Gulf of Amvrakia, about twenty sailing miles from Preveza. This time the winds were feckless and as they drifted aimlessly overnight off the ancient Corinthian port of Vonitsa the slaves were put to work rowing through the night. (Those were the days.) The next morning was one that only autumnal Greece could light: sunrise over the hills of Agrapha to the south, flat shimmering pink Gulf seas ahead, golden marshlands off Salaóra to the north, endless layers of blue above and a fine breeze behind, insomuch as they reached the delightful little landing of Loutraki mid-afternoon.

It has been seldom on this voyage that one has found a place now more or less intact and much as Byron and Hobhouse—Hobhouse in this case—described it then. Loutraki is one such, 'situated in a pretty, deep bay at the southeast corner of the Gulf. There is a custom house, and a lodge for soldiers, surrounded by a high wall, except at the water's edge.' The bay is still pretty and deep, the customs house is an occasional, rather reluctant, taverna—next to a yew tree with an Orthodox shrine built into the split at its hollow—and the base of the high wall is still there too. Along the shore are Gulf fishing skiffs, brightly painted, nets at the ready, run up on the beach and pointing hopefully out to sea.

No attempt has been made to prettify the working fishing village, and it seems amazing it has not all been turned into some ghastly holiday complex. That night two hundred years ago the party tented on the shore rather than lodged and the scene must have looked like a medieval invasion. Hobhouse ee-awed: 'the scene at night-time was not a little picturesque, a goat being roasted whole for the Albanians. They assembled in four parties round as many fires, and the night being fine they sang and danced to their songs round the largest blaze after their manner. Several of these songs turned on the exploits of robbers, one beginning thus "When we set sail a band of thieves from Parga—we were in number eighty-two."' They were in fact all ex-robbers, as Ali Pasha's strategy for a newly captured territory was to enlist the robbers into his army, thereby killing several birds with one stone. Their revelry that night might have had special gusto to warn off other robbers, for 'fifteen days past, thirty-five robbers made their appearance close to the house and carried off a Turk and a Greek, the former of whom they shot, and the latter of whom they stoned, on a small green spot at the bottom of the bay (by way of bravado, as we heard). This night, including the guard of the place, our company amounted to sixty-seven people.' As one can imagine, all this was the very grindiest grist for Childe Harold's mill, now three weeks into its first draft, and keeping its author occupied nightly.

The next morning Childe Harold and his troupe of servants and warriors weighed camp, found some horses at the Loutraki staging post for the principals and with the kilted, fearsome, fearless foot soldiers marching and singing beside them set off into outlaw country, the fringe of Ali Pasha's thiefdom, the magical Dytikian hills. If Albania had been grand wide open landscapes, horizontal rather than vertical gestures, red and purple and blue, Dytiki was close bound, clusters of forested hills rising and rising, the views ascending and descending and ascending again, green and brown and golden at these hints of a southern autumn.

They spent the first night fifteen miles south of Loutraki at Katouna where they were lodged in the village primate's house. Hobhouse noted 'there are but a few houses, but those good, and a school-house.' All that remained was lost in the 1953 earthquake, but the school house has not only been rebuilt but expanded enormously and the mid-afternoon roads are busy with school buses to-ing and fro-ing their charges from the nearby villages. The central square above and on top of the town is full of chattering, flirting, laughing, pouting and posing young Greek boys and girls, and around the square they bustle from the Sugar Café Club to the Café After Bar, dropping in at the Piccadilly Internet Café before topping themselves up at the Fast Food Perfecto, although one has to say that the Union Now! bookshop seems rather short of customers. Katouna is full of mountain air and the optimism of long futures.

I need to work out where to go next on the re-Tour. I was particularly keen to find out about the next village, which Hobhouse called Machala, a name missing from the modern maps. This is not uncommon as many place names changed after independence, and the riddle is normally solved by finding a local person who knew someone slightly older who knew someone slightly older still who remembered the name as it was. The unravelling of clues as one retraces Byron and Hobhouse's footsteps can easily become an end in itself, and the sleuth with his nose to the ground and his tail in the air becomes like a bloodhound fixated by the dying whiff of a tricky kipper. In this case the kipper was particularly whiffy because of Hobhouse's enigmatic description of their lodgings in Machala, or however it is now called. 'This house in which we are lodged is like a squire's house in the Wiltshire downs, a little in decay. There are two courts, one before and the other behind, with a terrace, the whole being surrounded with a strong high wall which shuts out the prospect, it is true, but shuts out the thieves likewise, who always infest this country.'

In a new town in Spain or Portugal Byron and Hobhouse would always head for the monastery because they could talk in Latin to the monks, a process I had tried with embarrassingly poor results with an African monk in a convent in Estremoz in Portugal. The Ancient Greek they had learnt alongside Latin at school was of little use here as the monks had lost their contact with Hellenistic Greek, which is used in Orthodox services today, and anyway they had by now acquired the Greek Andreas Zantakis as part of the group for conversing locally. Some monks spoke Latin, rather perversely as Ancient Greek came before Latin as the sacred language of Christianity, the early Roman Church being a colony of Greek Christians. Only a few days before I had read that Napoleon remarked that the introduction of Christianity itself was the triumph of Greece over Rome; the last and most signal instance of the maxim of Horace, *Graecia capta ferum victorem cepit* (captive Greece took its rude captor captive).

Two hundred years later the equivalent of Latin as the traveller's Esperanto is English, and so rather than seek out the nearest monastery where the incumbents would worship in Latin I had learnt to seek out the nearest Internet café where the incumbents would surf in English.

'Machala? Machala, you say?' the student at the Piccadilly counter asks. He shouts in Greek into the room. Soon all eyes and ears are on our conversation. I show a constellation of teenage eyes the Michelin map, Hobhouse's entry and my own attempt at Machala in the Greek alphabet. I explain it must be within a day's walk of here. But no one knows; slowly their enthusiasm dies, heads are shaken, shoulders are shrugged, internetting is resumed.

If the internet crew doesn't know about Machala I think it is time to revert to Byron's ecclesiastical friends. On the other side of the square from the students' bars and cafés is a large ochre traditional-style, but newly built, Orthodox church. A very dapper woman in a green and white cardiganed uniform is leaving as I approach. I can decipher the words 'Traffic' and 'Police' on her knitted sleeve.

'Machala? Machala? Machala?' she muses, 'no. Come.' She waves me to follow and in a side street off the square she takes me into a laundry-cum-dry cleaner. There is a flurry of words and gestures, an unfolding of maps and notebooks, a rally of village names, and after a minute a consensus is reached.

'Fities,' she announces. 'You want Fities.' The dry cleaner has already found it on my map. He points to it; it is indeed where it might well be, a day's march in the direction of Messolonghi. She takes me out to the street. 'Car?' I point to the blue and dayglo Smart in the square. 'No parking,' she looks up teasingly, 'go end this street,' she points to the opposite side of the square, 'end street right. Right. Straight Fities.' We smile, I thank, she laughs 'no parking' once more and wags her finger at the car as we wish each other goodbye.

The road to Fities would seem unchanged since Hobhouse wrote: 'Road through a *lovely* woody country. Mounting the hills just before Machala, the prospect widens, and a plain enclosed to the west with high mountains to the east. Also the view is very grand—a lake and the Archelöus river, winding through a woody plain. In this country there are fewer villages, and as far as travellers, we have met none, but the houses are better than in Albania.' The closer one comes to Fities the more the road becomes a track, and then the track, still climbing gently, clears the woods and one is left with an eagle's view of the plains. One just needs a well armed, white kilted, gold and crimson robed, fiercely loyal, singing and marching private Albanian army escorting one's own eccentric entourage to complete the illusion of vertical time, and to feel like Byron must have felt there and then, master of the moment, the King of Dytiki.

In tiny Fities the 'squire's house in the Wiltshire downs' is easy to find; at least either it is long gone or it is one of three strong candidates, three substantial dwellings that are over two hundred years old. One is restored and freshly painted, and the other two in various states of disrepair. As I am snooping around, the slightest of old women, with the blackest dress and whitest face, appears. By sign language and shared sounds it seems the smart house is owned by someone in Athens. The other two? She gestures into the distance, owners somewhere else, not Athens.

The seat of the Wiltshire squire soon becomes obvious. What was once 'a little in decay' is now turning from decay to dust. The 'high wall' no longer shuts out the prospect or the thieves, but what is left of it still forms the boundary. Someone at some stage has made the two courts into one, and the terrace remains, although now reverted to Fities flora and fauna. I am soon talking myself into buying it, how high to build the wall, where to extend the terrace, how to be a Wiltshire squire, all very satisfactory. The moment refuses to let go, and as a message in a bottle I give the old Greek lady my card and point at the ruin. She looks puzzled. I fish a €10 note out of my pocket and wave that at the house and my card, her face lights up, the drachma has dropped!, but at the time of writing the house still belongs to owners somewhere else, not Athens.

From Fities they started the gentle descent towards the flatlands, the mangrove swamps and salt marshes that lead to and then surround Messolonghi. Two hundred years ago one had to approach Messolonghi from the north by punt, from the salt marsh island town of Etolica, built as Hobhouse said in 'the Venetian fashion'. The illusion of Venice in the offing continues as one nears Messolonghi as reeds, then stilts, then stilts with seats, then stilts with shelters, then stilts with shacks grow out of the salt flats. Punt was the only way to arrive then, and it is still an alternative way for tourists to arrive now, and so the brigade became marines as they entered Messolonghi.

They were met by the British consul who thought Byron was an ambassador and insisted on speaking to him in French. Funnily enough I was met by the British consul too, although at the time I only knew her to be the president of the Messolonghi Byron Society. Her name is Rosa Florou, and knowing this little bundle of Greek energy as I now do I'm surprised she isn't just president of the Messolonghi Byron Society, the British consul and a director of the National Bank of Greece, but also prime minister of Greece and Greek ambassador to the United Nations, as well as the current incarnation of the goddess Demeter.

Messolonghi is like a shrine to Byron's memory and Rosa is the high priestess. She takes me to the temple, Byron House, a handsome square three-storey building on reclaimed land on the shore of the salt flats. Built by the Greek state in 1991, with an enormous bronze statue of our man outside, it also houses the Byron Research Centre, dedicated to the 'study of Lord Byron and Philhellenism'. The top floor library has first editions onwards of works by Byron, letters from and to Byron, lives of Byron, books about Byron and his philosophy, Byron and his women, Byron and his radicalism, Byron and his contemporaries, Byron and the Romantics, Byron and mythology, Byron and religion, Byron in Italy, Byron in Switzerland, Byron in Greece, but nothing, thank heavens, about Byron and his Grand Tour. There is one empty space on the shelves, and Rosa promises to keep it free, but I think she says that to all her boys.

Every year the Byron Research Centre runs the International Byron Student Conference and in autumn 2009 hosted the annual International Byron Society Conference, with hundreds of delegates from the Byron Societies of thirty-five countries from Albania to Uruguay. There the international Byronistas presented no fewer than seventy academic papers, visited Athens University and Byronic and ancient sites, were handsomely wined and dined, and all organised by the redoubtable Rosa.

We tour the town. No one knows where he stayed for those two nights in 1809; the town was destroyed in the War of Independence and most of its inhabitants massacred by the Turks in the Exodus of 1826 when those still alive in the town tried to break through the besieging Ottoman lines, but were betrayed and slaughtered. Those who remained blew themselves up rather than be taken alive by the Turks. The War is remembered in the Garden of Heroes in the town centre, an ironically enlivening Valhalla of philhellenes from every corner of Europe, and in the centre of them all, in pride of place, the only Hero accorded a full statue, is the figure of a proud and defiant Byron, hero still to the Greeks. Under the statue in a silver urn are his lungs. Nearby is a cross which stands where Byron died on 19 April 1824. Modern analysis suggests he died of an infection brought on by Mediterranean tick fever, probably caught from one of his pets, either Lyon the Newfoundland or Moretto the Bulldog. That alone would have been feverish but survivable, but the doctors and prevailing wisdom insisted on bleeding him with leeches and he was drained of over half his blood, and a combination of the fever and blood loss led to a slow, but by all accounts, peaceful death by dog and doctor.

Keeping the conversation flowing with Rosa requires no effort at all. Over dinner she is a wellspring of Byron anecdotes. Every Byron researcher or player makes the pilgrimage to Messolonghi, and to visit Messolonghi is to be entertained by Rosa. She recently had a Channel 4 film crew in town. Rupert Everett, an actor who was playing Byron for a docudrama, asked her if she is in love with Byron.

'How crass!' she reports. 'In Greece we cannot say this. You cannot be in love with a ghost. I am content to say I love his spirit, but Everett is an Englishman.'

I ask her what she loves about his spirit.

'We Greeks love his spirit because he loved us. No one else did. We did not love ourselves. We did not know who we were, what we had once been, what we could become. Only Byron saw this, and gave his life for it. He was our rallying cry. We love his spirit because he saw what we could be and the world followed him.'

Now over a jolly dinner, as Rosa is fine shaving a recently wriggling eel and I am whirling a particularly recalcitrant spaghetti puttanesca around a fork is not the time to qualify any of this, and anyway if it's a feeling it has its own truth away from facts and figures. The facts and figures would suggest that Byron had a marginal practical effect on the War of Independence, certainly compared to Lord Liverpool and in particular Foreign Secretary and then Prime Minister George Canning. They drew up the Treaty of London in 1827 whereby the Great Powers suggested to Turkey that as Greek independence was a self-fulfilling prophecy a war over it was in no one's interest. When the Turkish and Egyptian fleets failed to withdraw later that year

Admiral Codrington sank them in the Battle of Navarino and Greek independence was assured.

I ask her if, as it seems to me, Byron's life had reached a stage by Messolonghi in 1824 where death was the only logical conclusion.

'Yes, he had lived thirty-six years but also you could say a hundred years. Some people measure a life by the quality of their heartbeats. Don't forget that at the time the two most famous men in Europe were Napoleon and Byron. They lived more in a month than most people live in a lifetime.'

'Some people say Byron was the world's first celebrity,' I suggest, 'and that he gave his celebrity as much as his life to Greece. His death here united the Greeks around the cause as you said, but outside Greece it drew enormous attention to the cause, inspired Delacroix and the Philhellenes, and for the politicians made Greek independence an idea whose time had come, one they could not ignore. It's hard to suggest a modern equivalent, but say J. K. Rowling took up the cause of independence for Cabinda. At the very least it would go from page 35 to the front page.'

'Where's Cabinda? At least everyone knew about Greece,' she replies.

'Good point, I suppose there is no modern equivalent.'

'Diana and the landmines,' she says, 'yes, celebrity makes a difference, and you, do you love his spirit too?' she asks.

'No, not really,' I reply, 'I mean I don't not love it, it's just that I only really know him as a young man in the Grand Tour years, between twenty-one and twenty-three. His spirit, if we mean metaphysical spirit, was still young too, and being formed by all these extraordinary external experiences. I think this was the most exciting time in his life. He was new to the world and the world was new to him. The spirit that died here fifteen years later was, in a way, somebody else's.'

'He didn't really know Greece as Greece on this first visit,' she says.

'Not at all. On his first visit here he was still with Ali Pasha's escort and would have thought he was still in Albania, which in effect he was. His first contact with Greek consciousness, any talk of independence, was with Andreas Londos two weeks later. And it was the week after that he visited Delphi and came into his first direct contact with Ancient Greece and the myths and history he knew from school. He was a changed man as far as Greece was concerned a month after he passed through here on that first visit.'

I don't like to pursue it as it might upset Rosa with her two great passions, Greece and Byron, but it seems to me that Byron loved Greece and Greece loves Byron because they were both cauldrons of contradictions. Byron was a poet and a boxer, beautiful yet deformed, of masculine and feminine inclination, a republican and a social elitist who despised the attitude of the wealthy yet loved their wealth, an enormous commercial success who refused royalties, a radical who would outrage society in the morning and sup with it in the evening, the most loyal friend and the most careless suitor, a vegetarian and a marksman, a hater of humbug who perfected his own image, a lover of life who preferred it retold as legend. It was at this particular legends and myths crossroads that he met Greece, and the Greece he saw was noble legend against worthless life, where the sons of Apollo had become the serfs of the Turks, where those few who did know better forsook Athens for Byzantium, rhetoric for argument, practicality for idealism. To Byron Greece was above all an idea, an ideal, Aristotelian *nous*, and it inspired in his soul a passion that these kinsmen of Homer and Virgil should rediscover the glory that was Athens and Arcadia, that among the squabbling warlords and feckless *hoi polloi* a natural successor to Pericles would arise to lead them into a modern version of Plato's Republic. It was fortunate that Byron was not one to be weighed down by details.

Over coffee—and of course one must say Greek coffee and not Turkish coffee—followed by delicious Greek Delight, we discuss the riddle of Byron's succession. It goes like this. During the War of Independence many a long evening was taken up discussing, no doubt with the usual Greek fervour for political theory, the governance of Greece post-independence. The Napoleonic experience had destabilised political thought as it swerved from republic to empire to monarchy. The Great Powers, who in the political vacuum left behind by four centuries of Ottoman subjugation would eventually decide the new Greek constitution, had their own constitutional axes to grind, and political axis to protect. When the great day came in 1832 the Convention of London declared Greece should be an absolute monarchy. But who was to be the absolute monarch? There was no Greek pretender who did not immediately stir up equal animosities. There was no obvious European pretender either, nor any princely volunteers. Eventually, *faute de mieux*, the teenage Otto of Bavaria, second son of Ludwig I, was declared king, and he became King Otto of Greece. There seems no doubt that if Byron was still alive he would have been offered the role—they would have had to offer him the role—and the parlour game is: would the republican Byron have accepted the throne and become King George of Greece? Rosa thinks not, and I don't know our kid as well as Rosa does, but I think he would have accepted it like a shot, and taken it seriously too. The costumes! The pageant! The protocol!

But like Byron and Hobhouse two hundred years ago, my time in Messolonghi needs to be short, and like them I take the short sea passage over the Gulf of Corinth to Patras. Messolonghi brings home the degree of affection Greece still holds for Byron; Vyron is still a popular boy's name and in 2008 the Greek government declared 19 April, the anniversary of his death, a national holiday. Statues adorn every town he visited, plaques commemorate every house in which he rested. Byron Streets and Byron Squares are everywhere. Reasonably enough, the Byron whom Messolonghi remembers is the 1824 martyr and not the 1809 Grand Tourist. While at Messolonghi, on his thirty-sixth birthday and three months before he died, he wrote this clear acknowledgment of all that had come to pass, almost as a memorandum to himself, and where he knew it would lead.

> My days are in the yellow leaf;
> The flowers and fruits of love are gone;
> The worm, the canker, and the grief
> Are mine alone!

The Sword—the Banner—and the Field,
Glory and Greece, around me see!
The Spartan, borne upon his shield,
Was not more free.

Awake! (*not* Greece—she *is* awake!)
Awake, my spirit—think through *whom*
Thy Life blood tracks its parent lake,
And then strike home!

Tread those reviving passions down,
Unworthy manhood;—unto thee
Indifferent should the smile or frown
Of beauty be.

If thou regret'st thy youth, why *live*?
The Land of honourable Death
Is here—up to the Field! and give
Away thy Breath.

Seek out—less often sought than found,
A Soldier's Grave—for thee the best,
Then look around, and choose thy ground,
And take thy Rest.

Chapter Eleven

FROM PATRAS TO ATHENS, MYTHS AND ORACLES

22 NOVEMBER – 24 DECEMBER 1809 | 25 APRIL – 23 MAY 2009

*ℒ*ike Byron, Hobhouse, Fletcher, Vassily, and Georgiou the dragoman, the whole party recently joined by one of the Albanian guards, Dervish Tahiri, the more compact Strathcarron entourage of the writer and his wife left Messolonghi for Patras by boat. The Byron contingent were rowed all the way on a windless day, initially through the shallows and marshes which surround the town, the Strathcarron contingent relied on dear old Mr. Perkins to chug them along the channel, newly dug and banked through the salt fields.

On the way one still passes a waterborne village which remains much as Hobhouse described it. Shacks built on sticks rest on the water like so many wading spiders, and the fishermen surround their plots of marsh with wattle reed fences against the lapping waves. Wooden dinghies, seemingly overburdened with the paraphernalia of nets and buoys, rollers and pulleys, bob up and down at the end of these amphibious gardens. Two or three shacks have evolved into enjoying windows and doors, incongruously garish paint schemes and plastic roofs and porches. Outboarded dories are tied to a leaning post. As one glides past one automatically thinks 'how charming', but fears the reality would be 'how ghastly'.

At Messolonghi I had to meet the mayor for a photo-opportunity —his photo-op, I might add. Churchill said the Greeks were five

million people with five million opinions, and as Byron was to discover fifteen years after his first visit here two Greeks who agreed about anything were seldom to hand when you needed them. Whenever one wanders into a Greek bar and is distracted by the blaring telly, hard to avoid unless one is auditorily challenged, there always seems to be the same scene playing on the screen. Across the bottom half will sit a panel of half a dozen pundits discussing the *cause du jour*. Above them the screen will split into close-ups of whoever is talking at the time. There are always three of them, regularly there will be four, if you are lucky five, and there's no reason to suppose that from time to time all six talking heads will be talking heads at the same time.

I mention all this because at the meeting with the mayor there were always several conversations going on at once, various randomers like me wandering in and out, the raising of voices, and then the conciliatory gestures, the beating of breasts and then hugging of shoulders. When he had worked his way back to me, the mayor, a delightfully congenial red-hot socialist called Angelos, asked how I found Messolonghi. I said that I thought the fishermen's shacks on the way in from the Gulf were wonderfully evocative, but this was enough to set him off on a rant about the unfair development of uncontrolled capitalism. Later I found out that some of the more commercially minded fishermen had discovered the benefits to be had from eco-tourism, and turned their shacks into bijou cabins, and hence the doors and windows, garish paint, leak-proof roofs, hammocks in porches and smart new dories. Half the mayor's room was following the conversation, and when one of them translated it the other half joined in and pretty soon we were in a living metaphor of Greece as twelve million splinter groups who occasionally and with great reluctance form uneasy and short-lived coalitions; but the rancour has no depth, and moments later dissolves into querulousness, then apathy—but not for long!—then an opinion, then someone else's opinion, a brief respite, take a deep breath and off we go again.

But I digress. Patras. They made the considerable detour to Patras in the hope that waiting at the consul's house (the last British one before Constantinople) would be news and letters from England,

and in Byron's case remittances from Hanson. They had already met the Greek-born English Consul, Samuel Strané, in Malta and more recently here in Patras on their one-hour stopover eight weeks earlier, but unfortunately he had no packages waiting for them. There was, however, hope: he reported that the next convoy was expected within days, and they were welcome to lodge for as long as they liked. In the event they stayed twelve days in Patras, and only left when the convoy eventually arrived empty handed.

To spread the load of hospitality Strané introduced them to his cousin Paul, and pretty soon Byron and Hobhouse were involved in a tug-of-consuls: consuls, moreover, who represented countries at war, as on cousin Paul's flagpole flew the colours of France, Sweden and Russia. Both consuls outbid each other to entertain their visitors, but it seems that cousin Paul pulled harder and they stayed under Napoleon's protection, and dined on his Imperial extravagance, while waiting for the convoy.

Byron was anyway by this stage engrossed with the first draft of *Childe Harold's Pilgrimage*, and as always his creative impulses were aroused best at night. Hobhouse, in his diary entries for his time in Patras, seems rather bored and lonely. He amused himself with inconsequential day trips while his travelling companion slept the days away and worked through the nights. At least Hobhouse—and Byron—were consoled by the return to civilisation, writing that 'after a long disuse of tables and chairs, we were much pleased by these novelties.'

Cousin Paul kept a good kitchen too, and entertained lavishly. One evening, a fellow guest, a Greek doctor, told the story of Ali Pasha and the French General Rosa. The latter had gone to Ioannina to marry. We know not why. Ali Pasha took umbrage, possibly because he had not been the guest of honour. He invited the general into his palace as a guest for further celebration, had him seized and carried on a mule to Constantinople where he died of fury and a broken heart in prison. Byron must have filed the story under 'Plots', for this is the DNA of *Don Juan*, with Ali Pasha as Lambro and General Rosa as Juan.

Patras doesn't sound like it was a place to tarry, unless one was absorbed all night writing an epic poem or waiting for mail in a packet. The Irish traveller and writer, Edward Dodwell, who was in Greece five years before Byron, wrote that Patras

> was like all Turkish cities composed of dirty and narrow streets. The houses are built of earth baked in the sun: some of the best are whitewashed, and those belonging to the Turks are ornamented with red paint. The eaves overhang the streets and project so much that those opposite houses almost touch each other, leaving but little space for air and light, and keeping the street in perfect shade, which in hot weather is agreeable, but far from healthy. The pavements are infamously bad, and being calculated only for horses; no carriages of any kind being used in Greece.

Although Greece's third city after Athens and Thessalonica, Patras today is rather unsure of itself. Its main point of pride is its leading role in the Greek War of Independence, when in 1821 the Greek flag was raised for the first time on Greek soil. The Turks responded by razing the town, leaving only the old Venetian castle which still overlooks it, and which is now its only grace, still intact. When the Turks were finally forced out—by the French as it happens—in 1828, the city was rebuilt on a grid pattern, but the earthquake of 1953 was as devastating as the Turkish revenge and the city now retains the grid but is saddled with horrible 1950s concrete architecture. One needs to keep one's eyes at street level, for here can be found the bars and cafés enlivened by its large university population. It's a city for evenings and nights and weekends, but only, one would hazard, during term time.

Before leaving Patras Byron had some housekeeping to attend to, having finally lost patience as well as too many piastres with the dishonesty of Georgiou the dragoman, who was dismissed for untold robbery and replaced by Andreas, a Greek of the English consul Strané's employ who spoke Turkish, French, Italian and choirboy Latin. The latter he had learnt as a chorister in St. Peter's in Rome, an item on his CV of which Byron would have approved.

If Patras has an identity crisis, their next stop, known as Vostizza to Byron, Vostizi to Strané, Aiyion in the Greek guidebook, Aigion at the port, Egio on the Michelin map, Egion in the *Admiralty Pilot* and Aigio to the locals has so many identities a crisis seems inevitable. The town now is entirely nondescript, the victim of two recent earthquakes and botched rebuilds. If earthquakes here are like buses in London one hopes that the next rebuild will be more sympathetic.

But stranded they were in whatever-it's-called for over a week by foul winds. For Byron this was time well spent: the nights belonged to Childe Harold and the days to Andreas Londos, their host at Vostizza and the spark for Byron's Greek consciousness.

Londos was the Cogia Pasha, the prime minister to Ali Pasha's son Veli Pasha, who governed this part of the Peloponnese on his father's behalf. At the time he was only nineteen, so more or less Byron's contemporary, 'tiny with a face like a chimpanzee and a cap one third of his height'. He was already a devoted student of politics. Hobhouse noted that: 'We could in an instant discover the Signor Londos to be a person in power: his chamber was crowded with visitants, claimants, and complainants; his secretaries and clerks were often presenting papers for his signature; and the whole appearance of our host and his household presented us with the singular spectacle of a Greek in authority—a sight which we had never before seen in Turkey.' When Byron first arrived Londos was reticent about any political discussion, as Byron was after all the guest of, and recent visitor to, Ali Pasha himself. But as the week wore on they became closer, and by the time the entourage left a week later a life long friendship between the two lovers of Greek identity had taken hold.

Twelve years later Londos led a Greek insurrection at Patras which became the outbreak of the Greek War of Independence. He was a leading figure throughout the struggle, and is now a national hero whose portrait hangs in many a Peloponnese bar and bus station, but at the time, after the struggle had been won, he backed the wrong faction in the Greek roulette of independence politics and the subsequent and inevitable civil war. He had contact with Byron again throughout the War, and Byron wrote to him that 'Greece has ever been to me, as it must be for all men of any feeling or education, the promised land of valour, of the arts, and of liberty through the ages.' In his journal Byron wrote that 'Andreas Londos is my old friend and acquaintance since we were lads in Greece together.'

~

Foul winds eventually turn fair and on 14 December 1809 they hired a ten-oared galliot, hoisted a lateen sail and crossed the Gulf of Corinth from whatever-it's-called to the north side. By the evening they had reached the charming inlet and port now known as Galaxidi, the jumping off point for Delphi. They disembarked and found an inn, where they had to 'turn two parties out of two rooms half filled with onions'. As usual Fletcher made Byron's and Hobhouse's beds, before joining the rest of the entourage in the lesser room where they tucked down as best they could, although poor Fletcher was not a happy valet having 'a cheek, tooth and headache and catching twenty lice'.

Today Galaxidi is a delightful low-key, low-rise harbour, and fully returned to the prosperity it enjoyed before the Ottoman occupation. The hilltop church—its red cupola the first sight of Galaxidi through the binoculars—welcomes one in from the southern horizon. Outer islands show the way, one even just sports a church, and others just a vineyard. Some kind soul has built a monolith on a potentially treacherous reef, and one turns hard to port after passing it and straight into the harbour.

Like Patras it played a leading part in the War of Independence, and like Patras it was revenge-sacked by the Turks for its troubles. Its history has always involved the sea, and there is now an excellent Nautical Historical Museum tucked away in the cobbled backstreets, with a replica figurehead from *Cutty Sark* outside. The museum's resident dog looks like a goat, all the signs and literature are only in Greek—normally annoying but for some reason here rather refreshing—and the gift shop is now slightly emptier than it was before the writer's wife's visit earlier this morning.

The harbour that the Byron galliot pulled into is now the much smaller fishing harbour, a charming inlet lapping on the pavements of identikit tavernas, where the food really is a secondary consideration to the setting, peaceful in the near and spectacular in the far. Byron first saw Mount Parnassus from Vostizza on what must have been a particularly clear autumn day, and our first sight of:

> Oh, thou Parnassus! whom I now survey,
> Not in the phrensy of a dreamer's eye,
> Not in the fabled landscape of a lay,
> But soaring snow-clad through thy native sky,
> In the wild pomp of mountain-majesty!

was from the Taksis Taverna in the clarity of an early May summer morning. It was one of those occasions when Byron and the writer met through time.

As elsewhere throughout the Mediterranean the larger commercial fishing boats berths are making way for those intended for visiting yachtsmen. It's a question of unsentimental economics: a yacht brings in more euros to a port than a trawler. The nutrient poor Mediterranean has never been rich in fish—even the Romans used to complain about poor catches—but recent advancements in fish finding technology and the flagrant disregard for conservation by the fishermen themselves has meant that large-scale commercial fishing in the Mediterranean is now financially unsupportable. The trawler fishermen we met in Greece were all Egyptians (Egypt's fishing industry was destroyed by the Aswan Dam), and they looked like they had had enough too. There has subsequently been a revival of small-scale, almost hobby, fishing by one or two men in small open boats, and it is these dozens of skiffs and dories that now fill the Galaxidi harbour in which Byron arrived, while the larger harbour developed after the Second World War for old-style commercial fishing is smartened up and awaiting visiting yachts like *Vasco da Gama*.

Like Byron and the entourage we only stayed one night as Delphi beckons as powerfully as ever. Leaving Galaxidi, heading north and east the landscape changes immediately: to the west all is fertile, cultivated and populated, then just over a small ridge the valley which leads up to Delphi is barren in comparison, barely green, with boulders tumbling ominously down the slopes. One's eyes are drawn up, and there is Mount Parnassus glowering down at her subjects below. Over the next days we are going to see a lot of each other. I don't know if it's something I said but she never seems to approve. There are gods galore living in Parnassus's cleft at Delphi, Zeus himself, Apollo of course, and yet it's the spirit of snow-capped Mount Parnassus that seems to dominate.

Long before the worshippers of Greek gods came here it had been holy ground for the Mycenaeans, and before them the worshippers of Gaia, the earth goddess, daughter of Chaos and mother of Heaven. I was looking for the mystical cleft in one of Mount Parnassus's folds, the geological statement which once seen has explained to visitors from the beginnings of time why the gods would meet here.

And have you noticed how the gods always live in the most inconvenient places? Machu Picchu in Peru, Mount Kailash in Tibet, Mauna Kea in Hawaii, Uluru in Australia, all major expeditions, acts of faith, as if the gods want to be sure you really want to visit them. At least Zeus was less demanding: looking for the centre of the universe he released two eagles from its opposite poles, and after great flights through the ether they met on the slopes of Mount Parnassus, high above the Gulf of Corinth. Later Apollo made the site his seat, and taking the form of a dolphin (*delphis*) to guide Cretan sailors to him, renamed it Delphi.

Greek gods like Apollo differ from humans mainly in being immortal. For Ancient Greeks there was no afterlife; this was it. The gods had every human frailty: some were jealous, others were seductive, most could be devious, unpredictability was only to be expected, and cussedness not unknown. Perhaps it was cussedness that attracted them to Delphi.

Apollo's worshippers built his temple to align with the midsummer sunrise and midwinter sunset, and within it, at the exact spot where Zeus's eagles had met, at the navel of the planet, they set a sacred stone. Over that stone they built an inner sanctum, a temple for an oracle, and for a thousand years the Delphic Oracle, the mouthpiece of Apollo, would be consulted once every moon cycle. The oracle herself, always called Pythia, would be a fifty-year-old virgin (in greater supply then than now) at the start of her tenure and would hold the job for life. The sanctum happened to be built on north/south and east/west fault lines, and the *pneuma*, the breath of the earth, arising from them would induce trances to help with prophecies, which were either intentionally or pneuma-tically given as ambiguities.

In Byron's time the only way up to Delphi was via the town of Crisso, resting peacefully below the site on Parnassus's early slopes, and from there to take the ten-kilometre, thousand-metre-high horseback ride up to what was the village of Castri which occupied the site. Most visitors today hardly notice Crisso at all as they sweep past it on the highway which approaches the new town of Delphi, half a mile and tucked around the corner from the famous old archaeological site of Delphi itself. Byron was rather impressed with one aspect of Crisso: apparently the women were of such easy virtue that he suggested that it would have been better to build a temple to Aphrodite than Apollo. In spite of conscientious research the writer is unable to confirm.

Not having a horse, and a thousand-metre climb in May being a long one for Shanks's pony, the writer took the easy option and drove. At first all was well as the track was a road of sorts, and a bit four-wheel drive-y in parts, but I had a hire car so that bounced and groaned up just fine. But then suddenly, about half way up, a road works sign on trestles blocked the road. I had to get out and walk after all, safe at least in the knowledge my car blocking the road wasn't going to cause a traffic jam. Actually the climb is not too strenuous with Parnassus pulling you along, and an amble on the way down with the Gulf views to settle the stomach. Wild flowers, goats' bells and the scent of burnt almonds escort you along the track, and when you pause to take a breath the world pauses with you. Byron saw six eagles here, although Hobhouse later ruled that they were vultures.

Reading about their visit now, one has the feeling that Byron and Hobhouse were rather unimpressed by their first brush with the antiquities of Ancient Greece. Hobhouse wrote that 'divested of its ancient name this spot would have nothing very remarkable or alluring.' So often as one re-visits Byron's Grand Tour one cannot help feel that the places have changed for the worse, but Delphi stands out as an exception. In 1809 the site was occupied by Greek shepherds and goatherds and their respective flocks, but they were not Greek in the Hellenic sense of understanding the word and they made no connection at all between the columns and ruins in which they grazed their flocks and among which they sheltered for the night and any ancestors. After a week of patriotic political stirrings with Andrea Londos, and then a visit to Greece's disinherited past—a past still glorious in Byron's Classics educated mind—we can now see in Byron's verses and letters the first stirrings of his Greek national consciousness.

The first ancient sites they passed were the Sanctuary of Athena and Temple of Tholos and then at the base of the cleft the Castalian Spring, the very spot where Apollo prevailed, Pegasus landed, the Muses quenched their thirsts and generations of blocked poets have sought their inspiration. Byron took the powers of the waters seriously, drinking it 'from half a dozen streamlets, some not of the purest, before we decided to our satisfaction which was the true Castalian, and even that had a villainous twang.' A guide showed them around the ruins, making wild claims about the oracle's domain, Byron noting that 'a little above Castri is a cave, supposed the Pythian, of immense depth; the upper part is paved, and now a cow-house.' Of course it was nothing of the sort.

If Byron and Hobhouse were underwhelmed by the remains at Delphi the writer must admit to being rather overwhelmed, partly because it was one of the few occasions when a modern tourist complex had been done sympathetically. The village of Castri remained on the site Byron visited until the whole complex was bought by the French government for their archaeologists in 1891. The 'mud poor' villagers were moved to a new place, called Delphi, half a mile around the corner. Castri was excavated and the site evolved into what we can see today. The new museum is located discreetly, the car parks are out of sight, the signs are low and explain just enough of what each ruin was, the tour guides don't shout, the ropes guiding one along the approved route are barely noticed. Perhaps if my friends could return now they would be, well, if not overwhelmed, maybe just plain whelmed.

I had contacted a guide for the visit to Delphi, Penny Unger, a friend of a friend of Gillian's, who had been a fellow guide at the V&A Museum and who had married a Greek and settled in Amfissa, the nearest town to Delphi. We meet in the café of the Acropole Hotel. Penny is younger than I had expected, conspicuously of childbearing age, and blonder. She wears large purple spectacles on a chain. The spectacles go on and come off regularly. Around her shoulders is a thin cardigan, on her feet sensible boots.

She could only have a cut glass English accent: 'Now do you want to see anything in particular?'

'Yes,' I say, 'Lord Byron was here two hundred years ago. I have some quotes from him and some notes from his travelling companion. He was a naughty boy and carved his name in a pillar. There are some pretty good directions...'

'Ha!' she gasps, 'do you believe in coincidences?'

'Not normally. I'm more of a synchronicity merchant on the whole.'

'Yes, quite so, just yesterday my friend Apostolos from the municipality said we should do something special to celebrate the anniversary of Lord Byron's visit.'

'He knows the cow's cave, the pillar, everywhere they went?' I ask.

'He does,' she smiles and delves into her bag. She looks around the empty café and lowers her voice, 'Apostolos knows everything.' Moments later she is on her mobile to him: 'Apostolos...' that's all I can understand directly but am not surprised when he appears a few moments later.

We jump into Apostolos's people carrier and soon arrive at the Castalian Springs. They are now fenced in because of the danger of falling boulders. 'Two hundred years ago no problem one or two visitors at the Springs, now...' and he makes signs for a landslide. We leave there and walk down to the ruins of the monastery. Several dozen pillars lie randomly in the grass. A path of sorts surrounds them. Apostolos knows his pillars and heads straight for the one with

Byron's scratched graffito. We squat down beside him. He points to some faint indentations. I move through different angles, up and down, side to side, and with the sun at a certain angle, me at another, the pillar at another, my Polaroid sunglasses on, his finger pointing precisely at a point on the pillar I can just about make out a B. Later in his office he shows me one he had prepared earlier, with a dusting of powder brushed over and yes, m'lud did indeed vandalise a pillar at Delphi.

Back at the site, after she has whisked me round the museum, in rather sprightly style for one so pregnant, I ask Penny if she felt that they had done an Elgin.

'What do you mean?' she asks suspiciously.

'Well, it's as if they have taken the best bits from the site and put them in the museum. Galling enough if the museum is in London, but worse here when it's on site.'

She looks me over, as if to see if I can be trusted with a state secret. Evidently I can and she says, 'not all the pieces are from the site. This site I mean. Some from other sites. So reproduced.'

'You mean they're replicas?' I ask.

'Well not exactly replicas in that sense, but there was not much left here lying around, what with the Dorians and Nero and Constantine. And then the Turks. Complete philistines. Half of Amfissa comes from here. Well not half, but you know what I mean.'

At the top of the site is the stadium where they held the Pythian Games, the forerunner to the Olympics—although the Pythians had to compete in the nude, so depriving themselves of sponsorship opportunities. At this point Penny has an earnestness attack and we part, but flippant is as flippant does.

And so the Byron entourage left Delphi for the short journey to Athens. They passed though Livadia, Thebes—now Thiva—and Skourta, 'a miserable deserted village' then and a miserable polluted town now, all the way without much interest or incident. If the road was unexciting then it is duller now, and the land becomes a featureless Athens suburb soon after Skourta; Thebes is particularly disappointing, there is no sign of Oedipus or his mother, still less

Dionysus or his vineyard. I looked everywhere, but Thebes feels like it has never recovered from its destruction by Alexander in 335 BC. Thus they proceeded through Ottoman outposts until on Christmas Eve 1809 they found an inn ten miles short of the small and unimportant provincial town of Athens, the glories of which had been the subject of so many hours of Classics study, into which they rode unnoticed and bemused the following day, Christmas Day, 1809.

Chapter Twelve

ATHENS, THE GRAND TOUR DAYS

26 DECEMBER 1809 – 5 MARCH 1810 | 9–31 MAY 2009

*B*yron hasn't changed much over the last two hundred years, but Athens is someplace else entirely. Transport him forward to any of the other places we have visited so far, to Lisbon, fairytale Cintra, Sevilla, to Jerez or Cadiz, the dreaded Gibraltar, Cagliari, barren Malta, even sad Tepelenë, and he could soon guess where we are, but—unless he were standing underneath the Acropolis—Athens would be unrecognisable.

His first view of Athens was from Phyle, then a pine-clad hill but now a locally resented gypsy encampment. His enthusiasm was aroused immediately: '...the plain of Athens, Pentelicus, Hymettus, the Aegean, and the Acropolis, burst upon the eye at once; in my opinion, a more glorious prospect than even Cintra.' No such view exists today. The plains have become off-white concrete suburbs, the view to the Aegean has been long lost to smog, through which only the faintest outline of the Acropolis can be seen if one knows exactly where to look, and then looks hard.

Of the Athens of two hundred years ago we know quite a lot from the contemporaneous accounts and from some of the engravings mentioned in Acknowledgments. It was a small and rather unimportant provisional town, the fiefdom of one of the Black Eunuchs at Constantinople, ranked only 43rd in the Ottoman hierarchy of cities. It was run as a corruptocracy by a *voivode* or governor, Suleyman Aga, who was expected to submit to the Porte in Constantinople not only the taxes from the city but his personal tribute to the eunuch from whom he bought the rights to govern. He himself was assisted by a *disdar*, a military governor, whose fiefdom was the Acropolis. He in turn had to pay the *voivode* for his appointment, and so charged the curious and the collector for access to the Acropolis. He and the likes of Lord Elgin—of whom more later—soon built up a mutually reliant relationship.

The city spread from the Acropolis to the north-west, in what is now Monastiraki, and held about twelve hundred dwellings, some of them houses, many of them shacks and shanties. The best of the dwellings went to the four hundred Turkish families and their slaves, then to the three hundred Albanians families and the remainder to the Greeks to manage as best they could. The Turks and Albanians decorated the outside of their houses with marble pieces from the antiquities lying abandoned all around them.

In addition to these more local residents there lived eight Frank families, a Frank being the Turkish term for a non-Greek Orthodox Christian. The Franks were mostly consuls, who doubled up as usurers and traders, and all were under the ultimate protection of the French consul. In addition to all these there was a steady stream of Frank visitors like the Byron entourage, a stream that grew into a river with the rising tide of philhellenism—it wasn't until ten years later that Hobhouse himself became a founding member of the London Greek Committee. All in all the Christian residents had a surprisingly lively social life, especially in winter when there was even a ball or two, and the state of war or peace between the consuls' home countries did not seep through to any unpleasantness in Athens—where as far as the Turks were concerned they were all just Franks together anyway.

Samuel Strané in Patras had given Byron the name of the widow of his ex-fellow consul for possible lodgings in Athens. The widow had a sister, Theodora Macri, and she not only had the two adjoining consuls' houses to rent in what is now Agias Theklas, but three daughters, Katinka, Mariana and Theresa, aged from fifteen to twelve. These soon became Byron's 'three graces' with whom he engaged in 'hours of dancing and buffoonery', and Theresa was to become 'Maid of Athens, ere we part/Give, oh give me back my heart.'

Byron and Hobhouse were strangers in town but were soon visited by the Neapolitan painter, Giovanni Battista Lusieri, who had been hired by Lord Elgin to be his advisor and supervisor for the removal of the Parthenon antiquities. Lusieri, tall, talkative, witty and worldly, was to become one of Byron's closest friends over the next two years; he was also the uncle of Byron's soon-to-be ultimate boyfriend, Nicolo Giraud. As a result of his work for Lord Elgin he knew the sites of Athens and Attica better than any other Christian there at the time, and in spite of his work for Lord Elgin he shared Byron's despair at the removal of the finest pieces from their homes; but he also agreed with Hobhouse that better they were in London than Paris, or being ground down to make a Turkish house, bath house, or mosque.

Every traveller to Athens needs a Lusieri, and mine is a very fine fellow called Andreas Makridis. We had stumbled across each other on the Internet when he had seen some correspondence about this project on the International Byron Society forum. He is a Greek equivalent of a lobby journalist, and knows everybody in and everything about Athens. He is also a great Byronist and anglophile, a sort of reverse philhellene. The first time we met I had just breezed in from Albania and was catching the first flight out the following morning back to Malta. He picked me up on his motorcycle and we toured the wine bars of Plaka, the most amusing quarter of Athens. I seem to remember having a 4.30 a.m. call for a taxi to the airport, and surviving till midnight until we somehow weaved our way back to the hotel. He then rode back to the wine bar to finish the half bottle still left. As I say, a very fine fellow, and the perfect guide.

The main point of visiting Athens two hundred years ago, and for many still the main point of visiting Athens now, is to be among the archaeological sites of Ancient Greece. Here one either falls into the Byron or Hobhouse camp: for Byron they were ruins which had to be seen but which made him distracted; for Hobhouse there were antiquities which were a pleasure to see and which made him marvel. The writer, I'm afraid, falls into the Byron camp. Hobhouse would wander around a site taking measurements, noting compass bearings, making notes, and drawing sketches. Byron would stay on his horse and ruminate, summon up some couplets for later and move on. Hobhouse saw them with his head; Byron saw them with his heart.

And the ruined antiquities, to term them diplomatically, would have meant something to them, far more than they do to nearly all visitors today. Both had been schooled thoroughly in the Classics—Byron was introduced to Latin at the age of six at his school in Aberdeen, and there is no reason to suppose Hobhouse's education would have been any different. By the time they met at Cambridge three years ago they were totally familiar with the legends and language of Ancient Greece. When they rode across the Temple of Olympian Zeus they would have known that it was started by Peisistratus in 550 BC and completed by Hadrian in 131 AD, and they would have known why it was built in the first place and what had happened to it in the intervening 700 years—unlike the writer who has just had to look all this up in the Attica Guide.

They soon reached a practical arrangement for their visits to the sites. Byron had by this time finished the first draft of *Childe Harold's Pilgrimage* canto I and had started drafting canto II. This meant he was up most of the night and asleep for most of the day. Hobhouse would set off in the morning with Lusieri, and walk around the antiquities recording what he saw. In the late afternoon he would collect Byron, they would saddle up—Byron couldn't really walk very well over the rubble anyway—and ride out for a highlights revisit of the sites that Hobhouse had seen earlier.

Unlike Lusieri, who appreciated the treasures artistically, and Hobhouse, who viewed them academically, Byron saw them as symbols of the futility of even Man's highest achievements. If they had just been found in isolation, like Stonehenge, the futility would have been stark enough, but now the very treasures were surrounded by the direct descendants of these giants who were now living in serfdom, and even worse, in hopelessness under ignorant and oafish oppressors. The tables had not just been turned, but even at their zenith shown to be ultimately meaningless, that even the most virtuous circles are subject to decay and death. His exasperation and frustration at the fall, the pointlessness of all that had gone before, cry out in anger—and wisdom—at the start of the second canto on which he was now working every night.

> Ancient of days! august Athena! where,
> Where are thy men of might, thy grand in soul?
> Gone—glimmering through the dream of things that were:
> First in the race that led to Glory's goal,
> They won, and passed away—is this the whole?
> A schoolboy's tale, the wonder of an hour!
> The warrior's weapon and the sophist's stole
> Are sought in vain, and o'er each mouldering tower,
> Dim with the mist of years, grey flits the shade of power.
>
> Son of the morning, rise! approach you here!
> Come—but molest not yon defenceless urn!
> Look on this spot—a nation's sepulchre!
> Abode of gods, whose shrines no longer burn.
> E'en gods must yield—religions take their turn:
> 'Twas Jove's—'tis Mahomet's; and other creeds
> Will rise with other years, till man shall learn
> Vainly his incense soars, his victim bleeds;
> Poor child of Doubt and Death, whose hope is built on reeds.

Where did Lusieri take Hobhouse and Hobhouse take Byron? I don't intend to give exhaustive explanations of the sites as they are now, only to observe that apart from no longer being accessible they themselves are much the same now as they were then; it's everything else that has changed. Many of the sites are now lost in the endless drabness of suburbs, and therefore unreachable within a reasonable band of patience and care for one's health. Re-visited here are the main sites they visited then within the walls of the old city, which anyway are the ones the curious are most likely to visit now.

But first to observe that if Byron despaired at what had happened to Greek civilisation then, he would undoubtedly despair at what has happened to its capital now. The major changes have come about between the ancient sites: the endless construction and the concrete dust, the sharp angles of cost effective architecture, the noise and pollution of rushing cars egged on by impatient drivers, the fencing in and locking up of the sites themselves to contain the meandering and the inquisitive, the shuffling queues and the competing babels, the curio shops with nothing curious, the tavernas with identikit menus and prices, all served up for the tourists who prefer to read about what they are walking past rather than seeing what it has now become.

The main danger in central Athens now is the warren of pedestrian areas. These are signposted by a blue circle with a white image of a walking parent holding a child's hand. These signs seem to have two meanings; 'Pedestrian Area' and 'Motorcycle Shortcut'. The sport of the latter is to aim directly at the former, employing as many revolutions as his engine will manage while simultaneously encouraging his horn to blow a lively staccato. As the latter also do not have to wear crash helmets they have the additional advantage of being able to shout abuse at any of the former who do not clear a path at once. There's no point in complaining as the police are the worst perpetrators, and have the additional amusement of being accompanied by wailing sirens.

The Stadium, to which they rode out on several occasions, is the most altered site from Byron's day. Early nineteenth-century engravings show the foundations of the white marble three-sided arena, which was completely rebuilt to host the first of the modern Olympics in 1896. It was then given a wash and brush-up for the 2004 Olympics. The shape is said to be the same as in 330 BC, and most pleasing on the eye it is too, almost a *trompe-l'oeil*. They say it will hold 60,000 but it seems far more intimate than that. The fourth side is protected by a voracious main road, and the only athletics to be seen today is the Pedestrian Sprint; instead of a starting gun a green man lights up once every five and a half minutes and the runners have six seconds to cross two carriageways of three lanes each. Once the green man becomes a red man, all bets are off and any motorist who dawdles to give a pedestrian merely walking a sporting chance of survival is subjected to horns of abuse from behind.

The quintessentially photogenic Stadium has recently been 'improved' on its open side and is now almost impossible to photograph. I suggest we hire a helicopter. Andreas replies that one would not be too anti-social to take to the air as a helicopter hovering at camera height would hardly add to the noise and fumes. In the meantime tourists wriggle around the gates trying to find an angle. Lawrence Durrell observed that a good pair of binoculars is a far better friend than a camera, but here there will never be any lenses more useful than the ones in your eyes.

Andreas and I then walk through a park to the Temple of Olympian Zeus. ('Here, son of Saturn, was thy favourite throne! Mightiest of many such!') Since Byron's day one of the seventeen columns—out of the original 104—that he saw has fallen down and now lies like a chopped-up sausage on the ground. For some reason this mightiest of monuments, still awe inspiring in its misplaced confidence, has hardly any visitors. Andreas suggests it is because it requires the most imagination. The site has recently become used by Hellenistic neo-pagans, but somehow one suspects their hearts are not really in it, and once the cameras have gone, and before the police arrive, they wrap up their robes and togas and revert to being annoying students.

This visitor regrets not being able to actually enter any of the sites, but it is particularly vexing to be kept well away from the Temple of the Winds at the end of the Roman Agora. It is now surrounded by wrought iron railings and its rusting unornamented metal doors are shut tight and, should a pole-vaulting enthusiast manage to jump the spikes, padlocked. It must have been marvellous to ride as Byron could through the stones and altars and pedestals of the Agora and just tie up your horse outside the temple and wander in. Built in 100 BC by the astronomer Andronicus, the sides of its octagon show the direction from which the eight Greek winds, well known to sailors, blow. What is really remarkable—again especially from the sailor's point of view—is the accuracy of the eight compass points, as mysterious as remarkable because the first navigational use of the compass, by the Chinese, was not recorded until 150 years later. It was a full thousand years later before compass use became common practice in the Mediterranean. The Ancient Greeks knew a thing or not about large-scale geometry too: from outer space the Parthenon, the Temple of Poseidon at Sounion (we are going there later in the chapter) and the Temple of Aphaea on the island of Aegina make a perfect equilateral triangle.

Originally the temple also had a wind vane and hydraulic clock, but by the time Byron visited it the temple had already been substantially vandalised, and the Turks had given it to the Whirling Dervishes for their whirling worship. What has not been vandalised has now been sanitised by the Department of Archaeology. I feel more exasperation for the genius Andronicus and what the moderns have done to him than for the mighty Zeus, who was, after all, only a god.

Byron and Hobhouse's favoured site was the Theseum, partly because it was the nearest one to the Macri house and partly because it was, and still is, the best preserved of the temples. Its scale is also much more manageable; no mighty monument to Zeus this, but to Hephaestus, god of metalworking, and Athena Ergane, goddess of pottery and handicrafts. This was clearly the artisan quarter then and is now on the western edge of the warrens of western Monastiraki. Well before the Ottoman invasion it had been used as a Christian church, dedicated to St. George. The Turks occasionally used to frighten the congregation with live target practice, and the bullet holes can still be seen on the walls. St. George's became the cemetery for the Christians who died in the War of Independence, and here Byron wrote an epitaph in Latin to his fellow officer George Walden. Unfortunately it is no longer a church, or anything, the Gauleiters at the Department of Archaeology preferring to keep it locked, its spirit crying out to be a place of worship again.

Enough traipsing for one day. Andreas and I repair to Vassilos Bar in Plaka, and in the spirit of philculturism he has a large Famous Grouse (just called a 'Femmus' in Greek) and I have a small ouzo. I can't help but bitch about the way the sites are displayed, and Andreas agrees.

'They are overprotected,' he says, 'and poorly displayed. The archaeologists are overcompensating for the centuries of neglect.'

'I've always thought sites like the Sistine Chapel or the Taj Mahal, or indeed the Theseum or the Temple of the Winds right here, should have a two-tier structure. Let's say they are open from nine to five for free when the mass of tourists from cruise ships and coaches, who have no idea really where they are, could read and shuffle their way through in roped off lines. Then from five to six, or even seven, the site is open to those who want to wander around slowly, or sketch, or research or just sit and soak it up.'

'You'd have to pay,' says Andreas.

'OK, but I'd happily have paid €10 back there to sit quietly and pray in the Theseum. Those of us like you and Hobhouse could look really closely at the details of the place without being shuffled along, and those like Byron and I could just sit quietly, doing nothing, taking it all in.'

'Well that's not going to happen here. The arckies even wanted to pull this whole area down, pull all Plaka down, because it was built on old Athens. The worst that can happen to an Athenian today is that someone discovers a relic near your home, or actually worse you want to change a house and need permission. It can take twenty years. They nearly stopped the Olympics and delayed the Parthenon Museum by five years. They're still squabbling about it now.'

Ah yes, the Parthenon, the highlight for Byron and Hobhouse then and still the highlight for any traveller now. Hobhouse had to wait for two weeks before being allowed to visit it, or more precisely it took him two weeks to summon up enough tea and sugar to bribe the *disdar* to let him in. Lusieri smoothed the way and Byron soon followed.

As bad luck would have it when we visit the Acropolis most of the Parthenon is covered in scaffold and plastic sheeting. The whir of marble cutting machinery just about drowns out the drone of Athens below, the dust from it just about covers up the smog. It is being lovingly restored by craftsmen recently schooled in the old way of making marble joints and cement. For the first time I can sense the Athenian's anger at the loss of the Marbles; up until then it had been an abstract argument, but the columns look sad and depleted without their trappings, as though a favourite aunt had just been mugged of her jewellery. Byron had already written a tirade against Lord Elgin before he had left England, and even seeing the Turks using the Caryatids for target practice did not move Byron to Elgin's 'saving the treasures' argument. 'Not the point,' says Andreas. Anti-Elginism was a cause to which Byron was increasingly and passionately drawn, and one which would occupy him and the writer on their returns to Athens half a year later.

We deliberately choose to enter the site as late as we are allowed, both to miss the bulk of the cruise ship brigade and to catch the columns in the sunset. It is a successful strategy, although approaching sunset we are all shooed off as the site is formally closed by half a dozen Greek soldiers. It is a most incongruous sight, as they funny-walk from the Acropolis up to the entrance of the Parthenon. Then on level ground they march in tramp, in great big studded army boots. I cannot help myself and shout out 'Mind the marble!', as Andreas asks 'where are the arkies when you need them?'

~

After a month or so in Athens the Byron entourage set off on a clockwise tour of Attica, the province in which Athens sits, and after a week or so Andreas, Gillian and the writer set off after them as best we could. The first piece of advice is never rent a thing called a Hyundai Getz; the only thing it getz is on your nerves, and the only thing you getz is a pain in the back and a numb bum.

For both tours the first stop is the Pendeli Monastery, twenty miles north-east of Athens. In olden days the mountain on which the monastery rests, Mount Pentelicus, was famous for its springs and forests but the mountain also holds most of the marble with which ancient Athens was built and this has led to its southern slopes having been dramatically disfigured. Mining is now illegal, but Andreas assures us it still goes on at night.

The monastery is famously prosperous because it claimed land ownership for the northern slopes of Mount Pentelicus, and after independence the government honoured the land titles. The slopes are now covered in houses stretching down to the north-eastern suburbs. Although no one could argue that the area around the monastery is the paradise now that it once was, and certainly must still have been in Byron's time, the monastery and its own grounds are wonderfully serene and peaceful.

The monastery is just about open to visitors, and one wanders freely into a ground floor Orthodox bookstore and out again into the cloisters. Some monasteries have become tourist stop-offs—bad luck on the monks who chose to live their lives in seclusion but find themselves as tourist attractions—but this one, as worthy as any of a visit, has escaped. The Byzantine chapel in the central courtyard is an octagonal gallery of the darkest icons and fiercely gruesome martyrdoms, all haloed by the most elaborate chandelier we have seen.

There is a considerable building project here and interestingly none of the monks is taking part, all the work being done by outside contractors. The writer has attended ashrams in India as well as several meditation retreats in England, and an integral part of the practice is manual work. The idea is not just to save money by doing the work internally, but as a spiritual exercise in placing consciousness on what is happening in real time right in front of one, otherwise known as here and now. But here and now there are no monks, and when Andreas asks why they are not working he is told 'oh, they are resting.' There is not much sign of the modern world: where the Byron visitors would have tied up their horses is an early seventies Datsun Cherry, in what was once bright red but is now day-old smudged lipstick. Outside all is taking its lead from the monks and resting, and even the plentiful birdsong seems like unnecessary agitation.

After a lunch of fried eggs the Byron tour left for Marathon. While Hobhouse fretted about trying to find the scene of the famous battlefield where the heavily outnumbered Ancient Greeks heroically defeated the Persians in 490 BC, Byron became overwhelmed by the poignancy of the scene. He later told Trelawny that while Hobhouse 'had a greed for legendary lore, topography, inscriptions, pottering with map and compass at the foot of Pindus, Parnes and Parnassus to ascertain the site of some ancient temple or city. I rode my mule up them. They had haunted my dreams from boyhood: the pines, eagles, vultures and owls were descended from those Themistocles and Alexander had seen, and were not degenerated like the humans. I gazed at the stars and ruminated; took no notes, asked no questions.' Later, remembering the scene in *Don Juan* he wrote some of his most famous lines:

> The mountains look on Marathon—
> And Marathon looks on the sea;
> And musing there an hour alone,
> I dream'd that Greece might still be free.

Marathon now stirs no such passion, even in one wanting passion to be stirred. The plain of Marathon is a heavily developed coastal strip and actually reminds the writer of the other Marathon, the capital of the Florida Keys. This could be a case of reverse symbiosis, the first example of a European town copying its American namesake. Nothing here is more than twenty years old, whereas Marathon in Florida was certainly around in the time of the film *Key Largo*, and must have pre-dated Key West. Both Marathons are coastal, both have two lane highways running for several miles through them, both have service roads and stores running along the highway, both have revolving ads on stilts above factory stores and square car parks, and both have exposed overhead electric and phone lines. One doesn't need to ask with which town either Marathon is twinned. One wonders what the archaeologists are going to make of this mysterious aberration in two thousand years time.

But salvation is at hand for lovers of the sublime, for at the end of Attica, twenty miles but twenty eons from the tawdriness of Marathon, lies Cape Colonna and the magnificent Temple of Poseidon at Sounion. Byron arrived here one day after his twenty-second birthday. In the evening he saw the sunset dance through the columns and his horse reached the peak as the sun set over the dark green islands opposite leaving the sea as pink as the horizon. In the splendour of this setting he walked over the very stones where Plato had held his conversations, carved his name in the very temple above the ledge from where King Aegeus leapt to his death.

> Place me on Sunium's marbled steep
> Where nothing, save the waves and I,
> May hear our mutual murmurs sweep
> There, swan-like, let me sing and die.

That is from *Don Juan*, and from *The Giaour*:

> Fair clime, where every season smiles
> Benignant, o'er those blessed isles,
> Which, seen from far Colonna's height,
> Make glad the heart that hails the sight,
> And lend to loneliness delight.

Because it is two or more hours outside Athens, the Temple of Poseidon receives far fewer visitors than the sites in the city. Because it is a fair climb up from the car park base camp to the temple itself even fewer go all the way, the less energetic or more corpulent preferring to let their telephoto lenses do the work. Once there, and again the suggestion is to be there as late as possible, one senses the temple to be rather plaintive in its old age, as though it has said to Poseidon, the god of the sea: I have done my best, I was drawn by the best architect, I was made of the best marble, I was founded on the highest cape, I was host to the best philosophers, but your sea is still as young and strong and wilful as ever. It was impertinent of a mere mortal to reach for your immortality, and now I slowly decay back into the marble dust from which I arose.

They spent another month in Athens retracing old footsteps. Byron was becoming restless; he had 'done' Athens, at least the polite Athens, which is all he could do with Hobhouse in tow. He had been excited by the Ali Pasha adventure, and wanted to be closer to the diplomatic world—perhaps with an eye on Destiny—the real one in a centre of power, with ambassadors and sultans, not consuls and primates which was all provincial Athens had to offer. In Athens everything revolved around Constantinople, and to Constantinople, with its added prospect of fresh conquests, he was drawn like to a magnet. They had heard on the grapevine that Robert Adair, the British ambassador in Constantinople, was to be sent home, and that a frigate was on its way to collect him. The frigate would have to wait for its *firman* or travel authorisation in Smyrna—now Izmir. If they could reach Smyrna, they could reach Constantinople, and on a Royal Navy warship, complete with uniformed midshipmen, and on a diplomatic mission. In Piraeus they found the HMS *Pylades* sloop-of-war under Captain Ferguson, itself on a courier diplomatic mission to Smyrna. Hobhouse hastily made the arrangements for the entourage to join her, and within the week they had gone.

But first they had to say goodbye to the Macris, especially Byron had to say goodbye to Theresa. Two nights before leaving Hobhouse wrote that 'Theresa 12 years old brought here to be Deflowered, but Byron would not.' Byron later wrote to Hobhouse that 'the old woman Theresa's mother was mad enough to think I was going to marry the girl' and yet in a journal he wrote that 'I was near bringing Theresa away but the mother asked 30,000 piastres!' But life did not work out too badly for Theresa. As the Maid of Athens she had the fame of being the subject of 'the most romantic poem by the most romantic poet', and on a more mundane level she lived to 85 years, having married another Englishman, James Black, who presumably stumped up the 30,000 piastres, but who also presumably fell short in the poetry department.

Byron wrote that 'I like the Greeks, who are plausible rascals, with all the Turkish vices but without their courage. Athens is a place which I think I prefer to any I have seen.' He would return, and so will we.

Chapter Thirteen

FROM SMYRNA TO CONSTANTINOPLE, SEARCHING FOR HECTOR AND LEANDER

6 MARCH – 13 MAY 1810 | 1–19 JUNE 2009

*A*t the time of Byron's visit to the seat of Ottoman power Smyrna was the commercial capital of the empire, and Constantinople the political capital; a similar situation to which Istanbul and Ankara find themselves in today. Smyrna, now called Izmir, had for millennia the benefit of being situated in one of the great natural Mediterranean harbours, while to reach Constantinople—as we shall see—entailed a tiresome and unreliable sail through the Dardanelles against wind and current. Smyrna, with Mediterranean traders to its west and Arabic traders to its east, had been the principal port of what was for eight thousand years and until fairly recently called Asia Minor. Byron and Hobhouse would have noticed, and we do today, the Genoese forts atop each of the islands that act as stepping-stones on the approach to the Bay of Izmir.

The voyage from Piraeus on the sloop-of-war HMS *Pylades* took only four days; Byron's luck with the fickle Mediterranean weather, and this was in March, held once more. Apart from Hobhouse and Fletcher his entourage was now steady at the two devoted Albanian guards, Vassily and Dervish Tahiri, and Andreas Zantakis, the Greek translator Byron had collected in Patras. For new company they had an interesting fellow passenger in Dr. Francis Darwin, whose father had written *The Botanic Garden* and whose nephew, Charles, was to write *The Origin of Species*. The voyage was uneventful except for the flogging, which Hobhouse noted laconically: 'A man flogged for stealing. Three dozen. Not as bad as I thought.' Well, yes.

The evidence suggests that the entrance to Izmir has become far more painstaking over the centuries due to movement of the seabed caused by earthquakes, and by silting caused by damming and deforestation ashore. As they approached the port, weaving between the shallows, Dr. Darwin suggested it would all soon be silted up entirely, and if the current port of Izmir had not made constant efforts at dredging channels to keep the port alive, Darwin's prediction would surely have been correct.

We settle in the centre of the bay off the town quay, about half a mile south of where the *Pylades* anchored. It is not a happy scene. The water is the colour of school dinners, either the Brown Windsor soup with congealed fat floating on top, or the coffee-flavoured blancmange that wobbled its way down hungry young throats. To make matters worse, the sea, even in the inner harbour, is a juvenile mass of delinquent waves stirred up by the speedboat-ferries which form the best part of public transport along the shore. Occasionally some soup splashes over the coamings onto the cockpit sole, or onto the captain and first mate if caught unawares.

If the crew is less than enamoured with the quay at Izmir, *Vasco da Gama* is even less so. She is not a happy lady, demanding frequent hose downs, and as we have a mutually dependent relationship I am only too happy to oblige. We look after each other, and she knows that I know that she is not quite as inanimate as some might think; in fact she can be, and often is, a bit of a madam. For instance, she definitely prefers lying to starboard tack rather than port tack because she knows it gives her the right of way. Actually she's got a bit of a fixation about right of way, even getting a bit huffy when having to change course to avoid undisciplined supertankers. She occasionally likes a bit of rough—as it were—and enjoys showing her skirt to pursuers. In particular she likes being bought presents, the recent clothes washing machine being a particular delight, but no trinket from a chandlery goes unappreciated. Unlike Johnny Cash she has even forgiven me for giving her a boy's name, but as I said to her the other day 'at least it's not Agamemnon.' Her humour has become rather droll of late, but then again as she said to me 'better droll than gallows.'

Smyrna then was easily the least attractive place on the Grand Tour, as is Izmir on the re-Tour. The Byron party stayed with Francis Werry, the English consul, and his wife on the north shore in an area where the Christians were confined. Hobhouse was 'surprised at the excellence of Werry's house—a long, narrow house, like the gallery and chambers of an inn. It has no breadth, but everything is English and comfortable.' The area is now known as Alsancak, but all traces of its Frankish times have long since been destroyed by one of the forms of pestilence—fire, war or earthquakes—that since time began have set up base camp along the Aeolian shore.

The best one can do to recapture Smyrna in Byron's day is visit the Ahmet Pristina City Archive and Museum. The city's tag line is 'we are 8500 years old' and indeed they are (the Archaeological Museum's version of 'up to date' is 1700 years ago). The illustrations show a narrow strip of two-storey houses along the paved quay, mosques less numerous than churches would have been further west, the Genoese fort still sitting proudly on the northern hill, camels as beasts of burden, no women, dogs scavenging, slaves scampering, ships along the quay where *Vasco* was being stroppy, and grandees on horseback under parasols. The guide mentions 'earthquakes' and shakes his down-turned hand as we pass along the museum from period to period; there have been seven hundred, from the catastrophic to the tremulous, since 1900 alone. A panel shows the cataclysmic onslaught of Izmir's quakes and tremors that have run the Richter scale a merry dance over the centuries.

'Well,' one thinks stepping out into the dazzling and humid smog 'you just cannot trust an earthquake to destroy only that which needs destroying.' It is quite the most unattractive place, a sort of Asian Minor version of Nuneaton, a monument to how unsettling concrete can be if left to run amok.

For purposes of damage limitation when the next 'quake quakes each building is limited to eight storeys, and as if in defiance of such defeatist talk each building sports the rightist of right angles wherever it can like jaws jutting out looking for a fight. Architects have downed beauty and become Concrete Cost Control Consultants. Even the minarets on the mosques are bare concrete. Because the flat coastal strip is quite narrow many of the new houses have been built on the steep hills of the suburbs. To live there must be a calculated risk, like farming under Etna, and is surely the only place where property prices fall as the hill rises. These suburbs don't just sprawl gradually as elsewhere but endlessly replicate themselves like amoebae in a Petri dish.

Byron found himself at his lowest ebb in Smyrna. He was betwixt and between himself. No news had reached him from England for over a year, and so he felt cut off both from the gossip of his London circle and news of his affairs from Hanson. He missed the sociability and classical resonance of Athens, and was now in the land of its oppressors with even fewer Frankish families to mingle amongst, and all of those only involved in trade. In Athens the Christians and Muslims were equally numbered and rubbed along after a fashion, but here he was cut off from contact with the Turks, confined to the quarter on the northern shore. He brooded that it was one thing to forsake the emotional bonds with Athens for the stimulation of its capital Constantinople, another to be stuck in the disease-ridden backwater of Smyrna with the prospect of a long moody summer ahead.

Worse still he had no way of knowing how long he would be marooned there. The HMS *Salsette*, a 36-gun frigate sent to collect the British ambassador to the Sublime Porte, Sir Robert Adair, had already been in Smyrna harbour for over a month waiting for its *firman*—its travel pass—from the Porte. She was commanded by Captain Bathurst, whom Byron found a bit rough and ready; but both Byron and Bathurst were to die for the cause of Greek independence—in Bathurst's, by then Admiral Bathurst's, case one of the few British casualties at the decisive naval battle of Navarino.

All agreed the *firman* could take weeks, months, as the Porte would not allow more than four Frankish ships—and only one from each Christian nation—at a time through the Dardanelles. He must have felt he could not even eat properly, as then and now the diet makes no allowances for vegetarians, an affliction Byron shared with the writer, and the squelchy cakes have limited appeal after the first two weeks. At least he had his work for diversion, and he completed canto II of *Childe Harold's Pilgrimage* late in March 1810.

As a further diversion Hobhouse organised a side trip to Ephesus, site of the Greek and Roman capitals of Asia Minor and the Temple of Artemis; the latter being one of the seven wonders of the ancient world. The trip was not a success. Hobhouse become ill, and Byron was out of sorts with the world at large. As we have already seen at Delphi and will soon see again at Troy, they visited the site at Ephesus before the major archaeological expeditions had uncovered them and there was precious little to see. Byron wrote that 'The temple (of Artemis) has almost perished, and St. Paul [actually it was St. John] need not trouble himself to epistolize with the current brood of Ephesians who have converted a large church built entirely of marble into a mosque.' In fact he must have seen another ruin he assumed was the Temple of Artemis, as all of it was still underground and would be for a further fifty years.

Ephesus is now back to being a wonder to behold, and the Temple of Artemis and the sleeping place of her Seven Sleepers nearby—the setting for the *Comedy of Errors*—at least imaginable in its fuller glory. The ruins are sensitively displayed and, wherever possible, accessible, an example the authorities at Athens should follow. The nearest modern town, Selçuk, is a half-camel half-tractor sort of place. Byron took a greater impression from the frogs and the storks and the jackals than from the ruins. The frogs are still in full croak in the ditch if you walk the kilometre from the station to the Temple of Artemis, and the storks have actually set up a nest on top of the one remaining pillar. The jackals have been somewhat domesticated, and their relatives roam around Smyrna at night, patrolling the alleys and lanes in packs.

Back in Smyrna good news awaited them: the famous *firman* had arrived. Only Mrs. Werry was disappointed at their departure, for like so many others, she had fallen for the beautiful poet young enough to be her son. She cried and made Byron leave her a lock of his hair. Hobhouse was not impressed, and noted rather ungallantly that she was 'pretty well at 56 years at least.' One can almost feel the entourage jumping with joy as they clambered onto the *Salsette* on 11 April, after a mercifully short three weeks in Smyrna. Two hundred years later the crew of *Vasco da Gama* jumped with joy too as Izmir faded into the horizon; and madam herself sprung to stations as soon as she was free of the sweaty quay and filthy water.

From Byron's point of view the most interesting crew member on the *Salsette* was one of the midshipmen, the fourteen-year-old Frederick Chamier. Chamier's grandfather, like Byron's, had been an admiral, and Chamier himself later wrote four naval novels, became a naval historian and left us his autobiography, *Life of a Sailor*, from which the following scenes are drawn.

I couldn't rustle up a midshipman for *Vasco da Gama*, and the last I heard about the only admiral's grandson I know he had set himself up as a food stylist in Dubai, but in the Smyrna Beer Saloon on the town quay I had come across a French sea-hitchhiker in his early twenties, a certain Théophane Jauzzion. He asked me to where I was heading.

'Istanbul, and you?'

'Tahiti. I am hitch hiking there. By sea. From Marseilles. To see my cousin, she works for the *protectorat*. You need crew?'

He is a big strapping lad, hairy too. *Vasco* had a couple of overnighters to do in the approaches to Istanbul, and a third person to share the watches, especially one to whom to delegate the graveyard watch, is always helpful. 'Always helpful,' I reply, 'but surely it's the wrong way for Tahiti.'

'Oh, never mind. I have been in Izmir too long. I think I can find another ship in Istanbul.'

'So you are under no time pressure, then?'

He gives a Gallic puff and pout, which I took to mean 'Non'.

Theo crews with us to Istanbul. He is amicable, reads philosophy and writes poems in his notebook, stares to himself at the horizon and is generally quite Byronic. It is soon after we leave Smyrna that we discover his one disadvantage: he sleeps for an inordinate part of the day, ten hours at a stretch, and the stretches only have short breaks between them. I tell Gillian I think he has necrophilia, she presumes I mean narcolepsy, and we agree that either would be inconvenient on watch, and—especially if I am right about his condition—particularly on the graveyard watch.

Navigating north-east under sail through the straits of the Dardanelles to the Sea of Marmara and onward to Istanbul, the Bosphorus and the Black Sea has always required, above all else, patience with the fates. Europe lies to the north and west; Asia to the south and east. A strong current flows south-west from the Black Sea into the Aegean, and to make matters worse the prevailing north-easterly winds follow and encourage the current as they funnel through the Dardanelles. Eventually the northerlies relent and one needs not just a southerly but a healthy one to overcome up to four knots of foul current. Even today, with the likes of our friend Mr. Perkins chugging away below, progress upstream is best described as leisurely.

It's an ill wind, so they say, that does no one any good, and Captain Bathurst's ill north-easterly off the Dardanelles those April days in 1810 certainly did Byron, Hobhouse, Darwin and Chamier some good; while the *Salsette* languished at anchor for seventeen days waiting for its fair wind they were able to search for the remains of the settlements of Troy, and later were all to add their opinions to the academic arguments raging about Troy at the time.

Back in Byron's day ivory towerists had been theorising about where and when the epic siege and final battle for Helen's hand took place, and even if the Trojans ever existed at all. Latest cat among the pigeons was Jacob Bryant, who ten years before had published his *Dissertation concerning the War of Troy*. This had proposed that there was no Greek expedition, no battle and not even the citadel of Troy itself, and even insisted that Troy was, if anywhere, in Egypt. What is certain is that in 1810 there would have been no evidence—beyond some random rocks and walls that one finds everywhere coastal in Turkey—of the recurring civilisations that had been created and destroyed on the site as it was not until 1865 that the English Troad farmer/American diplomat/Troy enthusiast Frank Calvert steered the German archaeologist Schliemann onto the land under which he believed Troy had stood.

It is way beyond the scope of this book to follow the archaeological machinations and lootings at Troy since 1865, save to observe that archaeologists by necessity destroy what they hope to prove and, in the case of Troy, at times appear to have been more preoccupied with an almost Homeric sullying of each other's reputations than unearthing evidence of advantage to the rest of us. Many too seemed to have had light fingers and big trousers. For those interested not just in Troy as it was but also in the archaeological subplots I can recommend the excellent *The Search for Troy* by the BBC historian Michael Woods. For those interested in the siege and battle for a whole civilisation I can recommend Robert Fagles's translation of Homer's *Iliad* with its wonderful introduction by Bernard Knox.

Reading Michael Woods's updated postscript was exciting for the crew of *Vasco da Gama*, as we seemed to be in the right place at the right time. The latest high-technology surveys place the tomb of Achilles at Besiktepe just behind Besika Bay, five miles south of the Dardanelles, where we are at anchor. Woods concludes the evidence suggests that, just like Byron, Xerces and Alexander the Great, the Greek fleet anchored in Besika Bay and landed on its beach on their way to Troy. Homer conjures up the scene of the Greek invasion fleet at Besika Bay I saw yesterday afternoon:

> Their ships were drawn up far from the fighting.
> Moored in a group along the grey churning surf—
> first ships ashore they'd hauled up on the plain
> then built a defence to landward off their sterns.
> Not even the stretch of beach, broad as it was,
> could offer berths to all that massed armada,
> the troops were crammed in a narrow strip of coast.
> So they had hauled their vessels inland, row on row,
> while the whole shoreline filled and the bay's gaping mouth
> enclosed by the jaws of the two jutting headlands.

Byron's first visit to Besika Bay and the plains of Troy is best described by young Chamier:

The next day I was nominally at work again in the cabin, when Lord Byron requested he might be landed on the plains of Troy: in point of fact, he had been gazing through a telescope on the scene of the brilliant actions of antiquity for hours before.

'I will take this young acquaintance of mine with me, with your permission, Captain Bathurst.'

'Certainly,' replied that excellent man; and in one minute my books were closed, the chronometer sights handed over for the benefit of others, and I down below, 'cleaning myself,' as the term is on board ship, to go ashore.

His lordship had his fowling piece handed into the boat, and we shoved off, all in high spirits. It blew a stiff breeze, and the boat surged her gunwhale in the water, as she lifted over the wave. The cockswain ventured to hint that she would go faster for having a reef in. This was strenuously opposed by Lord Byron, who was a capital sailor, and we arrived, safe and sound, though by no means dry, in the bay, where it is supposed the Grecian fleet was formerly hauled on shore.

His lordship being accompanied by two servants (Vassily and Dervish Tahiri)—presents from that furious monster, Ali Pacha; as Lord Byron called him, 'the mildest looking gentleman he ever saw.' These two were his constant bodyguard; and the attachment between master and men was reciprocal.

Troy and its plains were hallowed ground to his lordship, which I ventured to profane, by blazing away at every bird I saw; and while the poet was imagining the great events of former days, I was lost in the sweet hope of the next day's dinner.

We had a long walk round old walls, and I was tired enough when his lordship brought himself to anchor upon the tomb of Patroclus, producing a book, which he read with the utmost attention, occasionally glancing his quick eye over the plains. It was a Homer.

~

We are at anchor in Besika Bay too. To landward of *Vasco da Gama* the bay and beach are deserted, while on a slight gradient to the south a dozen wind monsters are whirring away. Homer said the plains of Troy were 'windy, windy.' Byron noted the 'The ringing plains of windy Troy.' Behind, to seaward, lines of supertankers, coasters, cruise schooners and warships position themselves to enter the Dardanelles. The captain and first mate on *Vasco da Gama* remark how alike the Trojan coast is to Dorset, or maybe more to the point as a large expeditionary invasion was mounted across its beaches, to Normandy. Theo is asleep and so cannot confirm.

I venture the two hundred metres ashore in the dinghy. There is no one in sight, and I cross over a dune and a dirt track and find myself in front of Besiktepe, the tumulus of Achilles. It's impossible to say if Byron stood here too, still less climbed the mound as I do now. But just in case he didn't, and to pay my own homage, I climb the one hundred-metre slope. Crouching on top of it, and after looking around to make sure no one is watching, I lie down on its summit and hug the hill. I tell Achilles, 'Om! Paramatmane Namaha'; I hear Byron say, 'I've stood upon Achilles tomb and heard Troy doubted; time will doubt of Rome'; Homer says, 'I told you so.' I pass on the messages.

Sorry about that, getting a bit carried away back there. Ashore too the similarity to southern England in August skews the expectations of ancient Troy. There are wheat and barley fields waving in the wind, oak and poplar trees guarding their shade, poppies showing off and butterflies playing in the sun, surrounded by dirt tracks plied by dusty tractors. In a field half a dozen Anatolian peasants are crouched in a circle, presumably for a çay break.

After a further kilometre or so, but still some way inland from what we now know to be Troy, I think it's time for this Byron mini-tour to turn back in a half circle to the shore. He would have had no way of knowing where the site we know today was, and anyway he could not walk over rough ground for very long. On the way back I come across a wall, which may or may not have been the one that Chamier referred to. Looking up, there is a new view of Achilles' tomb and it could be—perhaps should be if Elgin really wanted a *coup de théâtre* and international outcry—reposing among the other tumuli somewhere near Glastonbury.

On another visit, this time with Hobhouse and Bathurst, Byron heard that 'When the English came here in wartime, they asked us only for a draught of water—but the Russians, they burnt our town and took everything, as you see.' Later that week Byron's group was confronted by a posse of Turkish cavalry who thought they were Russians. As Chamier takes up the story:

> ... we came suddenly upon a squadron of Turks, all mounted upon spirited animals, and all as surprised at meeting Giaours, as we were at finding ourselves so near the true believers. However, in the distance... they imagined we were Russians; and... drew their sabres... their countenances betrayed their eager desire for the encounter. In the mean time, our party began to make all preparations for fight; and had it not been for Lord Byron's coolness we should have been minus a head or two before long; for the foremost of the hot-headed Turks waved their sparkling cimeters over their turbaned skulls, whilst those in the rear drew

forth their splendid pistols, and cocked them. No sooner, however, did they learn that we were friends… than they expressed their satisfaction in suitable terms, returned their sabres to their scabbards, gave a very oriental and elegant bend, and… trotted past us at a quick pace.

Now that we know so much more about Troy than they did then, it is hard to feel the strong emotions the questions about its reality, factual or mythological, stirred at the time. I agree *comitante comite Byrone* that if something is experienced in consciousness it is real. It may not be factual but it is still real, that is to say that something unfactual experienced in full consciousness is more real than something factual experienced in ignorance of consciousness. This is where one can easily mistake the lesser reality of facts with the greater reality of, well, reality. Ten years later Byron was to write:

> We do care about the authenticity of the tale of Troy. I have stood upon that plain daily, for more than a month, in 1810; and, if any thing diminished my pleasure, it was that the blackguard Bryant had impugned its veracity. It is true I read 'Homer Travestied' (the first twelve books), because Hobhouse and others bored me with their learned localities, and I love quizzing. But I still venerated the grand original as the truth of history (in the material facts) and of place. Otherwise, it would have given me no delight. Who will persuade me, when I reclined upon a mighty tomb, that it did not contain a hero?—its very magnitude proved this. Men do not labour over the ignoble and petty dead—and why should not the dead be Homer's dead?

He would not be surprised that he has had his cake and eaten it, and that his tombs did indeed contain mighty heroes.

All foul winds eventually turn fair, and after nearly three weeks at Besika Bay, the *Salsette* entered the Dardanelles, then called the Hellespont. Progress was predictably tedious and in the meantime Byron had hatched a plot to swim across the straits from Sestos on the European side to Abydos on the Asian side, all this in a conscious attempt to imitate Leander who swam across to meet Hero, priestess of Aphrodite. On 3 May, as the *Salsette* was anchored in a small bay south of Abydos his chance arrived. Bathurst soon calculated that with the strong current running alongside him Byron would have to swim four miles over the ground: the current would account for three of the miles, Byron's prowess for the other one. I'm sure he further reflected that Hero too had done her leeway vector projections before giving Leander his task.

In the years to come Byron said his Hellespont crossing had meant more than any other event 'political, poetical or rhetorical.' If so, and as we have become rather friendly of late, I think I had better have a go too and on 4 June one hundred and ninety-nine years later make my own attempt at crossing the Dardanelles.

First problem was and is that there is nowhere to anchor, or even tie up, near Sestos. We know that the *Salsette* spent several days at anchor in the bay behind Abydos, and the only conclusion is that Captain Bathurst sent Byron and his swimming companion, Lieutenant Ekenhead, over to Sestos in the jolly-boat, no doubt rowed by a team of heaving and reluctant 'volunteers'. Having deposited Byron and Ekenhead ashore at Sestos, the jolly-boat would follow them across, now needing just the occasional paddle, at a discreet distance. On reading this, and to hedge bets, I 'volunteer' Theo to be part of our own two-man attempt, albeit as a relay not solos.

Unfortunately one can no longer anchor at Abydos, which is now renamed Fort Abydos and is yet another Turkish military installation. So we hatch a plan whereby Gillian will keep *Vasco da Gama* steady against the current off Fort Abydos, and Theo and I will outboard over to Sestos in the dinghy, scramble into our Speedos, and take it turns to be in the water or alongside in the dinghy.

Byron was clearly not just a 'mighty scribbler' but a mighty paddler, having already swum across the Tagus in Lisbon—actually further than the Hellespont—and had recently been swimming several times a week in Piraeus. I'm not much good at swimming outside a bath, but Theo says he is a strong swimmer, and so he looks, although I am frightened he will fall asleep mid-channel. It is not long after setting off in the dinghy that we notice the obvious snag to our plan, a snag with which Byron did not have to contend: the endless procession of supertankers, coasters, cruise schooners and warships which we had seen positioning themselves outside the Dardanelles are now in line astern in this narrowest part of the straits; not only that, but an equal number of supertankers, coasters, cruise schooners and warships are heading the other way only a few hundred metres apart.

From dinghy height the channel at this narrowest point is a churning mass of wash and wake, never mind tens of thousands of tonnes of determined tankers steaming at twelve knots and the regulation five hundred metres apart. One doesn't need a calculator to work out that to try is to die—and so with a great pretence at disappointment we agree to abandon our attempt to follow in Leander and Byron's breaststrokes and further agree to complete several lengths of the next swimming pool as a forfeit.

Afterwards Byron was so exhausted he wondered if 'Leander's conjugal powers must not have been exhausted in his passage to Paradise.' He later wrote the light-hearted 'Swimming from Sestos to Abydos'.

By journey's end Byron had cheered up a notch and wrote to Drury: 'I see not much difference between ourselves & the Turks, save that we have foreskins and they none, that they have long dresses and we short, and that we talk much and they little... in England the vices in fashion are whoring & drinking, in Turkey, Sodomy and smoking, we prefer a girl and a bottle, they a pipe and pathic. I can swear in Turkish, but except one horrible oath, and "pimp" and "bread" and "water", I have no great vocabulary in that language.'

How would Byron have written to Drury today? Maybe: 'I see not much difference between ourselves & the Turks, save that they drink raki and we wine, that we are trying to smoke less and they are succeeding in smoking more, that we are told to be politically correct and they would not stand the telling, that our sexes prefer the other and their sexes—in company at least—each other's. They are misplacing their taboos, as did our Catholics of recent times. We go home in the early evening and they go home in the early morning; we have lost our manners and they maintain a courtesy beyond etiquette. The division of work between men and women seems entirely equitable in Anatolia if not in Notts.: the women work all day in the fields or as porters in the markets or as menders of the roads, while the men rest in the cafés drinking çay and playing backgammon, occasionally looking out to make sure the women are doing their jobs properly. At dusk the women go home, clean the house, make dinner, clear it up and repair the roof, and in their spare moments produce more children & so the cycle continues much as before. I know not much Turkish, save I have learnt that here "mullet" means a haircut & not a red fish to eat.'

The chances are that Byron never saw a Turkish woman, at least not one that wanted to be seen. Even now, a straw poll conducted along the quayside suggests only about one in twenty passers-by are people of the opposite—as it were—sex. In Byron's day the society of the Ottoman Empire was a virulent patriarchy, and now like the Ottoman Empire before it the patriarchy is in a long and slow decline forced on it by external events. Judging by the look of the young women and girls all the old ways, in style at least, will be gone in two generations. It would sound patronising to lament its passing, which is where we came in.

Talking of patronising, as we sail through the Sea of Marmara on the way to Constantinople let's let Hobhouse write a diary entry of a street scene from Izmir: 'ye streets are tolerably clean, and the dogs, plentiful, not given to misbehaving, overtly. Ye men are dressed in western shirts and trousers, save the beggars, who like ours are Roma and so dressed, men & women alike and oft with baby in arms. Of women we see some, and in generations some stroll in the shade in the evening. Ye grandmother will wear open sandals and patterned socks, the harem trousers—all colours not bright—but a lot of them. Floral prints. For her blouse another print, not matching, a large sleeveless cardigan—beige—and on her head a full and dark patterned hijab. The mother, women's shoes as we would find, black trousers, patterned shirt, smaller hijab but still all covered. For the daughter, she shops at Ye Gap and looks much as do our girls in London, west.'

As a parting gesture to cultural equivalency, and as an economy measure against hairdressing costs, I suggest to Gillian that she might like to sport a hijab too, but I only receive ye withering look for my consideration.

We are sailing through this full moon night tonight so that tomorrow at dawn we should see the sun rise over the Bosphorus to our starboard and the Golden Horn in first light to our port, all before Istanbul reawakens for another day. At midnight, as watch changes from Theo to Gillian, the first yellow glow of Byzantium, Constantinople and Istanbul lights up the horizon off the bows. The moon is happy and bright, the sea at rest and the sails full. We are all excited about the dawn; even Theo stays awake.

Chapter Fourteen

CONSTANTINOPLE, THE DIPLOMATIC ROUND

14 MAY – 13 JULY 1810 | 10–30 JUNE 2009

Like *Vasco da Gama* the *Salsette* arrived off Seraglio Point, at the entrance to the Golden Horn of Istanbul, at dawn. Looking over the rails Byron would have seen Constantinople's skyline much the same as we see old Istanbul's now. Walking over to the other rail the Bosphorus itself then was much as it is now, save for on its banks an almost empty Asian side and only the Frank district of Pera its European side.

As Byron gazed that morning on the massive city walls surrounding the Great Palace, now the Topkapi Palace, and the mosques of Sultan Ahmed, Santa Sofia and Sokollu Mehmet, eleven minarets in all, he already knew he was looking at a Forbidden City. Christians were not allowed in, except, as we shall see twice, in exceptional circumstances. The contrast with Athens could not have been more stark, for here indeed was Athens's domineering capital city, and unlike Athens the seat of current glory, its antiquities not in ruins but in daily use, its buildings massive in scale and merit and confidence. It was only later that Byron saw Constantinople as Byzantium and the glory that was Greece.

A fortnight later Byron rode around the outside Seraglio part of these city walls, which in 1810 stretched for twenty-two kilometres. He wrote to his mother: 'the ride by the walls of the city on the land side is beautiful, imagine, four miles of immense triple battlements covered with *Ivy*, surmounted with 218 towers, and on the other side of the road Turkish burying grounds (the loveliest spots on earth) full of enormous cypresses. I have seen the ruins of Athens, of Ephesus, and Delphi, I have traversed great part of Turkey and many other parts of Europe and some of Asia, but I never beheld a work of Nature or Art, which yielded an impression like the prospect on each side, from the Seven Towers to the End of the Golden Horn.'

In Constantinople proper they could not stay, so instead they were shuffled off to Pera, the area on the other side of the Golden Horn but still on the European side of the Bosphorus, an area the Ottomans had condescended to give the Genoese so they could trade with them without having to look at them and their disgusting Christian habits.

As Byron and Hobhouse were soon to discover it was not just the City that was Forbidden, but a whole host of proscriptions were also concocted by a rigidly stratified and decaying society. They were Franks, at the bottom of Ottoman society's pile, and so were fully exposed to its form of justice, and tempering justice with mercy was not an Ottoman concept then, nor much of a Turkish concept now. As they took their first steps ashore they saw two dogs eating a corpse.

We know not what the corpse had done, but we can be reasonably sure he was beheaded, probably arbitrarily by a janissary on the spot, and probably for some minor indiscretion. In those days we whisked them off to Australia, the Ottomans merely chopped off their heads; the reader can decide who had the brighter future.

By 1810 the Ottoman Empire was already two hundred and fifty years past its Suleyman peak, and was by then well frayed at the edges. It had also become a most unattractive regime, its aesthetic glories long past, its religious benevolence taken to the wrong conclusions, and its rule throughout its empire maintained by corruption, greed and random, and thus terrifying, cruelty. Ali Pasha's fiefdom of Albania was a metaphor for Sultan Mahmoud II's Ottoman Empire as a whole.

Soon after Byron saw the dogs eat the corpse he was walking with Hobhouse when they came across another corpse lying in the street. Hobhouse recorded that 'he was on his belly with his head off lying between his legs, face upwards. The skin was off his legs and arms by bastinado or burning. He had been a Greek *Cogia Basha*. His face was black and he seemed to have been dead a week at least.' The beheadings had their own subtleties: the head placed between the legs face down was the most demeaning while face up was a stage less demeaning, the head under the arm, left or right, the face this way and that, all had their subtexts. On another occasion Byron was walking with Chamier when they came upon an execution, and Chamier wrote that '...the beheaded criminal was lying in the front of the execution-office, with his head placed between his thighs, and only one human being near. Lord Byron looked with horror at the appalling scene. Not far from this exhibition stood a melancholy looking Turk, endeavouring to scare away some dogs; but his attempts were fruitless, for, unmindful of our presence, they rushed at the body, and began lapping the blood which still oozed from the neck. I never remember to have shuddered with so cold a shudder as I did at that moment; and Lord Byron, who ejaculated a sudden "Good God!" turned abruptly away.'

This decapitocracy was carried out with industrial scale and efficiency. Sultan Mahmoud II, whom Byron was to meet in six weeks time, took fright at the growing influence of the janissaries and decided to... decapitate them, not as a body—as it were—but literally one by one. In one single day twenty thousand janissaries were said to have been beheaded in the Beyazit Tower. Now a janissary was not some sort of conquered serf amazed he had lived as long as he had, but a big strong guard—that was the whole point of him—and one wonders what force it must have taken to line up twenty thousand, presumably reluctant, janissaries and make them stick their necks out for their executioners' convenience. A calculator will tell you that that's fourteen janissaries done for each minute, non-stop for twenty-four hours. One wonders: how many executioners did they need? How many swords did it take, how many swipes per head, how to keep the swords sharp? And then, having severed head from body, what to do with the heads? And the bodies? And the blood—surely there can only be so many dogs with a constant appetite.

I'm afraid I become rather transfixed by the whole episode—in a *grisly* kind of way as Dame Edna would say—and so go to the Beyazit Tower, now rebuilt in stone, to investigate. Strange and stranger still. The tower is one hundred metres high and only about fifteen metres across. It was known as the Fire Tower as it was used to look out for fires, of which there were many, and so alert the firemen accordingly. The tower is in the grounds of Istanbul University, scenes of recent riots when the socialist women students demanded the right to wear a headscarf, Ataturk having banned headscarves in public buildings ninety odd years ago; the very concept of reactionary socialist women students would have appealed to my friend Byron enormously.

Anyway, the upshot of this little local difficulty is that I am met at the university gates by a particularly scruffy looking young man I presume is an unwashed student. He tells me the grounds are closed, I tell him I'm a writer and want to see the Beyazit Tower, even if only to photograph it from the outside.

'You old student?' he asks

'No.'

'Old teacher?'

'No. Old, yes. Teacher, no'

He softens. 'Not difficult go tower. I am policeman. What you name?'

'Ian.'

'Mine Bulent.'

We shake hands and so my secret policeman's tour begins. On the way there, walking through lovely dappled parkland, I learn that the students have recently been provoked by Greek agitators, normally they are good women. I ask if there are many female students—only male ones are visible—and he says 'too many' but this often doesn't mean 'too many' but 'quite a lot'; I take it he means 'too many'. Nevertheless he is quite charming and helpful, as charming and helpful as only a secret policeman can be.

The tower is closed to the public but the big bronze Arabic-inscribed front gate is unlocked and he pushes it open and follows me in. The stairs rise steeply around the walls on to the first floor—there are four floors—but this door is locked and we can't go up any higher. Bulent points upwards and says 'Same, same'.

I think what must have happened—the only way it could have happened—is that the twenty thousand janissaries were lined up outside and pushed inside, like Tokyo commuters, by an overwhelming number of guards or soldiers. The press of bodies had only one way to go, to the top of the wooden tower. There are Aztec pyramid sacrifice overtones here. Once at the top, on the lookout platform, it would be quite easy for a team of executioners already there to wield their mighty swords and the heads would plop down to the ground below, in full view of course of the living janissaries awaiting their turn to the top of the helter-skelter. But wouldn't twenty thousand heads, never mind headless bodies, makes quite a mound? And how did the executioners change shifts, and swords? And who was rounding up the dogs to eat up the mess?

Sultan Mahmoud II, the one who ordered the Beyazit massacre, also assassinated his predecessor, Sultan Selim III, but the latter was no slouch in the beheading department either. It was a law that Franks could not wear yellow footwear. On Selim's first day in office he decided to leave the Great Palace incognito to walk in the streets.

He saw a Greek with yellow shoes and ordered his beheading there and then, and stayed to watch too. Another rule was that a Christian could not cross the street in front of a Turk. One evening Selim was out incognito again, and two Franks unwittingly did just that. Selim ordered the usual punishment but was hurriedly told that the man was an officer of the English ship HMS *Sea Horse*, and the lady a Greek of some renown, and that they meant no offence to an ally of the English. The officer was let free but the poor woman was given a good, well bad, cudgelling.

I'm sorry to bang on about this, but just one more, this one from the first sultan, Mehmet II, who rather set the scene. The artist Gentile Bellini was showing him his drawing *The Beheading of John the Baptist*. The sultan took one look at the severed head, and said something like 'no, no, they don't look like that, the skin wraps in, not spreads out' and ordered the janissary standing next to him to cut off the head of the slave standing next to *him*. It is not thought Bellini painted another beheading, in spite of this lesson in still life, as it were.

The death penalty was abolished in Turkey in 2004 as part of the European Union accession process, but there is still a certain menace in the offing. While Byron was appalled at the way the ruling class treated the lesser orders, the writer was appalled at the way they treat animals now, except, strangely enough, pigeons, which they see not as flying rats but as cuddly grey lovebirds who must be fed constantly in case they starve. One can still see the Ottoman inheritance everywhere in the military posturing and the love of bureaucracy. The largest, and still conscripted, land army in Europe flies the biggest blood red flags from every hilltop (one is never out of sight of an enormous blood red flag); submarines ghost up the Dardanelles, turn around and ghost back down again; camouflaged helicopters and worse crisscross the skies; there are at least eleven different police forces (twelve if you include the Campus Corps above); armed guards—modern janissaries—patrol inside and outside every shopping centre, museum and art gallery, public building and train station; and having navigated oneself through the sentries onto the train the ticket inspector is dressed like a five star general. The country sports a worrying level of nationalism. As for the bureaucracy, I won't bore you with the minutiae but it took five hours to check *Vasco da Gama* into the country, and I'm told it will take five more to check her out. The harbourmaster looks like an admiral of the fleet; the health inspector looks like he is about to operate; the immigration officer looks like an infantry commander; and the customs man looks like a royal marine. And the undercurrent of beheadings is still somewhere down in the psyche: I saw two graffiti of beheadings, both in red paint with blood spurting out of the recently opened necks, both with slogans against the imagined victim—one rather well drawn, as Hobhouse would have said. It's hard to put one's finger on it, but there is something profoundly unspiritual about the place, if one can be profoundly unspiritual.

I digress again. Having navigated the corpse and hounds—not the pub, the street scene at Pera—Byron and Hobhouse set about finding lodgings. Unlike in Athens where they had had to take up lodgings in a private house, in Pera several inns were established to cater for the wandering Franks. Hobhouse said their inn 'was situated at the corner of the main street of Pera, where four ways meet', but what with the fire of 1836, the catastrophic earthquake of 1896 and the general development of Pera into the fine area it is today all trace of their inn has long since disappeared.

Byron was keen to settle into the Diplomatic Round and his first call was to the British Embassy, known then as the English Palace. It had been built by Lord Elgin fifteen years before and was a copy of Broomhall, his stately home in Scotland. Other diplomats to the Porte suggested Elgin had the English Palace built on the highest hill in Pera so he could watch the movements of the Ottoman navy from his bedroom window. Unfortunately Elgin's embassy was burned to the ground in the 1836 fire, but was replaced over the next twelve years with an equally splendid building, the one still standing today, modelled on Sir Charles Barry's Reform Club in London. When it was reopened it was renamed the British Embassy, but everyone locally still called it the English Palace. After the 1923 republic was established, and Ankara deemed to be the capital, to soothe

Turkish—and presumably Scottish and Welsh—sensitivities, it changed its name again to Pera House, but of course everyone locally still calls it the English Palace. These familiar names have a habit of sticking around. As I'm sure Hobhouse, thumbs in waistcoat pockets, would have told all concerned, they were not in Constantinople at all but in Istanbul, and had been since 1453, but deaf ears would have heard his advice. Constantinople it was; just as if you were born and live there Bombay it is too, with the added satisfaction at looking quizzically at the browbeaten and ask 'where?' when they mention what locals call 'the M-word'.

At the English Palace Byron saw Stratford Canning, just twenty-four but already *chargé d'affaires* and under-secretary to the ambassador, Sir Robert Adair. The *Salsette*, which had been sent to bring Adair home, was anchored in view beneath them, and once she sailed Canning would be *de facto* ambassador. It was the start of his fine career as well as a delicate and active time in Anglo-Turkish diplomacy, especially as the British navy had fired on Constantinople the year before in retaliation for the Turkish interference on the French side in the Ionian Islands. Adair and Canning had negotiated the Treaty of the Dardanelles in 1809 which ended the Anglo-Turkish War, a sub-war of the Napoleonic Wars. As Lord Stratford de Redcliffe he would return four more times to Constantinople, ultimately as full ambassador. His cousin was the future prime minister George Canning, and between them the cousins Canning played significant roles in the struggle for Greek independence.

Adair, on the other hand, had rather blotted his copybook. Although a fine diplomat by day, by night he turned into something slightly stranger. Word around the diplomatic campfire was that he had gone troppo, which translated from the Australian means he had turned into an eccentric form of native, his eccentricity being summed up by the ditty:

> Adair delights his manhood to display
> From window casements, and across the way
> Woos some sultana's fascinated eyes,
> Convinced the surest argument is size

Hobhouse later heard from the French ambassador that 'Adair was a passionate man who disgraced himself by following the servant maids of Pera, which shocked the Mussulman gravely…'

I was particularly looking forward to having lunch with Canning's successor, the current consul general at the English Palace, Jessica Hand. A disadvantage of travelling away for a long time—and just as Istanbul marked the first year of the Grand Tour, so it marked the first year of the re-Tour—is falling out of touch with events back home, and if somewhere foreign for any length of time I always pop into the embassy to say hello and pick up the local sitrep. No matter how many Margaret Becketts they throw at them, the Foreign Office staff are always last pockets of resistance. The embassy and ambassador had to follow the capital when it moved to Ankara, leaving the consul general with the English Palace by day and the vitality of Istanbul by night. The ambassador no doubt regrets.

Apart from her current posting, she shares with Canning multilingual abilities and professional entanglements with the Russians. Russia's shifting alliances with the French and Turks occupied Canning right up to the Crimea War, and Hand, having just spent three and half years in Moscow, foresees the consequences of us ignoring Russia's current strategy of European energy monopoly and control, and sees us doing just that. She has a mid-career, no-nonsense air, and we both agree that there's no point in trying to jolly the Russians along and that the only thing they understand is a good clip round the ear—not her exact words at all, I hasten to add.

We discuss the current preoccupations of the Anglo-Turkish relationship: EU accession, the hijab question, and—inevitably—the Iraq debacle. I report on my lunch the previous day with a Turkish grandee who is helping me with meeting family members of the ex-sultanate and who seemed to be particularly well connected and informed. The Turkish dilemma boils down to how *grise* should be the military's *éminence*. He made some interesting points: the government is at heart fundamentalist and becoming worse and the army secular and becoming impatient, and the dilemma for the progressives is that while they are naturally wary of the coup-inclined generals and military dictatorships, they need the generals to keep the sharia-inclined headbangers in line. For the secular traditionalists, and the country is split down the middle, it is the generals who represent continuity while the headbangers snuggle up to the mullahs, and as for the religious traditionalists, well their preferred options are degrees of theocracy. Nothing is what it appears, and dilemmas abound. In this context the hijab issue assumes an importance way beyond a piece of silk that covers the head, for as one can see everywhere in central Istanbul once that goes, everything else follows.

Everyone intelligent I've ever met has been horrified by our involvement in Iraq, and for the staff in the Foreign Office it has been an easily and well-predicted disaster which will take generations to overcome. The attaché in Tirana told me that every meeting with an Albanian official starts with a tirade against Bush and his running dog Blair, and Albania is not devoutly Islamic. Jessica confirms the dodgy dossiers, the lies to parliament, the deceptions of the public, Bush and Blair praying together, all made it look to Islamists like the Tenth Crusade. To me it was all about that moment when Blair received a standing ovation in Congress, and the look in his eyes on close up TV; we went to war for his vainglory. Jessica saw the scene too.

For those working at the English Palace all this has added piquancy because the building itself was bombed in a terrorist attack in 2003 which killed sixteen souls, and of course many more Muslims than Christians. Meanwhile the Bush/Cheney masterminds were promoting their policy of 'soft Islam', whereby Turkey, being softly Islamic compared to its neighbours, would do Bush's bidding in the region. As Jessica points out, you can no more be softly Islamic than a little bit pregnant, and the regional reaction to this bright idea and the hostile noises coming from the EU about accession are pushing Turkey towards its neighbour Iran.

I could not help but ask about her, our, current ambassador. 'Nick Baird?' she asks. 'That's the one,' I reply, 'and I really think he should smarten himself up. On your website he is pictured in an open neck shirt and calling himself Nick Baird. Now I'm sure off duty all his friends and family call him Nick, but his proper name is Nicholas and if on duty he is to represent HMG in a country where a headscarf is a can of worms he should certainly wear a suit and tie; to do otherwise makes him look like the sort of twerp who doesn't understand what duty means at all. Turkish men are notably well dressed, even if often in a uniform. I think it shows a lack of respect to turn up representing our country looking like a Friday afternoon in Basingstoke and using a nick-name, as it were.'

By a subtle twist of the eyebrows methinks she agrees, but decorum forbids etcetera, and I'm sure this sense of decorum means that when she is an ambassadress she will not be calling herself Jessie and sporting a boob tube.

The languid Ottoman sense of time and protocol meant that Byron had a long time to wait until he could leave Constantinople. As soon as the *Salsette* arrived, Adair had sought Sultan Mahmoud II's permission to take his leave, but before an audience with the sultan was granted there had to be a dress rehearsal with the vice-sultan. These things took time; two months of labyrinthine negotiations between seeking permission for an audience with Sultan Mahmoud and the actual audience itself.

But in the meanwhile there were exotic diversions. Whereas Athens had been as devoid of entertainment as any other small provincial town, in the capital there were endless amusements. They saw near-naked greased men wrestling (a tradition that continues), Whirling Dervishes whirling (since banned by Ataturk along with beards, fezzes, the Arabic alphabet, and—incidentally—women covering themselves up), and an early version of Madame JoJo's (of which there are a dozen of current version). In a classic piece of Hobhouse shock-horror we hear they 'went to a wine house of Galata. Hearing music, went into a room like a hall with a gallery all round it. This was a wine-house and here I saw a boy dancing in a style indescribably beastly, scarcely moving from one place, but making a thousand lascivious motions with his thighs, loins, and belly. The boys Greek with very thick and long hair. An old wretch striking a guitar and singing kept close to the dancer, and at the most lecherous moments cried out. Also they spread a mat and, putting on a kind of shawl, performed an Alexandrian woman's dance and seemed as if kissing. One of Mr Adair's Janissaries, who talks English was with us. I asked him if these boys would not be hanged in England. "Oh yes, directly. De Turk take and byger dem d'ye see?"'

But Byron's favourite days out were to ride north of the city to the beautiful Valley of Sweet Waters, and in particular to visit Lady Wortley Montagu's old house high in the village of Belgrade. The house itself has long been lost and the valley formalised as the Belgrade Forest National Park, and a visit there jumping on and off ferries along the Bosphorus makes for a fine day out from the scurry and scuttle of Istanbul. In Byron's time Lady Wortley Montagu's old house belonged to the embassy's chief dragoman, and Byron must have loved wiling away his time in the house where one of his favourites used to live.

Mary Wortley Montagu had been the wife of the ambassador ninety years before Byron's visit, and her friendship with Alexander Pope and her letters from Constantinople had drawn Byron to her. These letters have now been gathered into the book *Turkish Embassy Letters* and make delightful reading. Her style of writing is the opposite of e-mails, from the days when people could say 'today I'm going to write to my sister,' and 'today' meant all day. The letter would then start 'Dear Lady Mar, it is not without fulsome joy, my dear sister, that...'

She had great curiosity about the Orient and learned Turkish and would wear a veil and so disguised enter the Forbidden City. She became friends with various sultanas who colluded in her disguise and led her past the eunuchs into the city's hamams and harems, and so she wrote with a uniquely feminine perceptive view of Ottoman life. Incidentally, none of the sultanas was allowed to be Turkish, so with each generation the Turkish-ness of the sultans diluted. She came to see Islamic women not as the glorified slaves portrayed at large but as pampered enchantresses liberated from earthly pursuits and able to spend nearly all their time at leisure with occasional interruptions to become involved in the various stages of the child rearing process.

She was under no illusions about the vipers' nest that was harem politics; how the 'wrong' princes were regularly strangled; how the sultan's mother chose her son's entertainment, and the rewards that flowed back and forth should a son accrue; how the sultanas ran eunuchs and slaves to spread poison and intrigue. The Turks took to Lady Mary too, and the best portrait of her hangs in a kind of foreign heroes' gallery in the Istanbul Library.

Interestingly enough something in the Montagu gene pool has an affinity with Istanbul as a remote relative, Lord Montagu Douglas Scott, younger brother to the Duke of Buccleuch, is one of the most prominent Istanbul residents and, I hear on an unimpeachable grapevine, one of the world's leading Orientalists. It's rather fun having a triple barrelled name, like having a six cylinder motorcycle or twelve cylinder car, so delightfully unnecessary and so completely essential. My passport is bad enough, but with all his names and titles his passport must go on forever. We spent a delightfully Anglo-Oriental evening together. He came to Turkey thirty years ago on a school break, fell in love with the history, the culture, the people and his Turkish wife and has stayed here ever since. I tell him I know exactly what he means as the same thing happened to me in Kashmir, except religion and politics kicked me out and here I am circumnavigating, hedging my next incarnation bets, instead. I think it has something to do with re-incarnation, but being a sound Ottoman, John is not so sure.

He founded *Cornucopia* magazine, a cross between an Istanbul *Apollo* and a Turkish *Vanity Fair*, which is a magazine you don't throw away, indeed you collect, and a bit like a Rolls Royce or Land Rover most originals are still extant. Roumeli, that is Northern Turkey all the way from the Caspian to 'end of empire' and including Patrick Leigh Fermor's Roumeli part of Greece, reminds him of the England of yesteryear, all 'very Tin-Tin' as he puts it. I can see the point: England, especially for those of us brought up post-war in the last shadows of empire and officer, that England has gone forever, replaced by poly-this and multi-that and if one prefers a traditionally ordered, well educated, polite and intact society one needs to live in somewhere like Roumeli.

But, I say, I still just don't get it: the fondness other people have for Turkey. John clearly loves it and has made it his life, I met the Californian artist Trici Venola who came here five years ago and wants to stay forever, I met my neighbour's son Barney Fisher-Turner who loves it enough to stay, but I can't wait to leave. I suggest it's because I've always been on the wrong side of the Islam/Turkey divide: in India my sympathies lay with the Hindus and in Roumeli with the Greeks.

If Lady Wortley Montagu could flit unnoticed in and out of the Forbidden City, Byron and Hobhouse had to apply for permission to visit the famous mosques and the Grand Bazaar. They enlisted the support of Canning to deal with the Porte bureaucracy, and a month later their permits arrived. But this was not the private tour Byron would have expected, and he had to join a Cook's Tour of other Christians-under-sufferance, including Bathurst and Chamier and other officials from the English Palace.

It would be fair to say Byron was unmoved by the royal mosques, largely because by 1810 they had long since passed their glory; in fact they were dishevelled and neglected. Going on a tour with the other Franks would not have cheered him up too much either. Neither Byron nor Hobhouse passed much comment on the mosques, but Mark Twain, who visited a generation later, said that Santa Sophia was 'the rustiest old barn in heathendom'. He noted that 'the perspective is marred everywhere by a web of ropes that suspend dingy, coarse oil lamps. Everywhere was dirt, and dust, and dinginess, and gloom; nowhere was there anything to win one's love or challenge one's admiration.'

Fortunately it has all improved so much as to be unrecognisable. Santa Sofia is now the Hagia Sophia Museum and restoration is on a rolling basis. One can now sense it in its pomp as the Byzantine miracle; they say that just being there made one believe in a higher intelligence. I overhear a guide say that all mosques are round because of Santa Sophia and all churches have steeples because of the minarets on Aya Sophia, and that Gothic architecture came after the first crusaders saw filigree lace in Islamic designs and took the designs back to Europe. I'll have to check on that one tomorrow. The Sultan Ahmed Mosque is now the Blue Mosque, and seems to be fully restored. Byron, and Mark Twain, thought the Suleymaniye Mosque the grandest of them all, and at the time of writing this was closed for a major renovation.

They completed their tour of the mosques on 19 June, exactly a year to the day from when they left London on their Grand Tour. Funnily enough we are also in Istanbul on 19 June and that is also a year to the date from when we left Bucklers Hard on our re-Tour.

That last year, however, had taken its toll on Hobhouse's health, and he was now actively considering accompanying Adair all the way back to London, rather than spending the next winter with Byron in Athens. He had caught the clap in Cadiz while Byron was cavorting at the opera with Señorita Cordova; he had had a toothache since Smyrna; he had gone deaf for a week in Ephesus; and now in Constantinople he could not shake off what he thought was diarrhoea but sounds more like amoebic dysentery. Hobhouse had never treated the hardships of travel with Byron's equanimity, and would sidle over to Fletcher and join in the grumble about tonight's flea infested haystack. It might also have been grating on him by now that he was only there on Byron's borrowed generosity, and may have become tired of this subtly unequal relationship with Byron's coattails.

On 10 July 1809 Adair's big day with the sultan arrived. Fletcher must have woken Byron at 3.30 a.m.—or more likely Byron just stayed up until then—as by 4.30 a.m. he was ready in his full regimentals to join the embassy procession. It was ordered in line with strict protocol and hierarchy, and Byron wasn't the main attraction, which would have set his mood back as much as the early hour. At its head, on foot, in their finest uniforms were the one hundred embassy janissaries in two lines, followed by Byron's fellow swimmer Lieutenant Ekenhead on horseback leading twenty marching marines from the *Salsette*, and then a dozen embassy servants, in specially made yellow, gold and blue uniforms.

Next came Adair's detail, led by the embassy's Master of Ceremonies and Pisani, the principal dragoman, ahead of two more of the *Salsette's* officers leading fourteen sailors in two lines. The sailors—no doubt to much ribaldry from their shipmates—had been dressed up in red suits and fur hats, and formed an escort for Sir Robert on horseback. He was dressed in his best court dress, a bright green satin suit, and topped off with his turban of state. Only then did Byron appear, and on foot—insult after insult!—in a loose group with Canning, Bathurst, Hobhouse, the various consuls and functionaries from the embassy, the remaining officers from the *Salsette*, and lastly the British employees of the Levant Company.

At the eastern shore of the Golden Horn, the sailors and marines crossed in the *Salsette's* specially decked-out jolly-boat, Adair in the Master of Ceremonies' barge, and Byron and the others in another of the sultan's barges. As they passed the frigate, still anchored at Seraglio Point, the sun rose over the Asian side of the Bosphorus. The frigate herself was strung with colours and the yards manned, and as the ambassador passed she fired a seventeen-gun salute. Hobhouse reported that after the salute 'the sun, seen red through the clouds of smoke, and giving to these clouds a fiery red dun colour, presented a scene most indescribable.' As they disembarked the *Salsette* fired off another seventeen rounds, this time to salute Sultan Mahmoud as he made his own way, in magnificent splendour, to the Seraglio.

After half an hour they arrived at the first gate of the Topkapi Palace, the Baba Humayun or Sublime Gate. On their left was the Hagia Eirene or Church of the Divine Peace, founded by Justinian in 537 and now used by the janissaries as an arsenal. The procession swayed slowly up the hill to the next gate, the Baba-Salam, the Gate of Health and Felicity. Waiting for them there were the officers of the Porte, magnificently arraigned in silks and turbans.

Byron was absorbing all the splendour, and whole scenes from the day's events would make themselves known again in different parts of *Don Juan*. Through the next smaller court they saw the kitchens on one side, and ahead the Divan, where the sultan's advisers held their council, on the other. Waiting for them was the vice-sultan, and behind him a whole host of his advisers, officers, secretaries and treasurers, as well as ambassadors from other Ottoman territories. Adair was invited to sit next to the vice-sultan and through the whispered translations of dragomen the business was transacted. The procession route is easily followed today, although be prepared for lesser processions from the cruise ship contingent led not by uniformed janissaries bearing a standard but by gnomish men in shorts holding up a company clipboard.

At ten o'clock lunch was served. The ambassador and vice-sultan sat alone at an elevated table, and Byron, Hobhouse, Bathurst and Canning sat with high, but not highest, ranking, officers of the Porte. Lunch went on forever: twenty-two different courses, each consisting of only one food at a time, and at the end of it the assembled worthies were given a mass sprinkling of rose water.

After lunch a message arrived that the sultan himself was now prepared to receive the ambassador and his suite. Following the ambassador, Byron was led out to the third gate, the Baba-Saadi or Gate of Happiness. All the British guests were given long sleeveless fur coats—this was noon in mid-July—so that they would be fit to sit before the sultan.

The procession was now joined by the sultan's own janissaries and officers, and after some time spent reshuffling the pack of Porte officials and Frank guests in strict order of hierarchy, the vice-sultan led the way from the Divan. Byron had by now been relegated to the top of the third division. On either side of the vice-sultan were two officers of state carrying silver staffs which they banged on the ground with every step. The vice-sultan then entered the inner sanctum to be alone with the sultan; Adair along with Byron and the rest of the suite had to wait outside in their fur coats, closely surrounded by the sultan's and vice-sultan's janissaries.

After ten minutes they were summoned forth. Byron, like all the others, was assigned a white eunuch, and the eunuchs walked and then stood behind them, a strong hand on each shoulder, for the duration of the audience. Byron's became Baba in *Don Juan*. They proceeded in crocodile file through two more chambers, the first lined with pageboys wearing gilt caps and white dresses, another piquant image for Byron to absorb, the second chamber decorated with the most magnificent carpets. Opulence dripped from every pore of the chambers, but these were just appetisers for the audience room which was further adorned with pearls and silver and gold and precious stones along the walls, and the most exquisite inlaid mosaics on the ceiling. The room was packed with Porte dignitaries, attended by eunuchs and protected by janissaries, as were the chambers all around it. 'Baba' pushed Byron to the front row of the guests, only five or so metres from the sultan. His throne was, and still is, as long and deep as a king size double bed and the canopy made entirely of silver and pearls. He reposed on cushions of silk embroidered with gold and pearls. On his one side stood the vice-sultan and on the other an elaborately inlaid desk—a gift from the Moghuls—on which was a silver inkstand decorated with more precious stones and the prepared letter to King George III. All these, except the letter of course, are now in the adjacent museum, and it is staggering to think of them once being just everyday items.

Sultan Mahmoud II himself wore a yellow satin cloak with black fur borders, a diamond studded dagger across his chest, an elaborate white and blue silk turban with an enormous diamond star at his forehead topped by a tall straight bird of paradise plume. Etiquette demanded that the sultan not demean himself by looking at a Christian, and a Christian was not allowed the honour of looking at the sultan. The latter rolled his eyes, keeping both hands on his knees, occasionally stroking his beard, in a display of deliberate disinterest. However he did notice Byron, and years later when told that Byron was plotting against his rule in Greece remarked that he remembered the beautiful young Frank, and assumed he was a woman in disguise.

The business of the day was then conducted, but neither Byron nor Hobhouse could follow the whispered translations. According to protocol, the translating dragomen had to talk as softly as possible in front of the sultan, so not to offend his ears with any Frank words that might escape. Adair could only address the sultan through the vice-sultan, and he could only address the vice-sultan through the embassy dragoman whispering to the vice-sultan's dragoman. Should the sultan reply the tortuous exercise was repeated in reverse; this time he did reply with some words of respect to King George, and these were repeated and translated back down the line in reverse.

Adair then made the mistake of replying—one can almost hear the internal groans of all concerned—and as a Frank could not have the final word the whispered process started another cycle. At a given signal the eunuchs, all the time with their hands on the guests' shoulders, pulled the Franks up to stand and forwards to bow, and then with some haste led them back out through the antechambers and though the courts and chambers, and then with more than a little shove, out into the street—and considering what had taken place in the last four hours—all with remarkably little ceremony.

I am interested to find out what happened to the sultan's family after the republic was established in 1923. As expected John Scott knows it all. The heir to the sultanate, His Imperial Highness Şehzade Bayezid Osman Efendi, is now ninety-four and living in New York. He married an Afghan princess and reinvented himself as a businessman. Other brothers also married well: two to Hyderabads, which restored the family fortunes, another to an Egyptian princess, two more to American heiresses, one of whom rejoiced in the self-styled name Princess Adeline-Mae Osman Efendi. But as the generations passed so the House of Osman's fortunes dwindled and their collective spine buckled. The current generation can't even raise a smile in the Istanbul gossip columns. There is no monarchist movement at all, but then they were never really cuddly kings and queens in the first place, but arrogant despots, and at the end weak ones too. Nothing so demeans a despot as weakness.

That evening there was a full-scale embassy ball, and then all thoughts were turned to leaving as quickly as possible, and leaving only Canning behind. Byron and Hobhouse spent the next three days packing and settling accounts, and boarded the *Salsette* on the evening of 14 July. Byron and later Adair both received seventeen-gun salutes. With wind and current behind them they sailed quickly to the island of Kea, an important shipping terminus then but rather run down now, not pretty enough for the tourists and not near enough to Athens for commuting.

After a year and a month it was time for Byron, and now it's time for us, to say goodbye to Hobby. The *Salsette* would continue to Malta with Sir Robert and Hobhouse, while Byron, Fletcher, Vassily, Dervish Tahiri and Andreas Zantakis all took a ferry the thirty miles to Athens. Our friend's last diary entry reads: 'Went on shore with Lord Byron and suite. Took leave, *non sine lacrymis* of this singular young person on a little stone terrace near some paltry magazines at the end of the bay, dividing with him a little nosegay of flowers, the last thing perhaps I shall ever divide with him.' A month later he wrote to Byron: 'I kept the half of your little nosegay till it withered entirely and even then I could not bear to throw it away. I can't account for this, nor can you either, I dare say.'

Coincidentally it is also at Kea that we part from Theo. Like Byron we are heading back to Piraeus, and he is resuming his seaborne hitchhiking quest to Tahiti. There are no nosegays or tears, and I resist the temptation of giving him a six-pack of Red Bull, but a week later I find I'm missing our sleeping passenger rather as one would miss a rescue pet one has been house-sitting, and of which one had grown rather fond.

Chapter Fifteen

ATHENS, SATING THE INSATIABLE

18 JULY 1810 – 22 APRIL 1811 | 9–31 MAY 2009

*B*yron and his entourage, now without Hobhouse and so reduced to our old friend the long suffering Fletcher, the loyal Albanian bodyguards Vassily and Dervish Tahiri and the reasonably honest translator Andreas Zantakis, arrived back in Athens on 18 July 1810. The next day Byron wrote to his mother:

Dear Mother,

I have arrived here in four days from Constantinople, which is considered as singularly quick, particularly for the season of the year. I left Constantinople with (British Ambassador) Adair, at whose adieux of leave I saw Sultan Mahmoud... Your northern gentry can have no conception of a Greek summer; which, however, is a perfect frost compared with Malta and Gibraltar, where I reposed myself in the shade last year, after a gentle gallop of four hundred miles, without intermission, through Portugal and Spain. You see, by my date, that I am at Athens again, a place which I think I prefer, upon the whole, to any I have seen.

Malta is my perpetual post-office, from which my letters are forwarded to all parts of the habitable globe:—by the bye, I have now been in Asia, Africa, and the east of Europe, and, indeed, made the most of my time, without hurrying over the most interesting scenes of the ancient world. Fletcher, after having been toasted and roasted, and baked, and grilled, and eaten by all sorts of creeping things, begins to philosophise, is grown a refined as well as a resigned character, and promises at his return to become an ornament to his own parish, and a very prominent person in the future family pedigree of the Fletchers, who I take to be Goths by their accomplishments, Greeks by their acuteness, and ancient Saxons by their appetite. He (Fletcher) begs leave to send half-a-dozen sighs to Sally his spouse, and wonders (though I do not) that his ill-written and worse spelt letters have never come to hand; as for that matter, there is no great loss in either of our letters, saving and except that I wish you to know we are well, and warm enough at this present writing, God knows.

Yours, etc., etc.,
BYRON.

Byron initially lodged back with the Macri family, but now there was a slight awkwardness in the air. The time for buying the childe bride had flown, and there was nothing much more to be said. No doubt the three-daughtered Mrs. Macri, like an Athenian Mrs. Bennett, was already looking for other suitors, and having the uncooperative

English m'lord in residence merely clogged up the machinery. Whether Byron jumped or was pushed we will never know, but after a week with the Macris he left their lodgings and made for Patras, no doubt to see whether Strané had received any more remittances from the recalcitrant Hanson, as well as letters from friends.

A month later, in late August, Byron was back in Athens. His excursion to Patras had not been fruitful. Apart from the lack of fresh funds or letters, he had just about survived a nasty fever, which sounds a bit malarial, and endured some unwelcome openly sexual overtures from Ali Pasha's son, Veli Pasha, made worse for having Strané as a wide-eyed witness. Back in Athens Byron now found space in the Capuchin Monastery on the southern flanks of the Acropolis, in what is now the Plaka quarter.

Only the base of the monastery and the adjoining Monument of Lysicrates—a fourth-century BC patron of the theatre of Dionysius —remain, the building having been sacked by the Egyptian Ottoman Omar Pasha in 1824 as part of the reprisals for the Athenian uprising in the War of Independence. Byron and the monastery were to die within five days of each other fourteen years hence. The Capuchins themselves had spun off from the Franciscans in the sixteenth century because they felt the followers of St. Francis had become too comfortable in their practice. But in Athens, having built the monastery, they had struggled to fill it, hence its changed use as a boys' school-cum-hostelry two hundred years later. (Incidentally, the Capuchin monks' distinctive hooded habit gives us the word cappuccino.)

The monastery, where Byron was to spend the winter of 1810/11, was the ultimate Byronic haunt, the very opposite to the Capuchin ideal, the scene of what he described as his 'fantastical adventures'. Apart from his group the monastery held a friar who taught six boy students from the resident Christian families, and for the want of anything resembling a hotel, it served as a hostelry of sorts for visiting Franks. In the absence of monks the work was done by fallen Albanian women, whose 'favourite pastime was sticking pins into Fletcher's backside'. The combination of boys and fallen women, a nominal friar and revolving guests suited all of Byron's appetites perfectly. To Hodgson he wrote gloatingly:

> I am living in the Capuchin Convent, Hymettus before me, the Acropolis behind, the Temple of Jove to my right, the Stadium in front, the town to the left; eh, Sir, there's a situation, there's your picturesque! Nothing like that, Sir, in Lunnun, no not even the Mansion House. And I feed upon Woodcocks and Red Mullet every day.

To Hobhouse he wrote that: 'What with the women, and the boys, and the suite, we are very disorderly.' He was learning Italian from Lusieri's nephew, Nicolo Giraud. Byron was 'his padrone and his amico and Lord knows what besides. We are already very philosophical.' The Italian lessons included 'spending the greater part of the day in conjugating the verb embrace', but 'the lessons are sadly interrupted by scampering, eating fruit, pelting and playing; and I am in fact in school again, and make as little improvement now as I did then, my time being wasted in the same way. I wish you were here to partake of a number of wiggeries, which you can hardly find in the gun-room or in Grub Street.'

In the code Byron's Cambridge set used for sexual encounters, Byron noted that 'he had obtained over two hundred pl&optCs and am almost tired of them.' Pl&optC is an abbreviated form of '*Coitum plenum et optabilem*', a quotation from Petronius's *Satyricon*, meaning 'complete intercourse without limits', or 'no end of leg-over', as you prefer.

There is also no doubt that he found freedom in not having his bulldog Hobhouse in tow. In fact there was no one from his past, and he could safely reckon from his future, to witness the licentious scenes which took up where London in 1808 left off. In himself he couldn't decide whether he wanted Hobhouse to witness the shenanigans or not, and wrote: 'After all, I do love thee, Hobby, thou hast so many good qualities, and so many bad ones, it is impossible to live with or without thee.'

~

It is the intention of this book to follow in Byron's footsteps wherever possible, but in the instance of the Capuchin Monastery, and the goings-on within, one will have to ask to be excused. The monastery was razed and never recovered, so time spent inside is not possible. As for the goings-on therein, 'over two hundred pl&optCs' would put a severe strain on the writer's resources, would certainly raise the prospect of marital excommunication, a visit to the chiropractor and the mass depression of thousands of expectant Athenian virgins. In the spirit of forgiveness, I hope the reader will understand my position vis-à-vis the monastery cannot, in this instance, be missionary.

There is an excellent engraving of the Capuchin Monastery in the early nineteenth century to be found in the Finden edition of Byron's Travels mentioned in Acknowledgments. The site on which the monastery stood is now public space in the heart of Plaka; the Monument of Lysicrates alongside it still stands after nearly two thousand five hundred years. If one wanders up to the north end of Vyronus (Byron) Street one just falls upon it. The drawing was done from what is now the slightly elegant Café and Bar Daphne, looking directly up at the Acropolis. The public space in front of Daphne's is the yard in the foreground of the engraving and the monastery was where you can now see the benches and olive trees of a small park, into whose shady grove the Diogenes Restaurant has evolved. From Galt's memoir of his visit there we can deduce that Byron's apartment was behind and to the right of the monument looking at it from Daphne's.

Among his notable visitors was The Hon. Frederick North, who founded the Ionian University in Corfu. He insisted, as chancellor, that he and his students parade around in classical costumes. He failed to impress Byron who called him 'the most illustrious humbug of his age and country.' I'm sure Byron would have been more impressed by his direct descendant, Lord North, of the famous cricketing family, who when told that his sixth born was also a daughter rounded himself up and declared to the great umpire in the sky: 'My God, I've bowled a maiden over.'

He also met the wilful Lady Hester Stanhope, the younger Pitt's niece and political hostess. Now in her mid-thirties, she was on her way East with her lover Michael Bruce. It was not a meeting of minds. Byron knew his way around men, he knew his way around women, but this odd crossover had him on the defensive and he told Hobhouse that he 'did not admire that dangerous thing a female wit.' Hobhouse had met her himself in Malta on his way back and her way out, and found her masculinity most disagreeable: 'a violent, peremptory person.'

She did not rate Byron too kindly either: 'I think he was a strange character: his generosity was for a motive, his avarice for a motive; one time he was mopish, and nobody was to speak to him; another, he was for being jocular with everybody. Then he was a sort of Don Quixote, fighting with the police for a woman of the town. He had a great deal of vice in his looks.'

She wasn't mad about poets either: 'As for poetry, it is easy enough to write verses; and as for the thoughts, who knows where he got them?' Byron had the last laugh though, as the night before they sailed for Cairo, Bruce propositioned Byron after they had dined together. Byron declined.

Apart from amusing himself with the visitors to the monastery, and the 'Ragazzi' in its boys' school, Byron found that, especially in winter, the Christian families in Athens had a surprisingly active social life into which he was always welcomed. The leader, both by personality and Turkish approval, was the highly sophisticated French consul Louis François Sebastien Fauvel, and it was with Fauvel and his friend from his first visit to Athens, Giovanni Lusieri, that Byron spent most of his time. The three were, at first sight, an unlikely trio of friends. Byron was a generation younger than Lusieri who was a generation younger than Fauvel. The fact that England and France were at war was unlikely to worry either the French consul or the member of the House of Lords, matters of war and peace between nations being an inconvenience which need not bother them here. The fact that Fauvel had been sent from his previous post in Constantinople to try to outbid Elgin for the Marbles might have been of more concern, as Lusieri was Elgin's agent—and so working against Fauvel—and Byron was fiercely opposed to the destruction of the sites and the removal of the Marbles to London or the Louvre or anywhere else. But these practical differences were set aside as all three were each other's best company, sophisticated, erudite and creative (Fauvel was an artist too), and all this in common was too much to resist among the small Frank setting of Athens, 1810.

Byron had of course long objected to the very thought of removing antiquities from their surroundings. In 1807 the first collection of Elgin Marbles had been shown at Elgin's own Park Lane House. Byron had mocked Elgin in his satirical *English Bards & Scotch Reviewers:*

> Let Aberdeen and Elgin still pursue
> The shade of fame through regions of Virtu;
> Waste useless thousands on their Phidian freaks,
> Mis-shapen monuments, and maimed antiques;
> And make their grand saloons a general mart
> For all the mutilated blocks of art.

Hobhouse had rather feebly argued that British artists, architects and sculptors would benefit by having these illustrious pieces close to hand. Byron would have none of it: 'I oppose, and ever will oppose, the robbery of ruins from Athens, to instruct the English in sculpture, who are as capable of sculpture as the Egyptians are of skating.'

In one of the notes to *Childe Harold's Pilgrimage* Byron wrote: 'When they carry away three or four shiploads of the most valuable and massy relics that time and barbarism have left to the most injured and most celebrated of cities; when they destroy, in a vain attempt to tear down, those works which have been the admiration of ages, I know no motive which can excuse, no name which can designate, the perpetration of this dastardly devastation.' By now he had finished the first two cantos of *Childe Harold's Pilgrimage* and was working on *The Giaour, Hints from Horace* and *The Curse of Minerva*, the latter aimed squarely at Lord Elgin.

But, for better or worse, the Elgin Marbles are now in the British Museum and not in the Louvre, and the Elgin Marbles have been PC'd into the Parthenon Sculptures. Nevertheless Fauvel had been sending pieces back to Paris since before the French Revolution, and the 'Plaque of the Ergastines' frieze from the interior and the tenth metope from the exterior are among the treasures in Paris. I am curious to see why the French collection is not on the repatriation radar whereas the British collection is seldom off it. I am also curious to meet the current version of Louis Fauvel and so make an appointment to have lunch with the French cultural attaché to Greece.

Well, I could not have preconceived my preconceptions more incorrectly. Sitting at the restaurant I am expecting a musty old bullfrog, a *petit fonctionnaire* masquerading as a *grand fromage*, instead of which in breezes the fabulously glamorous Caroline Fourgeaud-Laville. She is wearing, one could almost say modelling, a printed silk summer dress; reddish light gold is the overall impression, and, although I didn't like to look too closely, the scenes are like an Hermès print of Andalusian folklore. She wears a necklace of gold rings and pearls and emerald earrings alongside emerald eyes; scarlet lipstick and an easy suntan with matching blonde hair. Various bangles jangle around her wrists. Byron approves immediately, in fact I can feel him giving me a nudge as we sit down.

I explain that Fauvel, at fifty-seven and a man prone to flushes, could hardly be less similar to his successor, and ask how someone just over half his age could represent France in such a culturally important city as Athens.

'I took a doctorate at La Sorbonne, and then taught there.'

'What did you study?'

'My doctorate was about Victor Segalen, who was a traveller-writer in the beginning of the twentieth century. The subject was about the boundaries he had inside him and also in his relationships with other people. It was quite surprising looking at him like that because he is considered a great traveller, a great captain—just like you, I am sure—who did everything and met everyone during his short life: he died when he was thirty-eight... young like your Byron.'

'And why the change from academia to diplomacy?'

'I needed to take a turning point—is that correct?—leaving culture for diplomacy, because I really love living abroad, discovering people, people like you! But the French system is far different from the British. Much more bureaucratic.'

'We have the British Council doing what you do.'

'Yes, we are much more centralised, so here at the Institut Français we run French courses and directly promote French artists. The British Council is even separate from the embassy, a different structure entirely.'

'And your perfect English?'

'It has to be these days,' she giggles with wide open enthusiasm. 'And my best friend here is Irish, the writer Lauren O'Hara.' She has been here three years, normally a full tour of duty, but has been asked to stay for an extra year, because 'my ambassador loves me.' Funny that. 'But on the other hand I love Paris, bookshops, artists and writers... they are necessary to my life at least like oxygen!'

We chat about Elgin and Fauvel. At one point I suggest that if Melina Mercouri had plonked herself for three hours gazing at stolen treasures and dreaming of Athens in the Louvre instead of the British Museum all those years ago Caroline's job here might be more diplomatic than cultural.

'But we only have a few little pieces,' she pouts.

This is not exactly how I remember a visit there, and anyway the Plaque of the Ergastines is hardly just a little piece, let alone the others. But I can quite see a Greek minister melting at the mere suggestion of their return: 'Oh, my dear Attaché,' he would say kissing her hand, 'by all means, you just keep your little pieces.'

Next I find myself regaling her with stories of my heroic struggle for the workers and students of the world during *Les Événements* of 1968. I was a student at Grenoble University, and we skied all week and rioted at the weekends. Cobblestones flew. Windows shattered. Placards jostled. Red was everywhere. *Les flics* (a particularly virulent form called the CRS) charged. We regrouped. Daniel Cohn-Bendit, ha! Then I notice a culturally dettachéd look in her eyes and realise she has not the foggiest idea of what I am talking about, hardly surprising as she was not yet with us then. Reluctantly I conclude there's probably not much point in telling her my Aretha Franklin story either.

Unfortunately even an Athenian lunch with a French diplomat eventually has to end, and we exchange cards and kisses and promise to stay in touch—which we have. It was charming, but at the end I am no clearer about how the French have managed to hide their marbles under a bushel. Luckily Andreas had arranged for me to meet the leader of the repatriation movement, none other the very same Melina Mercouri's brother and taker-up of the Marbles baton, Spyros Mercouri.

It's funny how *événements* turn out, because on our way to meet Spyros, Andreas and I stumble across a riot. Andreas works in the Parliament building in Syntagma, the central square of Athens. I take off my crash helmet to hear the thud-thud of tear gas guns, and phone Andreas 'there's a riot going on.' He replies he knows, he is looking at it from his desk. We arrange to meet in the subway, hoping for peace underground.

'What's happening?' I ask.

'It's Allah Akbar time,' he replies. Turns out there are tens of thousands of Muslim asylum seekers in Athens. Most Greeks think they're phonies but the EU won't have them sent home. The government puts them in blocks. There's no work, and even if there was no one would employ them. Some steal, and last night, during a police raid, a policeman opened a Koran to shake it out. Hence the riot.

You smell tear gas before your eyes feel it. We smell it. The wind has changed direction and is now swirling the gas down a level into the subway. 'You're a journalist, should be no problem,' says Andreas as we break into a mild trot. Outside, above, we hear sirens and more thuds. 'It's getting serious,' says Andreas. It is. Then we get hit by the pepper gas. There's no way of knowing where it's coming from and commuters in the subway are scared and somewhere way beyond distressed. We take an escalator to the level below. I tell Andreas his is a double or quits strategy. It's quits, but the horrible pepper taste and smell and itch and sting remain for the next half hour.

I know my way round tear gas but this is the first acquaintance with the pepper variety. I'm sure the police love it as much as the dysfunctional rioters hate it. Andreas tells me that in the previous winter riots outside the Parliament Building the wind changed direction and pepper gas got into the office vents. It was so unpleasant that the police were told to use tear gas first in future, and only pepper gas if things were turning ugly. Andreas suggests that was why we had tear first and pepper later.

Since Melina died Spyros has taken up the cause of having the Marbles returned to the Parthenon. It takes someone like Byron or Melina to bring a cause the attention it needs, and we swiftly agree that one of the main reasons the Greeks adore Byron is his disgust at what Elgin and others were doing. Spyros was sure Byron would certainly be on the committee. I was too polite to say: no, he wouldn't, the one body he would not embrace was a committee. And the point from that exchange is that Byron's and Melina's campaign was all about charisma and not committees. Spyros is a lovely chap, a real gentleman still best loved for his playboy past, but his proudest claim on the behalf of the Marbles was that there are now seventeen committees worldwide 'including a very fine one in Sweden.' At which point Byron would have drawn a swift sword.

I delicately point out that the committee in the UK is useless and he defends them by saying that they have no money. 'We'll soon sort that out!' Byron and Melina cry in unison as they hurry off to doorstep a hapless Minister-of-Something-or-Other.

But Spyros says he is optimistic on two fronts. 'Firstly you know we are opening the new Acropolis Museum next month and on Melina's instructions we have left a large space empty for the Elgin Marbles.'

'Is anyone from London coming?' I ask

'I'm not sure,' he replies, 'the London committee will be there and they may bring some guests.'

'And secondly?'

'Secondly the London Olympics might shame the British Museum into returning them. Do you follow the Olympics?' he asks.

'Not too much. I like the women's volleyball though.'

'And does Britain have a good team?'

'I don't know, I tend to support the Scandinavian teams.'

'And do you support the return of our marbles.'

'Yes, but I don't agree with Byron and Melina that they should never have been taken in the first place. They had already been terribly vandalised over the centuries. The Turks were crushing them for their houses and mosques, the Greeks didn't even know what they were, and the French... by the way, is there a committee for returning the pieces in the Louvre?'

'No, Melina never claimed them. Are there any?'

We say our goodbyes, and good lucks with his museum and my book. Methinks it's time to follow Byron to the Turkish baths.

~

In between bouts of flirting in the monastery, and flirting in company, Byron flirted 'thrice weekly' in the Turkish baths. These have been beautifully restored by The Museum of Greek Folk Art, and renamed 'The Bath House of the Winds'—they are next to the Temple of the Winds—with the enticing tag line of 'Museum of Personal Hygiene and Toilet.' In spite of its name the institution remains largely unvisited, but luckily, as it transpires, is managed by an enthusiastic Byronist and careful English speaker Sylvia Michelis.

In Byron's day it was a one-storey building, and men and women used it on alternate days. It was then expanded upwards and used by men and women accordingly. I ask Sylvia to show me the part Byron would have used.

'You know Ottoman baths were far more than just bathing rooms.' I tell her about Hobhouse calling them 'the coffee houses of the East.' 'That's right, especially for the women who were only allowed out alone to come here. Now, here is the men's changing room.'

We are in a square room about ten metres across with a marble floor and wooden benches. The light comes from small round skylights in the domed ceiling.

'When was it last used?' I ask.

'In 1965. It's just not a Greek pastime. You like Turkish baths?'

'Yes, I was hoping this one was working too. I loafed around the one in Bayswater in London when I lived there, but that was more Eastern European Jewish than Turkish. Men and women have different days there too, but I went to one in Munich and they all piled in together. Why is it not a Greek pastime?'

'We are too active. Have you heard the expression "to live like a pasha"?' I haven't. 'It is to be passive, sitting in the shade, fat belly, smoking the pipe, slaves around to bring this and that.'

I tell Sylvia that I had noticed in the drawings that all the bath attendants were black, and ask how that came about. 'They were slaves, there was a slave market every month near the Stadium until Independence when the Christians banned it. The baths would buy black slaves and train them as attendants and masseurs.'

'And the Turks, they had slaves here too?'

'Of course,' she replies, 'but they would have Christian slaves, white ones, the paler the more prestigious.'

I tell her the story about Fletcher and the bastinadoed Spaniard. Byron or Hobhouse had been insulted on their way for a swim at Piraeus (imagine that now!) and complained. It turned out that the transgressor was a Spanish slave, and the slave was given fifty whacks across his feet, all witnessed by Fletcher who reported back gleefully that the unfortunate man had 'shit his breeches'. The slave's owner found out and wanted him killed—presumably he wouldn't be able to stand for a week or two. The authorities refused the owner permission and the slave lived to serve another day. But the extraordinary point was that there should be a Spanish slave in Athens in 1810. The traders were the pirates of the Barbary Coast, the city-states of Tunis and Algiers, which were just about still part of the Ottoman Empire, albeit run with a loose rein. When they stole a ship they would take the crew as slaves and sell them in one of the markets of the Ottoman Empire. If shipping had been light they would raid the coastal towns of Spain or Italy, a tactic which had the additional advantage of procuring female slaves. Fletcher's bastinadoed Spaniard was either a merchant seaman or town dweller who had been taken by Barbary pirates.

Back in the Tepidarium Sylvia conjures up an image. 'The Turks would have two or three white slaves in attendance, bringing them fresh water, tea, coffee, new clothes, pipes, whatever they desired. They would spend an hour or so here, then go next door,' we walk through an archway, 'into here, the Caldarium, the hot room.'

'This is where the action was.'

'Yes, the steam would roll off the walls. Those marble slabs there are where they were massaged. This is a common room, and off here were private rooms.'

'For special services?'

'I imagine so. Maybe you have Byron in mind?'

'I wouldn't put it past him,' I say, and an image of him and a young black slave behind closed doors flashes across the mind. 'But he did not have slaves himself, and there is no record of his Albanian guards accompanying him. He was probably the only Christian to visit here.'

'He would use the baths' slaves. Not a big problem,' she says as we walk back through the changing room. Our tour is over. Sylvia showers me with gifts: brochures and a video, and the Museum pen from the Visitors' Book. I promise to send her a copy of this book, which I will. Sylvia, if you are reading this sentence now, thank you again.

But by now, the spring of 1811, Byron's thoughts were turning home. He had perhaps just run out of steam as he was running out of money. He had already sent Fletcher back to England with letters and papers to prepare the ground. He was pleased to be rid of his valet for a while: 'the perpetual lamentations after beef and beer, the stupid bigoted contempt for anything foreign, the insurmountable incapacity of acquiring even a few words of any language.'

Above all he left Athens committed to the Greek cause, a cause that the Greeks did not yet know they had, and of course a cause for which he was to die. He wrote that 'at present they suffer all the moral and physical ills that can afflict humanity. Their life is a struggle against truth; they are vicious in their own defence. Now in the name of Nemesis! For what are they to be grateful? To the Turks for their fetters, and to the Franks for their broken promises and lying councils? They are to be grateful to the artist who engraves their ruins, and to the antiquary who carries them away; to the traveller whose janissary flogs them, and to the scribbler whose journal abuses them? This is the amount of their obligation to foreigners.'

A month later, with a heavy heart, he boarded the packet for Malta, unaware of the fresh horror of incarceration that awaited him there. His second last deed in Athens was to pay-off his Albanian guards, Vassily and Dervish Tahiri, the latter taking it especially badly, refusing payment and crying continuously. Byron would always remember their fierce loyalty, and was moved by this last display of emotion 'which contrasted with his native ferocity, and improved my opinion of the human heart.' His last deed before leaving Athens was to take on two new Greek servants, who he felt would be more suited to the restrained atmosphere of London society.

Chapter Sixteen

MALTA, HEADING HOME

30 APRIL – 2 JUNE 1811 | 30 SEPTEMBER 2008 – MARCH 2009

*B*yron and his pet Nicolo Giraud, together with his new Greek servants Demetrius Zogroffo and Spiridion Sarakis, disembarked from the *Hydra* in Malta's Marsamxett Harbour on 30 April after an eight-day voyage from Piraeus. In his portmanteaux were 'four Athenian skulls—a phial of Attick hemlock—four live tortoises—and a greyhound.' Ironically, in view of Byron's detestation of Elgin and all he stood for, the cargo on board the *Hydra* contained more 'Elgin Marbles', in this case a capital and drum from the Parthenon, a Doric capital and an Ionic column from the monastery at Daphne, as well as a colossal sepulchral cippus. A further cargo was to be found in one of Byron's portmanteaux, the manuscript of *The Curse of Minerva*, his savage *j'accuse* to Elgin for the theft of Greece's monumental heritage, in which Byron explains to the Greeks that Elgin came not from England but 'from Caledonia, land of meanness, sophistry and mist.'

His entourage's arrival was duly noted by the Port Officer in Malta: '30th April 1811. English ship *Hydra*. Captain William Waggood, 44 members of crew. 9 passengers. Among them a certain Lord Byron and servants. From Athens in 18 days with a cargo of marbles for England without a license because Consul unavailable. Awaiting permission to perform quarantine.'

Ah, quarantine. Every traveller's worst dread, where the perfectly healthy were imprisoned in close conditions which could have been designed to make them equally unhealthy in the three weeks of confinement. But Lord Byron or no, like all travellers from the East he was unceremoniously sent into quarantine in the local lazaretto, a bit like an unpassported pet being offered up on arrival at Heathrow.

All ports then had their lazarettos but Malta had a Lazaretto, an imposing two-storey sandstone structure of cells and courtyards, surrounded by colonnades and pivoted around capitals. The location still is perfect, the prime waterfront position on Manoel Island looking over to Valletta across Marsamxett Harbour. Ancient history is the view. One view across the harbour was the Chapel of St. Roque, the patron saint of plague protection, which the Knights had built with a wide open frontage so worshippers from the Lazaretto could follow the service and so be spared spiritual isolation too.

Curiosity about the Lazaretto leads me to the site but it is rather rustily padlocked, more a token than a serious attempt at securing the plot. I think about giving the old lock some percussive engineering but then see a large notice board with the diagram of the Lazaretto-to-be and the architect's telephone number. The following morning, a sprightly, trendily unkempt young architect arrives with an equally rusty key, but we find the lock broken open anyway.

'Hello, I'm Edward Said,' he says and we start the tour. He is full of enthusiasm for his new project. The Lazaretto is not one building, but a collection of palaces, warehouses and customs offices that were sequestered by the Knights in 1663 to make a quarantine centre for their newly acquired slaves and an isolation centre for those other slaves in transit. By the time the Byron party arrived history had moved on and it was wealthy passengers and their servants who slept where slaves once slept. It turns out that Edward is a bit of a Byron buff too.

We turn a corner and there is a large triangular space, totally flattened.

'What happened?' I ask.

'Bombed by the Luftwaffe in 1941,' he replies.

'Not very sporting of them, any particular reason?'

'A very good one actually. In the war we turned this into HMS *Talbot*, a submarine supply base.'

'Ah. And what was it before?'

'This was called the Profumo Office. Here they used to fumigate everything that belonged to the inmates.'

One can imagine Byron, who as we have seen always sported a huge baggage train, himself fumigating as all his letters and manuscripts, books and journals, finery and mementos were smoked and hung to air like so many kippers. But in an age and place where strange and unknown diseases were random and rampant, when the last plague in Malta was in living memory, such precautions could not be gainsaid.

Nevertheless Byron, already feverish, found the whole experience ghastly from top to bottom. For a start it was annoyingly democratic: it was one thing to have Nicolo Giraud pouting and whining in the next cell, but to have the two Greek servants slouching around in adjoining cells was clearly intolerable. Then the place was run by the worst sort of British martinet, a crazed Ulster Protestant enthusiast called Colonel Bryant MacBrearty, who rejoiced in the title of Superintendent General of the Palace, Captain of the Lazaretto and Adjudicator of His Majesty's Quarantine Regulations. Byron's detestation of crazed Protestants was only equalled by MacBrearty's detestation of foppish poets. Regulations were strictly enforced, much to MacBrearty's delight, including the ultimate sanction 'Death without the Benefit of Clergy.'

We climb upstairs to look at the cells. There are about a dozen, each about three metres square, either side of a gloomy passage. The layout is repeated alongside and above. To the left lies a slightly larger cell, for captains, rich merchants – and by legend, Lord Byron.

'The inmates had to pay to stay here,' Edward explains, 'not just their board and lodgings but the wages of their guards too. The guards themselves were convicts.'

'So they would trade time off for hoping not to catch anything catching?'

'That's right, and you can bet they charged for every little extra too.' He leads me outside to the exercise yard. 'Here they took some air. There wasn't much to do except carve their names in the sandstone.'

'I've seen a photograph of Byron's graffito.'

'Yes, it's long been washed away by the rain and sun, I'm afraid.'

Even if Byron had known that Cardinal Newman, William Makepeace Thackeray and Benjamin Disraeli were later to suffer similar inconveniences as Lazaretto alumni in future years his mood would not have lightened. Made worse actually, he would have told himself he was just being used, and brutally, as an experiment for the drifters and chancers who were to follow in his wake.

Next Edward shows me the Parlatorio. 'Visitors and salesmen could only be received here in the Parlatorio. They had to stand on opposite sides of the hall with guards in the middle to keep them apart.'

Cardinal Newman had one such visit on Christmas Day 1831, and he noted 'the strange dresses, the strange languages, the jabbering and the grimaces, the queer faces driving a bargain, without a common language, the solemn, absurd guardians with their staves in the space between them, the opposite speaker fearing nothing so much as touching you, and crying out and receding at the same time.'

The tour over Edward and I repair to the Royal Malta Yacht Club for a well-earned lunch. I explain how Byron was not well when he arrived, having contacted an ague, which sounds like an unreliable cousin of malaria, further east. He described the ague to Hobhouse: 'A villainous quotidian tertian it killed Falstaff and may me. It returned in quarantine in this infernal oven and the fit comes on every other day, reducing me first to the chattering penance of Harry Gill, and then mounting me up to a Vesuvian pitch of fever, lastly quitting me with sweats that render it necessary for me to have a man and horse all night to change my linen.'

When he could find pen and paper his mood was maudlin. He jotted down *Four or Five Reasons in Favour of a Change* in his life:

1 stly, at twenty-three the best of life is over and its bitters double.

2 ndly I have seen mankind in various Countries and find them equally despicable, if anything the Balance is rather in favour of the Turks.

3 rdly I am sick at heart (and then misquoting Horace's ode *To Venus*) Nor Maid nor Youth delights me now.

4 thly A man who is lame of one leg is in a state of bodily inferiority which increases with years and must render his old age more peevish & intolerable. Besides in another existence I expect to have *two* if not *four* legs by way of compensation.

5 thly I grow selfish and misanthropical, something like the jolly miller—I care for nobody—no not I—and nobody cares for me.

6 thly My affairs at home and abroad are gloomy enough.

7 thly I have outlived all my appetites and vanities—aye even the vanity of authorship.

Eighteen days later he was released from the Lazaretto; several hours later Edward and I stagger off in our various directions. At least I only had to enjoy a siesta; Byron now had to face the dire task of two very different adieus: a finale to Constance Spencer-Smith and a coda to Nicolo Giraud.

He had feared the worst with the former, feared that she would be there waiting for him, her passion, unlike his, still in bloom. She had written to him only weeks before their rendezvous in Malta: 'I should feel happy to repeat to you how much I am sincerely yours.' One can imagine Byron's lack of joy at being reminded in writing of Anglo-Saxon emotional rigidity and formality after the freewheeling and spontaneous light-heartedness further east. Constance, Florence, who had seemed so free and wilful, so exotic to him on his way out of England, now seemed prim and needy, and demanding a part of him he had long left behind. He had anyway some time before quite recovered from his New Calypso's charms, writing of their affair in Athens in January 1810:

> The spell is broke, the charm is flown!
> Thus it is with life's fitful fever:
> We madly smile when we should groan;
> Delirium is our best deceiver.

Yet a meeting with the lady there had to be, a scene that had to be obliged, and he told Hobhouse 'the Governor... was kind enough to leave us to come to the most diabolic of explanations. It was in the dog-days, during a sirocco (I almost perspire now at the thought of it), during the intervals of an intermittent fever (my love had also intermitted with my malady), and I certainly feared the ague and my passion would both return in full force.' What this diabolic explanation was history does not relate. Most Byronists conclude he shocked her with explanations of his sexual ambivalence, possibly throwing in an unmentionable disease; my feeling is that there was no diabolic explanation, doesn't seem like his style, just awkwardness and illness on his part and anxiety and intelligence and maturity on her part, and obvious conclusions, with relief and sorrow accordingly, drawn all round.

Byron feared the worst after their meeting as well, and noted that when she wrote her memoirs he would 'cut a very indifferent figure; and nothing survives of this most ambrosial affair, which made me on occasion risk my life, and on another almost drove me mad, but a few Duke of York*ish* letters and some baubles....'

His last and most dreaded act on Malta was to part from his Greek delight Nicolo Giraud. Nicolo was beside himself with grief, sobbing gratuitously and pledging undying, unswerving devotion to his master. As usual, as with Constance Spencer-Smith a few miles away, once Byron had parted with his passion, his passion parted too. Although Nicolo Giraud was to write to him in Latin, Greek and English ('I pray your Excellency to not forget your humble servant which so dearly and faithfully loves you', 'My most precious Master, I cannot describe the grief of my heart at not seeing you for such a long time. Ah, if only I were a bird and could fly so as to come and see you for one hour, and I would be happy to die at the same time.' etc, etc) Byron had moved on to passions new and Giraud's Labrador love was never answered at all, let alone with fondness or affection. Nicolo was to finish his schooling in Malta at Byron's expense but left for Athens after a few months after falling out with the monks; 'I never did like monks anyway,' he wrote in one his letters to his *padrone* back in England.

It was hardly surprising then that Byron left Malta with what he called his 'hudibrastics', the poem 'Farewell to Malta':

> Adieu, ye joys of La Valette!
> Adieu, sirocco, sun, and sweat!
> Adieu, thou palace rarely enter'd!
> Adieu, ye mansions where I've ventured!
> Adieu, ye cursed streets of stairs!
> (How surely he who mounts you swears!)
> Adieu, ye merchants often failing!
> Adieu, thou mob forever railing!
> Adieu, ye packets without letters!
> Adieu, ye fools who ape your betters!
> Adieu, thou damned'st quarantine,
> That gave me fever, and the spleen!
> Adieu, that stage which makes us yawn, Sirs,
> Adieu, his Excellency's dancers!
> Adieu to Peter—whom no fault's in
> But could not teach a colonel waltzing;
> Adieu, ye females fraught with graces!
> Adieu, red coats, and redder faces!
> Adieu, the supercilious air
> Of all that strut 'en militaire'!
> I go—but God knows when, or why,
> To smoky towns and cloudy sky,
> To things (the honest truth to say)
> As bad—but in a different way.—

Farewell to these, but not adieu,
Triumphant sons of truest blue!
While either Adriatic shore,
And fallen chiefs, and fleets no more,
And nightly smiles, and daily dinners,
Proclaim you war and woman's winners.
Pardon my Muse, who apt to prate is,
And take my rhyme—because 'tis 'gratis.'

And now I've got to Mrs. Fraser,
Perhaps you think I mean to praise her—
And were I vain enough to think
My praise was worth this drop of ink,
A line—or two—were no hard matter,
As here, indeed, I need not flatter:
But she must be content to shine
In better praises than in mine,
With lively air, and open heart,
And fashion's ease, without its art;
Her hours can gaily glide along,
Nor ask the aid of idle song.—

And now, O Malta! since thou'st got us,
Thou little military hothouse!
I'll not offend with words uncivil,
And wish thee rudely at the Devil,
But only stare from out my casement,
And ask, for what is such a place meant?
Then, in my solitary nook,
Return to scribbling, or a book,
Or take my physic while I'm able
(Two spoonfuls hourly by the label),
Prefer my nightcap to my beaver,
And bless the gods I've got a fever.

The five-week journey back to England was deeply depressing. He knew he would have to deal with debts and creditors and the hypocrisy of polite society. He did not know how *Childe Harold's Pilgrimage* would be received; he had greater hopes for *Hints from Horace*. He wrote to his friends and mother, talking up his plans, trying to be cheerful. When he couldn't cheer himself up any more, he levelled with Hobhouse: 'Dear Hobby, you must excuse all this facetiousness which I should not have let loose, if I knew what the Devil to do, but I am so out of Spirits, & hopes, & humour, & pocket, & health, that you must bear with my merriment.'

~

The feeling is shared. I should have been behind him trudging up the Channel, back to the Big Grey. The original idea was to follow Byron home, deal with the publishing, and then set off again in the spring—this time across the Atlantic in the wake of my favourite author Patrick Leigh Fermor. The great man had written his first book, *The Traveller's Tree*, about his early post-war travels around the Caribbean and *Vasco da Gama*, Gillian and I were to island hop in his footsteps.

I blame it on the Lazaretto. Reflecting quietly in Byron's cell a few days after Edward's tour, thinking about Byron's seven reasons not to be cheerful, I came up with seven of my own and they all related to returning to England and the realities that would have to be faced; realities that could be easily avoided by staying away. I thought about the Strangelove/Rumsfeld rumination: 'There are known knowns. These are things we know that we know. There are known unknowns. These are things that we know we don't know. But there are also unknown unknowns. These are things we don't know we don't know.' I knew that the known knowns were bad enough and the unknown unknowns were all likely to be ungood and make me unwell.

Also, our relationship had changed. The first inkling was on the promontory at Kea where Hobhouse and Byron parted. Until then I felt that Hobhouse was keeping an eye on Byron, keeping him in some sort of orbit, but after Hobhouse left Byron was fluttering vulnerably and I worried, as a father to a son, about him. This was a new emotion, and I must admit that up to Kea I felt detached: Lord Byron was a bit too pleased with Lord Byron for me to be drawn willingly towards him. But after Kea I wanted to be closer, in part to protect him from himself, in part because the tables had turned: he was now following in my footsteps, early-twenties debauchery-wise, and I felt protective, albeit helplessly protective. Sitting in his cell in 'the infernal oven' in the Lazaretto I knew that if I followed him back to England I'd be sucked into his world like so many others and I'd follow him out again to the Alps, the Adriatic and the Aegean.

There was one other reason not to follow Byron home: Mark Twain. In Athens I bought a wonderful reference book called *Travellers' Greece*, about literary visitors to Greece when it was still an Ottoman province. Many writers contributed: apart from Byron and Hobhouse and many others, there were chapters by Bulwer Lytton, Chandler, Chateaubriand, Lady Craven, De Pouqueville, Lear, Melville, Lady Stanhope, Thackeray, Trelawny—and Twain. The latter stood out as being brash and wry, and freshly observed. His visit to Greece was part of his own Grand Tour—this one as a journalist to the Holy Land, also Ottoman controlled, and resulted in the book *The Innocents Abroad*.

And so as *Vasco da Gama* sailed past the Lazaretto and out of Marsamxett Harbour we parted our ways. Byron turned to port for the long dread back to England and we turned to starboard for the promise of the Holy Land, for the prospect of having one's lotus and eating it. I remembered Hobhouse on Kea, 'taking leave of this singular young person.' We had no nosegay on board to divide with him, only some stalks of thyme, but I offered them to his westbound wake—also *non sine lacrymis*. It had been fun.

~

The Grand Tour was nearly over, and heading into northern climes all around him Byron saw grey seas, grey skies, and soon there would be grey people with their grey conventions. Finally, on 11 June, the party was over. He disembarked at Sheerness; still, it could have been worse, it could have been Gravesend.

Epilogue

LORD BYRON, POST-TOUR

14 JULY 1811 – 25 APRIL 1816

*A*very different Byron arrived back in England on 14 July
1811 from the one who had left Falmouth twenty-five months
earlier. In the days when all experiences had by necessity to be first
hand, he returned having mingled with despots and spies, tyrants and
ambassadors, prostitutes and paedophiles, grandees and brigands.
He had seen for himself war and execution, beauty and squalor,
snobbery and serfdom, sites of myth and sites of wonder. He had been
shipwrecked, adored, humiliated and castigated. He had explored
within himself the depths of licentiousness and decadence to which he
could sink without shame, along with the summits of the sublime and
creativity to which he could rise without effort. And if he suspected
before he now knew he could write and write beautifully, write like
the angel he wasn't, write about emotions he would never feel and
write about life's ways with an ease and fluency he rarely experienced
once his pen was back in its well. The Grand Tour had given him
the raw material of experience with which to fashion *Childe Harold's
Pilgrimage*, the manuscript of which was in his portmanteau, and
whose publication was to lead, event by event, over the next five years
to his rise to the heights of fame and adoration—what his wife called
Byromania—and to the depths of disgrace and exile.

He disembarked at the port of Sheerness, not the most poetic of
landscapes then or now, and a portent of what lay in wait for him in
London: debts, homophobia and death. In spite of some promising

CHILDE HAROLD'S Pilgrimage.

J.H. Jones fecit.

Canto 1.   Stanza 39.

IN 4 CANTOS,
*
LONDON.

Printed & Published by W. Dugdale, Russell Court, Drury Lane.

1825.

offers Newstead remained unsold, the Nottinghamshire mines were still in a legal quagmire and his debts were stubbornly unresolved—and in fact worsened by the Grand Tour. In the meantime London had become gripped by a fashion for homophobia. While homosexuality in general and sodomy in particular were still illegal, the degree of enforcement rose and fell to no particular rhythm. When he had left two years earlier there was some degree of tolerance in the air, but now the tide had swung and men were being imprisoned and pilloried with excrement. His friends were quick to point out the dangers, Hobhouse in particular warning him of the changed climate and off loose talk or explicit written references to what Hobhouse himself had seen on the Grand Tour.

But if debts could be imagined away and homophobia avoided by discretion and bisexuality, it was the four deaths which brought him back to the realities of life in England after the frippery of the East. The first to go was his mother, who died after his arrival at Sheerness but before he could see her again at Newstead. She was only 46, but overweight and overanxious. Although, like his father, he got on best with his mother from afar, her death hit him hard. He made the arrangements for a lavish—and of course unaffordable—funeral, which he himself could not bear to attend. Then two old friends died: from the Harrow days John Wingfield and, worse, his witty and articulate Cambridge friend Charles Skinner Matthews, drowned slowly in distressing circumstances. But emotionally the worst loss was John Edleston, the chorister with whom he fell in passionate love at Cambridge, and who was always to remain as Byron's ideal of boyish beauty and desire.

Back in London his interests were poetic and politic. His new publisher, John Murray, was enthralled by *Childe Harold's Pilgrimage* and was preparing the presses. Meanwhile Byron had taken up the cause of the Nottinghamshire frame breakers in their fight against new machinery for his maiden speech in the House of Lords. He spoke lucidly for their plight and against the Tories' plan for dealing with that plight: 'I have traversed the seat of war in the peninsula, I have been in some of the most oppressed provinces of Turkey, but never under the most despotic of infidel governments did I behold such squalid wretchedness as I have seen since my return in the very heart of a Christian country. How will you carry the Bill into effect? Can you commit a whole country to their own prisons? Will you erect a gibbet in every field, and hang up men like scarecrows?' The Bill was defeated by one vote, in Byron's mind his vote.

Childe Harold's Pilgrimage was a sensational success across Europe from the first edition, and the success snowballed with each reprint in each translation. Readers were transported to exotic places, to balmy climes and endless days, to dangerous foes and daring deeds, and came to feel that they too were there with Childe Harold. The Spenserian stanzas were ideally suited to the long narrative: the stanzas easy on the eye, the rhymes and rhythms easy on the ear, and each stanza reading like a paragraph in a novel. The secret of the epic was its accessibility to readers sophisticated and less so, the very beauty of the language, the lilting emotions it stirred, the longing for a life that would never be lived and the daring for a passion that would never be felt. Women in particular responded to its magnetic hints of the erotic and to the tastes of the exotic, the romance of the settings, the vulnerability of the players and the tenderness of the very words. The autobiographical nature of the poem was clear. Who was Childe Harold? Who is Lord Byron? Soon the fan mail started, and Byron pronounced: 'I awoke and found myself famous.'

Famous indeed. The toast and the talk of the town. The international success of *Childe Harold's Pilgrimage* and the fame attached to its success immediately propelled Byron to the highest reaches, the most exclusive *salons*, of London's political and cultural society. The deaths and homophobia were to be put aside, and as if to show he was alive and heterosexual Byron embarked on a giddying series of affairs and dalliances and flirtations and courtships and conquests. Unfortunately when it mattered most he chose unwisely—could hardly have chosen less wisely—for among the most prominent of these were three totally disastrous relationships, with Lady Caroline Lamb, with his half-sister Augusta Leigh and with Annabella Milbanke, who became Lady Byron.

The centre of intrigue was Melbourne House in Whitehall, the headquarters of the Whig hierarchy. Lady Melbourne was forty years his elder and had, in the vernacular, been around the block a few times. A born survivor, she had reinvented herself many times from *courtisane* to *femme fatale* to *confidante* to *grande dame*. She was just too late to have been the inspiration for Madame de Merteuil in the recently published *Les Liaisons Dangereuses*, but could easily have been her. She took to Byron immediately, seeing in him an endless source of scheming, scandal and intrigue. He took to her immediately too, seeing in her humour, wise counsel and discretion—the perfect preceptress. Their uninhibited letters still remain the best biography of his 'years of revellery', and reveal a lot of his character in those days. He had been propelled by his fame into a world which his minor title would not alone have admitted him. He was by nature shy with strangers and always self-conscious of his lameness. Lady Melbourne allayed his doubts and bolstered him and guided him. At his first visit to Melbourne House he met Lady Melbourne's daughter-in-law, the fateful Lady Caroline Lamb, Caroline's mother Lady Blessington—another piece of work in her own right—and Caroline's husband's cousin, the fatal Anne Isabella—Annabella—Milbanke, the future Lady Byron. If only he had known then what a vipers' nest he had just fallen into he might well have turned on his heel, but the reality was that his fate, of which he was never in control, made him fall in even faster.

His life in London soon became a parody of an Oscar Wilde parody of a William Congreve restoration comedy. With Lady Melbourne directing the cast and extras he was soon partying at Lady Holland's, Lady Westmoreland's, Lady Cowper's and Lady Davy's; flirting with Lady Rancliffe, Lady Jersey and Lady Forbes; cavorting with the Princess of Wales and Princess Caroline of Brunswick; Guinevere-ing with Lady Wedderburn-Webster and when not proposing to her sister Lady Annesley faux-proposing to Lady Leveson-Gower; scandalising with Lady Shelley; overnighting with Lady Heathcote; warding off Lady Falkland; coinciding with Lady Rosebury; nestling with Lady Holland and nesting—in several trees—with the redoubtable

Lady Oxford. Some good came of it: at Lady Sitwell's he met his stunning cousin-in-law Anne Wilmot, and the next morning, according to legend with a pounding hangover, he remembered her through the haze and wrote the three verses which start:

> She walks in Beauty, like the night
> Of cloudless climes and starry skies;
> And all that's best of dark and bright
> Meet in her aspect and her eyes:
> Thus mellowed to that tender light
> Which Heaven to gaudy day denies.

As the most eligible bachelor in London society in that summer of 1812 Byron could have chosen any one of these socially suitable and well financed, and mostly virginal, women to court and marry, but being Byron he chose a train crash instead. Lady Caroline Lamb was—where shall we start?—emotionally neurotic, trouble with a capital T. But then, albeit to a less violent extent, so was he. They were pulled at each other like a collision, and he found her as she found him: passionate, erratic, unstable, irascible, treacherous, capricious, bisexual, jealous, obsessive, compulsive and possessive. She famously wrote after their first meeting that he was 'mad, bad and dangerous to know'; he could with even more justification have written the same about her. She also presented more practical difficulties: she was married, and married well to a future prime minister, frequented the best *salons* in London, was five years older than Byron, and totally, unabashedly, ostentatiously indiscreet. She wrote of Byron, with some prescience, a few days after they met, 'that beautiful pale face is my fate.'

Their open affair scandalised London, and even Lady Melbourne, and Hobhouse, were soon trying to backpedal them. But they were inseparable: in private exchanging bloodied pubic hairs, cross dressing, Byron (unwisely in retrospect) confessing his homosexual exploits East, and she role playing accordingly; in public attending balls and receptions as one, and as one shouldn't. But soon even Byron felt their relationship spiralling out of control as she shifted from obsession to jealousy, and then from jealousy to treachery, and treachery to blackmail and forgery. She had always been unhinged, but now as he was hinting at a tactful separation the door had come off altogether. Her infatuation and cold revenge would carry right through to his own marriage separation and beyond.

Having survived, just, the emotional ballistic missile known as Caroline, Byron then found himself reunited with his half-sister Augusta. They had not seen each other for four years, since before the Grand Tour, and had hardly known each other as children. She was five years older, married to her rather dull army cousin, and often alone. They hit it off immediately, and spent hours and days and weeks and months talking and laughing about being a Byron. With Augusta, as with no other woman before or after, he was totally relaxed. She knew exactly how to handle his moods, mostly by laughing them off, which in turn caused him to laugh at his own absurdities too. He wrote to Hobhouse: 'We never yawn or disagree; and laugh much more than is suitable to so solid a mansion [Newstead]; and the family shyness makes us more amusing companions to each other than we could be to anyone else.' He had found his soul mate, and she had found hers.

They became closer and closer, living in increasingly idyllic isolation, and soon the hermits were forgetting the taboos of sibling celibacy and drifting inexorably into incest. The family had some form on this front as their father 'Mad Jack' had had an incestuous relationship with his sister Frances, herself the mother to Augusta's cousin-husband. One could say it was a family affair.

For Byron this was a respite of happiness and productivity. *The Giaour* had been published in editions of increasing length, and work continued apace on his new poem *The Corsair*. He would, as was his habit when composing, work well into the night, and brandy to hand often finished 200 lines before retiring at first light. It seemed that Newstead had at last been sold, even as they were living in it, and for the first time he would be free of debt. His plans now had shifted from a career in politics to more travel abroad, this time with Augusta, and he proceeded to outfit them for the journey, ordering swords, guns, desks, boxes, uniforms, saddles, beds and all the accoutrements of the famous Byron baggage train. He drew up plans for a replica of Napoleon's carriage. But then the Newstead sale fell through, and now faced with even higher debts he had to give up plans for the new journey eastwards.

Although Byron and Augusta were not themselves deterred by the taboo of incest, as suspicion spread and rumours crept others were less circumspect. It was his mentor Lady Melbourne—and again Hobhouse, his other soul mate, now back from military duty abroad and of whom Byron wrote at the time 'he is my best friend, the most lively, and a man of most sterling talents extant'—who pulled them back from the brink. We shall never know, but the deduction from timing and the decoding of letters to Lady Melbourne would lead one to suspect that Augusta's daughter Medora (born on 15 April 1814) was also Byron's.

Augusta herself was by now becoming aware of the whispering campaign and, determined to avoid a scandal, decided that the best course of action would be for Byron to marry. Lady Melbourne agreed, with the additional thought of heading off Caroline who had by now re-appeared from abroad and was circling above like a buzzard ready to swoop. Together Lady Melbourne and Augusta suggested to Byron not any of the eminently suitably ladies, most Ladies, with whom he had been disporting before the Caroline adventure, but Lady Melbourne's niece Annabella Milbanke. They had met a year before and exchanged pleasantries, and the routine light flirtation, but nothing more. They could hardly have been more different, but Byron did remember her with amusement and wrote to Lady Melbourne that he was 'intrigued by the amiable *mathematician*. I thank you again for your efforts with the Princess of Parallelograms, who has puzzled you more than the Hypotenuse. Her proceedings are quite rectangular, or rather we are two parallel lines prolonged to infinity side by side, never to meet.' Well, most of that was true, except the part that mattered—the last three words.

In Caroline he had escaped from the obsession of the most unsuitable woman in London with whom to have an affair; he now rebounded by pursuing Annabella, the most unsuitable woman in England with whom to tie the knot. Whereas Caroline bore her brain in her heart, Annabella hid her heart in her brain, and hid it very well indeed.

What on earth he thought he was doing it is hard to imagine; it was not after all that he lacked experience in conjugal relationships or judgement of others' characters. Three months before proposing he had described her as 'the most prudish and correct person I know', a description he would not expect anyone to bestow on *him*. It was not even as though she was easy to woo, living as she did in Seaham on the far north-east coast of England, a mighty trek from London today and a serious undertaking of discomfort and risk back then. She did not even have much of a fortune, being merely comfortably off when nothing less was commonplace. Nevertheless even though he had not seen her for a year he proposed to her, by letter, and she accepted but only at the second time of asking. To pursue her at all was the biggest error of judgement he ever made, and not to accept the first rejection the second biggest. If creation and destruction are two sides of the same coin, here was the proof. When Caroline heard of their engagement she commented that 'he would never be able to pull with a woman who went to church regularly, understood statistics and had a bad figure.'

Annabella was not in herself a bad person, not at all, but she had a personality that was prissy and pious and prickly and prim, an overconfidence in the rightness of her deductions and an unwavering belief that the deductions must be correct because they were hers. She would brook no dissent in her rigid beliefs, her rights and her wrongs. She would have made the ideal wife of the local clergyman, just as she was to make a disastrous wife to a poet prone to mood swings, atheism and alcohol.

It is possible that he was attracted to her for the very reason she was attracted to him; the chance to bring about the other's redemption, or at least reformation. Where she felt she was different from the other women in his life was that she, and only she, could save him from himself. Byron later mused that 'She married me from vanity, and the hope of reforming and fixing me.' There's an inbuilt part of the feminine psyche that wants to reform the rake. From Byron's view he may have felt the opposite needed to be applied; not exactly corrupting her, but at least liberating her from herself. She was after all the only woman playing hard to get—not that she was playing the game seductively or with wiles, but really was hard at heart and hard to get. Perhaps Byron mistook this as demanding a challenge from himself.

Byron found the courtship uncomfortable. It was not just the physical discomfort of visiting her so far away, but also the behavioural discomfort of playing the role of fiancé to an innocent and inexperienced girl. All his other lovers had been either married, or male, or clandestine, or offshore, or servants or spoke no English. Annabella, a young twenty-two, had not lived at all except through her books, and these were not fiction or poetry but textbooks and bibles.

Yet for better or worse, richer or poorer, in good health and bad, on 2 January 1815 marry they did. Hobhouse was the best man, and noted that 'never was a lover in less haste' as they went north for the marriage, 'the bridegroom more and more less impatient'. At the vow 'Byron looked at me with a small grimace'. Hobhouse felt he had 'buried a friend.'

The honeymoon, or 'treacle moon' as Byron described it, was a disaster, but merely set the scene for what was to follow. On the wedding night, Byron awoke, saw a candle burning on the other side of the scarlet bed-curtains, and exclaimed, 'Good God! I am fairly in Hades, with Proserpina by my side!' At least her feelings would not have been hurt; she would have had no idea to what he was referring.

Clearly Byron was far from faultless. She loved him, wanted to love him as she had read she should be loving him, and so when he was kind she overloved him. But he chose not to control his moods and when he was cruel, as was often, she was correspondingly devastated. She was after all a closeted, impressionable and highly inexperienced young girl and one whom Byron could have moulded any way he liked. But for all her brain power she was really still just a child in the world, and one with no idea how to handle a man, especially one who frequently behaved like a spoiled child himself. Her mind was literal, whereas he dealt in irony as a common currency. When he threw words around as he did she took each one literally and instead of laughing them off as the playthings they were, as Augusta would have done, she analysed every supposed nuance until her nascent inferiority complex had bloomed into a tearful neurosis.

They say no man is a hero to his valet. Fletcher, who had seen his master with dozens of women in hundreds of circumstances in all manner of moods, observed: 'It is very odd, but I never knew a lady not manage my Lord, except my Lady.' Caroline's mother, Lady Blessington, who had also come to know him well agreed: 'he gives the idea of being the man the most easily managed of any I ever saw; I wish Lady Byron had discovered the means.'

His lack of understanding of her predicament, one after all brought on by his own overtures, twice—this was no shotgun wedding—and his maltreatment of her was thoughtless and cruel, a display of hubris that inevitably led to nemesis. He never understood that the arithmetic of love is unique: two halves do not make a whole, only two wholes make a whole. One hesitates to be judgemental of what goes on behind closed doors, but cannot help be reminded of a more recent marriage between an experienced and egotistical man and an inexperienced and willing girl, where the man put his own gratification before the needs of the whole, and that too inevitably ended in disaster.

She came to believe that the only explanation for his disagreeability was that he was mad; an echo of Caroline's earlier prognosis. She then tried to read method into his madness, and when the two clearly did not fit she had nowhere to turn except the lawyers and her mother. Both egged her on for a separation in spite of Byron's belated attempt at thoughtfulness and all their friends prompting for a reconciliation. But to make matters even worse, her own inheritance had by then failed and the bailiffs had arrived. Events now moved quickly to a conclusion. On 10 December 1815 Annabella gave birth to a daughter, Ada. Hounded by debts and shame, Byron turned more heavily to drink and became even fouler. When Ada was six weeks old Annabella could take no more abuse and took her daughter and left to be with her parents. She and Byron never saw each other again.

She still clung to the hope that he would be proved insane and so prove her to be correct—and him redeemable in her hands. But by then matters had assumed their own momentum. Assisted by innuendos from her lawyers and malicious gossip from Lady Caroline Lamb and others—largely true it has to be said—rumours spread that he was a homosexual and a sodomite, a 'practitioner of incest', of loose morals, syphilitic, prone to alcohol and depressions and sometimes violence—and Byron's reputation was as ruined as his finances. On 21 April 1816, sixteen months after he had signed the marriage certificate, Hobhouse signed the separation on Byron's behalf, and four days later the latter left England, five years after he had first returned, but this time never to return again.

~

So, what are we to make of Byron on his return from the Grand Tour? He did not seem a happy soul as he careered from creation to destruction and back again. After the triumph of *Childe Harold's Pilgrimage* John Murray launched *The Giaour* and the *Bride of Abydos*, both to great acclaim. *The Corsair*, which followed next, sold 10,000 copies on its first day. *Lara* was slightly less successful, but still well received, as was *Hebrew Melodies* and the *Siege of Corinth*. But in between these creative highs he laid a trail of emotional destruction for others to clear up.

One is tempted to conclude that the poet of wonderful romance knew not himself of love—pure, unselfish, unconditional love. He knew it not as others did, with words beyond romance: 'Love is not love/ Which alters when it alteration finds,/Or bends with the remover to remove... Love's not Time's fool, though rosy lips and cheeks/Within his bending sickle's compass come.' He knew of passion—more or less permanently, one bout after another; he knew of romance—whenever he picked up a pen and allowed the words to do the work; he knew of lust—either way, as long as beauty was present. But pure love is light, just, bears no pressure or compulsion, offers no dark days or partiality. That love wants the best for everybody, it has a humour and tends its ways to bliss. It belongs to no one and everyone, it is a quality—*the* quality that transforms life into something deep and meaningful, the ultimate virtuous circle.

That love passed Byron by. His emotions were essentially selfish, and so he was driven by the duality of attraction and repulsion which reflected in a never ending series of contradictions. Just after his engagement to Annabella he thought—or maybe Hobhouse suggested—he should have his head examined. Literally. He visited a phrenologist who pronounced that the two sides of Byron's brain were uncommonly incompatible, in fact mutually incompatible. He was at war with himself, did not know if he was a genius or a werewolf, and so it was hardly surprising that he could not be at peace with anyone else and took pleasure in their subsequent suffering.

It is beyond the scope of this book to follow him into exile in the Alps and Italy and then on to death in Greece. His life remains as compelling a story as ever, and it is apt that the story should end in the birthplace of tragedy, of hubris, nemesis and catharsis which stalked him throughout his short life. It has been well observed that the best way Byron could have served the cause of the Greek independence was to die for it, thereby causing not just independence for the wretched Greeks but his own immortality as well.

And immortal he seems to be. He had that one magical, indefinable, unbuyable quality that no one could gainsay: what the self-same ancient Greeks called *kharisma*, gift of the divine. If sometimes one feels too bilious about Byron the man, a few moments 'in transport' alone with *Don Juan* will settle the stomach—it was written by Byron the poet, and he was someone else altogether.

Thanks and Acknowledgements

~

The re-Tour is over.

It has been fun, and it owes special thanks to the following people and books, both of which have helped it along the way.

'I am a mighty Scribbler.' So said the man himself and scribble away he certainly did. It has often been said that Byron was his own best biographer, and indeed his own writings have been the main source material for this book. When one considers that his publisher and friends destroyed a lot of the more contentious material after he died—supposedly to protect his own and others' reputations—one is tempted to conclude there must have been a whole team of mighty Scribblers, so extensive were his writings.

The best way to access Byron's writings is through Professor Leslie A. Marchand's *Byron's Letters & Journals*, all thirteen volumes of them. Marchand also wrote a three-volume biography in 1957, and the more accessible *Byron: A Portrait* in 1971, the book that inspired the re-Tour. On board *Vasco da Gama*, where space is limited, free internet access to the letters and journals can be found via The Project Gutenberg E-Book of *The Works Of Lord Byron, Letters and Journals*, edited by Rowland E. Protheroe on www.gutenberg.org. This also has excellent footnotes. Also on Gutenberg, for those with a strong stomach, is Ali Pasha's biography by Alexandre Dumas the elder.

More recent biographies than Marchand's are *Byron: Life and Legend* by Fiona MacCarthy and *Byron, Child of Passion, Fool of Fame* by Benita Eisler. Both are massive undertakings which are useful for checking facts and dates, but only the former ever really gets under the subject's skin: the latter is good for knowing where and when he had breakfast without knowing what he had for breakfast, or why or with whom.

I thought it only good form to read the young Byron's two favourite books: *Anastasius* by the artist Thomas Hope and *Vathek, an Arabian Tale,* by his early role model William Beckford. Both books are good ground for Grand Tour atmosphere in general and Byron on Grand Tour atmosphere in particular. Thomas Hope was a slightly earlier Grand Tourist, and his book brings to life the Orient that Byron would have found. Lady Blessington recorded that 'Lord Byron said he wept bitterly over many pages of it, and for two reasons—first, that he had not written it, and secondly that Hope *had* written it… a book, as he said, excelling in wit and talent as well as in true pathos.'

For those who want to find out more about Byron in general I can heartily recommend joining the International Byron Society (IBS). This is headquartered in the UK but has national societies and branches in thirty-five countries from Albania to Uruguay. Looking back, I am tempted to conclude I learned more from the local society in each country than from the biographies and all the other books I carted around. In particular I would like to thank Rosa Florou of the Messolonghi branch of the IBS who has built up a wonderful collection of Byron books in the library of Byron House. This is the best single research facility I found and I spent many a happy hour up there looking up and out over the lagoon.

Among the gems in Messolonghi are Finden's *'Illustrations of Byron', Volumes I to III*, published by John Murray, 1833, with their wonderful illustrations of the Grand Tour; *Greece in 1800, Engraving of an Era*, edited by Miltiades Makriyiannis, Ergo Publishers; *His Very Self and Voice* by Ernest Lovell, Macmillan, 1954; and *Byron and Greece* by Harold Spender, John Murray, 1924.

The other first-hand source is of course Byron's travelling companion John Cam Hobhouse. Hobhouse took extensive daily notes for his diary, and one can see, touch and smell the original in the British Library. It fair sent tingles down my spine to hold the very book that went on the main part of the Grand Tour. He eventually wrote a very much fuller account called *A Journey through Albania and other Provinces of Turkey through Europe and Asia to Constantinople in the Years 1809 & 1810*. A particularly helpful Hobhouse website is Peter

Cochrane's www.hobby-o.com. This must have been a real labour of love as he edits Hobhouse's work to make it Byron relevant and then has wonderful footnotes and cross references back to the text.

These sources mentioned above are all about the poet. For the poetry there are any number of editions, and my favourite is Professor Jerome McGann's *Byron: The Major Works*; Rosa told me to make sure to use the Oxford edition.

Two BBC presenters have written books that were useful: Jeremy Paxman's *On Royalty* was helpful with King Leka I of the Albanians, and Michael Woods's *In Search of Troy* was helpful, well, searching for Troy.

Looking across at the bookshelf I can also see that *The Accursed Mountains* by Robert Carver about Albania is well thumbed, as is Lady Wortley Montagu's *Turkish Embassy Letters*. Charlotte Higgins's *It's All Greek to Me* is an enjoyable reunion with Greek gods and myths. *Travellers' Greece*, edited by John Tomkinson, was useful for eighteenth- and nineteenth-century Ottoman Greek background. Another little gem is *Lord Byron's Iberian Pilgrimage* by Gordon Kent Thomas, published by Brigham Young University Press, 1983. I also tried Edna O'Brien's *Byron in Love* but it's fluff and nonsense and manages to miss the point about Byron *and* love.

Now, on a more practical level I am especially indebted to Imray Laurie Norie & Wilson Ltd, not for legal advice but for publishing the Imray *Pilot* series of yachtsmen's guides to the different waters of the Mediterranean. One should not leave berth without them.

Also useful, when things go wrong (oh boy!), is Nigel Calder's *Boatowners Mechanical and Electrical Manual*, and for when you go wrong Tom Cunliffe's *The Complete Yachtmaster* tells you how it should have been done.

And lastly, thanks to all the people mentioned in the book for their co-operation and enthusiasm, but above all thanks to Gillian for not hearing the pins drop or the pips squeak.

Index